'We live in a world in which technological development threatens to outpace both the legal and ethical frameworks which define the boundaries of what is acceptable. Established principles can seem outmoded, or even obstructive, when set against the siren attractions of new discoveries. Nowhere is this divergence more acute – or more relevant – than in the field of emerging military technologies. It is therefore essential that those with deep experience of the law, ethics, and technology encourage us all to pause and reflect on the likely consequences of these transformative scientific discoveries. It is not enough to wait and see what these consequences will be. Nor is it an exaggeration to say that these consequences could be so far reaching as to cause us to question what it is to be human and the value we place on human life. This is therefore a very timely book which deserves to be widely read by all those involved in any way in the development and implementation of emerging military technologies.'

Air Commodore John Thomas RAF (Retired), *President, International Society for Military Ethics in Europe (Euro-ISME)*

'I am delighted to be able to endorse this book. There are two main reasons for this. First, I have known George's work in the area of cyberwar and autonomous weapon systems for two decades now. In his work, George combines excellent analytical insights, the highest level of scholarly research with an in-depth knowledge of the defense and military organizations and the relevant technology he writes about. This is a great element, as most of the work in this area is often anecdotal research-wise and superficial in terms of the proposed analysis. The depth of George's publications alongside their clarity and linearity makes them an almost-unique contribution to this field of work. They appeal to experts, both academics and practitioners, and to students and junior researchers who want to delve into this area of work. The second reason is that his books and publications thus far have been seminal, and I believe this will also be the case for this book. This is because the book has a very impressive breadth covering from cyber to kinetic uses of digital technologies and focusing on the entire spectrum of ethics and governance from procurement to deployment. The questions that it addresses are central to the debate on the ethics of war as well as to effort to regulate state use of digital technologies for defense purposes . . . I could not recommend this book more.'

Mariarosaria Taddeo, *Associate Professor and Senior Research Fellow, University of Oxford, UK*

'Finally, here is a book that unifies the fierce but siloed debates over military robotics, AI, and cyberwarfare – connecting the dots, which aren't obvious. These revolutionary technologies are so crucial to the future of security and defense, well into the next century if not more. The author is one of the very few who could pull this off; he was there at the start of these debates, not only as an academic philosopher and military historian but also in the trenches of international policy discussions and military operations. In this book, theory meets real-world practice.'

Patrick Lin, *California Polytechnic State University, San Luis Obispo*

'Blending real-world insights with a thought-provoking advancement of human-centered ethical frameworks for conflict involving next-generation robotics, autonomy, and other breakthroughs, this book offers a vital contribution to the study of future warfare.'

August Cole, *non-resident Senior Fellow at the Atlantic Council, Washington, DC*

'I've had the great pleasure of working with and learning from Professor George Lucas for many years. His reputation at the service academies and, more broadly, within professional military education is beyond peer. His decades of research and writing have had a major and lasting impact on curricula worldwide. This book is destined to be required reading for leaders, practitioners, and even those with a casual interest in the field. Built upon years of scholarship enabled by a network of subject matter experts and the financial support of the Peace Research Institute Oslo, this book reflects on the leading edge of emerging military technologies. Few understand the ethical implications of emerging military technology in the way George does. As only an ethicist writing from experience within the institutions charged with grounding practitioners in tactics, techniques, and procedures regarding emerging military technologies could do, George Lucas clearly describes the trends associated with postmodern war and the implications for systems associated with its execution. His particular expertise in cyber operations figures prominently in this book and will introduce the reader to new and important insights. George's concluding chapter, however, makes this book stand apart. His deep connections with private sector leaders engaged in weapons development render fresh, uncommon perspective from key stakeholders in emerging technologies. Defense contractors and engineers are rarely asked about the moral implications of their efforts. Professor Lucas ensures their concerns are accounted for in this evolving and fascinating field.'

Joseph J. Thomas, *United States Naval Academy, Annapolis, USA*

'Defense and security professionals, policymakers, legislators, computer engineers, and all those interested in ethics, law, and emerging military technologies want to know where consensus is emerging around ethical norms that will serve for adequate governance. Professor Lucas's discernment of 11 principles is a potentially breakthrough advance that lays out "soft-law" guidelines – ranging from mission legality and a presumption against unnecessary risk to meaningful human control, product liability, reckless endangerment, and more. Foresight and warning in this field is difficult enough. This formulation of principles for engineering and research capable of attracting assent, and emerging from wide-ranging research, is simply brilliant.'

Esther D. Reed, *Professor of Theological Ethics, University of Exeter, UK*

'The disruptive and destabilizing impact emerging military technologies such as cyberwarfare and autonomous weapons systems will have on the conduct of conflict and combat is commonly presented by either those who wish to restrict their use or those who argue as to why their development is essential for national and international security. With a long distinguished career teaching ethics and *international humanitarian law* (the law of armed conflict) to present and future officers in the U.S. Navy, George Lucas is singularly gifted to embrace and bridge this tension while elucidating potential pathways forward. Unfortunately, recent events have underscored the inevitability of hellish high-tech conflict. George Lucas serves as our Virgil guiding us through the landscape of emerging military technologies with astute sensitivity as to how a degree of morality can be introduced into this worst of human habits.'

Wendell Wallach, *Senior Fellow at the Carengie Council for Ethics in International Affairs, Senior advisor to The Hastings Center, and scholar at Yale University's Interdisciplinary Center for Bioethics, USA*

'This book engages the mind-bending ethical complexities of emerging technologies that compel the reader to ask the penetrating questions of moral agency. Dr Lucas's work complements the prescient tasks of technology's impact on moral decision-making. How far will technology erode humanity's control of it? We do not have an ethics gap with technology innovation – we have an abyss between our regressing ethics and the exponential innovation of technology. Lucas, noting the "devaluation of norms" across the world, calls for an increased emphasis on ethics education, which often supersedes law. Laws are becoming a new moral baseline, where the practice of laws and ethics should be separate. Laws are there for those who do not have a strong grasp on morality and must be coerced by laws into doing the minimum. This cannot be the case when designing new weapons systems. Developers and engineers have an obligation to incorporate ethical frameworks in the process.'

Thomas E. Creely, *Creator and Director of the Ethics and Emerging Military Technology Graduate Certificate Program at the U.S. Naval War College, Newport, RI*

'George Lucas grapples with the profound ethical and legal challenges posed by contemporary armed conflict. An impressive and highly readable book on urgent topics such as robots, autonomy, AI, and cyberspace.'

Lonneke Peperkamp, *Chair in Military Ethics and Leadership, the Netherlands Defense Academy, the Netherlands*

'George Lucas has provided an ambitious and penetrating analysis of the legal and ethical dimensions of technologies that are reshaping the nature of modern military operations. He assesses the complex potential consequences of these technologies not only for society but for those who are involved in developing and deploying them. The result is a rich and deeply insightful work that draws on multiple disciplines to provide valuable guidance.'

Mitt Regan, *McDevitt Professor of Jurisprudence, Georgetown University Law Center, Washington, USA*

'George has done an outstanding job of taking the enormous body of literature on the topic of emerging military technology and developed a framework for understanding. Also, he does a superb job helping the reader grapple with the differences between human morality and the legal adherence that one would imagine should be built into emerging military technologies. His is a must read for people who want to think seriously about how technology should be used in warfare.'

Rear Admiral Margaret "Peg" Klein (USN Retired),
Dean of the College of Leadership and Ethics at the US Naval War College in Newport, RI, USA

LAW, ETHICS AND EMERGING MILITARY TECHNOLOGIES

This book addresses issues of legal and moral governance arising in the development, deployment, and eventual uses of emerging technologies in military operations.

Proverbial wisdom has it that law and morality always lag behind technological innovation. Hence, the book aims to identify, enumerate, and constructively address the problems of adequate governance for the development, deployment, and eventual uses of military technologies that have been newly introduced into military operations or which will be available in the near future. Proposals for modifications in governance, the book argues, closely track the anxieties of many critics of these technologies to the extent that they will proliferate, prove destructive in unanticipated ways, and partially or wholly escape regulation under current treaties and regulatory regimes. In addition to such concerns in domestic and especially in international law, the book addresses ethical norms in the professions involved in the design and eventual use of specific technologies, principally involving the professional norms of practice in engineering and the military (as well as biomedical and health care practice), which impose moral obligations on their members to avoid reckless endangerment or criminal negligence in the course of their activities. Thus, in addition to exploring the application of existing legal regimes and moral norms, the book examines how these professions might develop or improve the voluntary constraints on forms of malfeasance that are enshrined in their histories and codes of best practices.

This book should prove to be of great interest to students of ethics, military studies, philosophy of war and peace, law, and international relations.

George Lucas is Distinguished Chair in Ethics Emeritus at the U.S. Naval Academy and Professor Emeritus of Ethics and Public Policy at the Graduate School of Defense Management at the Naval Postgraduate School in Monterey, California. His earlier books include *The Routledge Handbook of Military Ethics* (2015), *Military Ethics: What Everyone Needs to Know* (2016), *Ethics and Cyber Warfare* (2017), and *Ethics and Military Strategy in the 21st Century: Moving Beyond Clausewitz* (2019).

War, Conflict and Ethics

Series Editors:
Michael L. Gross
University of Haifa
and
James Pattison
University of Manchester

Ethical judgments are relevant to all phases of protracted violent conflict and interstate war. Before, during, and after the tumult, martial forces are guided, in part, by their sense of morality for assessing whether an action is (morally) right or wrong, an event has good and/or bad consequences, and an individual (or group) is inherently virtuous or evil. This new book series focuses on the morality of decisions by military and political leaders to engage in violence and the normative underpinnings of military strategy and tactics in the prosecution of the war.

The Moral Status of Combatants
A New Theory of Just War
Michael Skerker

Distributing the Harm of Just Wars
In Defence of an Egalitarian Baseline
Sara Van Goozen

Moral Injury and Soldiers in Conflict
Political Practices and Public Perceptions
Tine Molendijk

The Empathetic Soldier
Kevin R. Cutright

Law, Ethics and Emerging Military Technologies
Confronting Disruptive Innovation
George Lucas

For more information about this series, please visit: www.routledge.com/War-Conflict-and-Ethics/book-series/WCE

LAW, ETHICS AND EMERGING MILITARY TECHNOLOGIES

Confronting Disruptive Innovation

George Lucas

Routledge
Taylor & Francis Group
LONDON AND NEW YORK

Cover image: © Getty Images – vadimrysev

First published 2023
by Routledge
4 Park Square, Milton Park, Abingdon, Oxon OX14 4RN

and by Routledge
605 Third Avenue, New York, NY 10158

Routledge is an imprint of the Taylor & Francis Group, an informa business

British Library Cataloguing-in-Publication Data
A catalogue record for this book is available from the British Library

ISBN: 978-1-032-22730-6 (hbk)
ISBN: 978-1-032-22728-3 (pbk)
ISBN: 978-1-003-27391-2 (ebk)

DOI: 10.4324/9781003273912

Typeset in Bembo
by Apex CoVantage, LLC

For my grandson **Erik Judy**

Aerospace Engineer in the Making

May he and his generation continue to reach for the stars, despite the dismal legacy we are leaving them here at home.

I wish to gratefully acknowledge support for this research provided by the Norwegian Research Council through a grant to the Peace Research Institute Oslo (PRIO).

CONTENTS

ABOUT THE AUTHOR

George Lucas is "Distinguished Chair in Ethics" Emeritus at the U.S. Naval Academy, and Professor Emeritus of Ethics and Public Policy at the Graduate School of Public Policy at the Naval Postgraduate School in Monterey, California. He has taught at Georgetown University, Notre Dame University, Emory University, Case-Western Reserve University, Randolph-Macon College, the French Military Academy (Saint-Cyr), and the Catholic University of Leuven in Belgium, and most recently served as the Vice Admiral James B. Stockdale Professor of Ethics at the U.S. Naval War College (Newport RI). His earlier books include *Ethics and Cyber Warfare* (Oxford University Press, 2017); *Military Ethics: What Everyone Needs to Know* (Oxford University Press, 2016); *The Routledge Handbook of Military Ethics* (Routledge, 2015); *Anthropologists in Arms: the Ethics of Military Anthropology* (AltaMira Press, 2009); and *Perspectives on Humanitarian Military Intervention* (University of California Press, 2001). His most recent books are *Beyond Clausewitz: The Place of Ethics in Military Strategy* (Routledge, 2019), and *The Ordering of Time: Meditations on the History of Philosophy* (Edinburgh University Press, 2020).

PREFACE AND ACKNOWLEDGMENTS

Much of the material in this book is drawn from articles either written solely by me or published jointly in collaboration with colleagues over the past several years (principally in law reviews and scientific, peer-reviewed journals). A considerable amount of material also comes from college and university seminars or guest lectures delivered as public presentations at conferences devoted to international law and international relations. All of these presentations and publications were aimed at exploring the various ways technological innovations in military weapons systems and combat operations presented challenges in the understanding and application of customary and widely shared moral norms or principles guiding individual and collective behavior, as well as in the interpretation and application of the extant bodies of law and legal norms enshrined in treaties and conventions or in customary practices applicable to military and combat operations carried out by nations in conflict. None of these materials is classified; all are fully in the public domain. In every instance, I have revised, edited, and updated previous material for publication in this book with the full permission and acknowledgment, where appropriate, of other colleagues involved in this research.

The opportunity to gather all these disparate bits together, however, came about through a generous multi-year grant from the Norwegian Research Council (NRC) to the Peace Research Institute Oslo (PRIO), which in turn graciously enlisted me as a project participant and funded a block of time specifically to work on finalizing the manuscript for this book as a contribution to that overall project. I wish to acknowledge and thank the NRC and PRIO for this support and specifically my cyber research team colleagues Prof. Greg Reichberg and Prof. Henrik Syse (PRIO), Professor Frank Pasquale (John Jay College of Law), Prof. Kirsi Heleveka (Norwegian Army Cyber Security division), and Col. James Cook (U.S. Air Force Academy) for their ongoing advice and support, and permission to include some of the results of our extensive collaboration on varieties of artificial intelligence and the impact of their uses on military operations (especially cyber operations).

Also, I have deferred on numerous occasions to the pathbreaking work of the Oxford Digital Ethics lab and its principal researchers, Dr Luciano Floridi and Dr Mariarosario Taddeo, to whose scholarship and leadership in this entire field I wish to pay special tribute. Dr Robert Sparrow of Monash University, as an acknowledged pioneer in this field, has been a frequent inspiration for my work. We collaborated on producing the lengthy report from which (with his permission) the fourth chapter of this book on automated maritime warfare is abridged, revised, and updated. Likewise, readers will note the heavy reliance throughout the book, even in disagreement, on the substantial work during the past two decades of Wendell Wallach (Yale University), Noel Sharkey (University of Sheffield), and Ronald Arkin (Georgia Tech).

Also, I wish to express gratitude to the following institutions for numerous invitations over the past decade or more to present seminars and guest public lectures on the topics now included in this book. These include the Australian Defence Force Academy (ADFA) and the Australian National University (ANU-Canberra); the U.S. Naval Academy, U.S. Air Force Academy, U.S. Military Academy, Naval Postgraduate School, and U.S. Naval War College; the Royal Military College (Kinston, Ontario), the University of New Brunswick's Brigadier Milton F. Gregg Center and Canadian Armed Forces Camp Gagetown; the École Militaire (Paris) and the French Military Academy (Saint-Cyr); Oxford University's Uehiro Center for Practical Ethics as well as the University of Warwick, the U.K. Defence Academy (Shrivenham), Bath University, the University of Exeter, and the Royal Naval College (Dartmouth).

While there is an enormous background of literature on this general topic and specific branches of it (e.g., military robotics), the principal source of supporting research and peer-reviewed scholarship for this book comes in the form of journal articles and anthologies, rather than monographs. Much as my earlier work on ethics and cyber warfare (OUP, 2017), this book is now intended to provide (insofar as possible) a *synoptic perspective and summative evaluation* of this large body of research from the unified standpoint of a single author. Some of the most significant of these prior collaborations have been collected in an earlier Routledge publication titled *Emerging Technologies: Ethics, Law and Governance* (Oxford: Routledge, 2016), co-edited by the aforementioned Wendell Wallach of Yale University, together with Gary Marchant of the Arizona State Law School. Both are well-known and highly respected scholars and authors whom I cite extensively in my own work. Wallach is the sole author of an important critical study of ethics, law, and technological innovation generally (although not focused exclusively on military technology) titled *A Dangerous Master.*[1] Prof. Braden Allenby, also at Arizona State University, has edited an anthology in the same Routledge series, "The Library of Essays on the Ethics of Emerging Technologies," specifically focused on important, previously published articles devoted to *The Applied Ethics of Military and Security Technologies* (Routledge, 2016). Dr Tim Demy of the U.S. Naval War College has collaborated with others on an edited volume of essays on this topic previously published in several issues of the *Journal of Military Ethics* (including some of my own earlier work). Demy's collection is also published by Routledge and is titled *Military Ethics and Emerging Technologies* (Routledge 2014).

Finally, I wish to call attention to the pioneering work of Dr Patrick Lin (California Polytechnic Institute and State University), one of the best-known and widely cited of those working at the intersection of technology, military applications of technology, and ethics. His work likewise encompasses several important anthologies (e.g., *Robot Ethics* (Cambridge Mass.: MIT Press, 2011) and *Robot Ethics 2.0* (Oxford UP, 2019), as well as numerous seminal articles for highly respected and widely read journals and magazines such as *Slate, Forbes*, and *The Atlantic Monthly*. Were it not for the extensive work and leadership of these many colleagues, there would be precious little to summarize and evaluate.

A Brief Meditation on Law and Morality

Finally, it bears mention that the synthesis and synoptic treatment in this book purport to incorporate the joint perspectives of *ethics* (moral philosophy) and *international humanitarian law* (the law of armed conflict). While I have worked extensively over the years in both areas, let me emphasize that I am not myself a legal scholar or expert in the fine structure or details of international law, nor do I wish to pose as one. Rather, I tend to approach these issues from the standpoint of a moral philosopher working in contemporary military ethics, understood as the *ethics of the profession of arms* itself, and of the tradition of historical debates over centuries among varieties of scholars and professional practitioners of arms, statecraft, and international relations (just war theory or the just war tradition (JWT)), out of which international law largely grew and whose moral norms and perspectives international humanitarian law (IHL) has now largely come to incorporate.

In the *Nichomachean Ethics* (Book VII), Aristotle contrasts the role of the lifelong cultivation of an ethics of virtue with the role of law, suggesting that among its many positive roles in teaching and embodying justice, the Law is also meant to govern and restrain the behavior of those incorrigible members of any community who, as he remarks, "lack even a tincture of Virtue." In other words, we might conclude that Law and the threat of punishment for disobedience constitute, in essence, the last resort for those individuals who just don't get it (i.e., who do not grasp the demands of morality).

In the general case, such a distinction might suggest that Law defines a *compulsory baseline* for behavior, separating permissible from prohibited behavior, and setting forth the requirements of justice to be observed by all (under the promised sanction of punishment). It is the *minimum acceptable standard* below which we must not slide. Morality, on the other hand, defines principles and virtues (ideals and best social practices) that ought to be cultivated by those who seek to flourish and attain excellence of character and moral agency themselves, while simultaneously nurturing the good life for members of their community through word and deed. In a darker sense, morality also trains its spotlight on actions and forms of behavior that, while not strictly prohibited by law, nonetheless are evidence of defect ("vice") and perhaps reveal a person in possession of a weak or corrupt character.

That at very least suggests that morality sets the high bar for human conduct, far exceeding the grudging agreement merely to "abide by the law" (under the presumed threat of coercion). That is part of the reason why – in time of war especially, when the general respect for the rule of law has collapsed or been seriously undermined – it is vitally important *not* to equate moral behavior (or the demands of the code of conduct of the profession of arms) merely with *compliance* with the law. That is true even when, as in IHL, legal stipulations such as distinction (the requirement to distinguish between combatants and civilian noncombatants and to refrain from deliberately targeting or harming the latter or their civilian objects) are heavily reliant on moral norms and principles (such as respect for basic human rights, human dignity, or considerations of humanity and compassion). When these moral instincts are already severely truncated and scarce amid armed conflict, it becomes all the more important not to extinguish them entirely, or wholly externalize them, by conflating them with legal compliance (what many sources and citations in this book, including the author, equate with "machine morality").

The purpose of IHL, as enshrined in portions of the United Nations Charter and the Hague and Geneva Conventions, is primarily to protect the vulnerable victims of war (noncombatants, refugees, and prisoners of war) from superfluous harm and injury and wholly unnecessary suffering by constraining the use of lethal force by adversaries justly or unjustly engaged in armed conflict with one another. IHL does not itself adjudicate their conflict but instead requires at a minimum that all parties to the conflict exercise lethal force only so far as required to attain necessary and legitimate military objectives.[2]

Less often remembered, however – especially by the combatants whose behaviors are thus constrained – is that the moral norms embodied in IHL historically arise within their own military practice, experienced both as abysmal failures (war crimes) and as noble aspirations and ideals (humanity, compassion), long before there was anything resembling contemporary IHL. Those customary laws and codes of the profession of arms are meant to protect combatants themselves, as well as unfortunate victims caught in their crossfire. That protection consists not only of shielding against cruel or superfluous bodily harm (should combatants become defenseless prisoners of war or otherwise rendered *hors de combat*) but also from what is currently called *moral injury*: severe damage to or loss of *their own humanity and capacity for moral agency* while mired within the most horrific and inhumane of circumstances. Personal rectitude and moral self-governance (honor, integrity) constitute the root meanings of autonomy, in marked contrast to the machine autonomy discussed at length in these pages. These precious commodities risk being seriously damaged, if not extinguished altogether, whenever we discount or ignore the role of morality or conflate morality with mere obedience to the law in time of war – especially when, as we so often do, we proceed to represent the law itself to military personnel merely as a set of seemingly arbitrary constraints imposed on the behavior of combatants by lawyers and diplomats in privileged and protected circumstances regarding activities with which the latter have little direct knowledge or experience.

Disrespect for international law by those who ought to be most willing to own it and be governed by it is thus the tragic result of attempting to equate or conflate law and morality. It is, sadly, the ultimate manifestation of those on all sides who just don't get it. In times of war, of course, there are quite a few individuals who don't get it or who forget who they are, the ends that they serve, and what they have learned in the practice of their profession. Thankfully, there are a great many more practitioners of the profession of arms who do not, but who, as Plato portrays it in the *Republic*, "remember themselves" and retain the knowledge of who they are, what they are properly about, and what the ideals and principles of the code of conduct of the profession of arms unvaryingly require of them.[3]

Nowhere is this better illustrated than in one of the central founding documents of IHL itself, the Lieber Code, a list of requirements and expectations placed upon military professionals (initially in the Union Army during the U.S. Civil War by President Abraham Lincoln and known as General Orders 100). That document enshrines deliberations regarding the ideals and limitations on proper military conduct in combat as discerned by a select committee of senior military practitioners under the guidance of Dr Franz Lieber, an influential German-American legal scholar at Columbia University who had himself served as a member of the Prussian Army during the Napoleonic Wars. Scholars often cite this document and its historical importance as a founding document in the evolution of international law. But just as often, they overlook its significance as a profound reflection, during a moment of historical exigency, by military professionals themselves concerning the ideals, best practices, and (most importantly) the *limits of acceptable practice* within their profession. This document served ever after as a Code of Ethics for members of militaries in the United States and Canada, as well as in Europe, Australia, and New Zealand. The Lieber Code is an act of remembering, or as Plato might say, "re-minding" – helping military personnel not to lose sight during armed conflict of who they were and what their collective enterprise represented in terms of the safety and security of their fellow citizens. Soldiers were not to risk forgetting themselves (e.g., by committing senseless atrocities) in the midst of the brutality of an inconceivably harsh, brutal, and bitterly contested "civil" conflict.

Our PRIO project, at its core, now seeks both to reinforce this ongoing effort and particularly to examine the manner in which warring with machines might also risk degrading, eroding, or de-skilling the human beings who constitute the members of the military profession through their ever-increasing reliance upon artificial intelligence and a purely calculative, compliance-based machine morality. Also, we seek to examine whether such increasing reliance might reinforce, rather than automatically degrade, the core virtues of the military profession and enable (as some scholars and practitioners maintain) an even greater adherence to the moral principles of humanity and compassion at the heart of contemporary international law.

To that end, and with due respect and deference to those whose legal expertise vastly exceeds my own, I nevertheless unapologetically attempt to retain a dual focus on both vital sources of practical wisdom, professional guidance, and moral rectitude in the discussions that follow.

Notes

1 *A Dangerous Master: How to Keep Technology From Slipping Beyond Our Control* (New York: Basic Books, 2015). Wallach is also coauthor (with Colin Allen of Indiana University) of *Moral Machines: Teaching Robots Right From Wrong* (New York: Oxford University Press, 2008).

2 See *Just and Unjust Warriors: The Moral and Legal Status of Soldiers*, eds. David Rodin and Henry Shue (Oxford: Oxford University Press, 2008).

3 See my discussion of "forgetful warriors" in *Ethics and Military Strategy in the 21st Century: Moving Beyond Clausewitz* (London: Routledge, 2020): 149–160.

References

Lucas, George R., Jr. *Ethics and Military Strategy in the 21st Century: Moving Beyond Clausewitz* (London: Routledge, 2020): 149–160.

Rodin, David; Shue, Henry, eds. *Just and Unjust Warriors: The Moral and Legal Status of Soldiers* (Oxford: Oxford University Press, 2008).

Wallach, Wendell. *A Dangerous Master: How to Keep Technology From Slipping Beyond Our Control* (New York: Basic Books, 2015).

Wallach, Wendell; Allen, Colin. *Moral Machines: Teaching Robots Right From Wrong* (New York: Oxford University Press, 2008).

INTRODUCTION

The Transformation of Contemporary Armed Conflict

Proverbial wisdom has it that law and morality always lag technological innovation. The more novel, exotic, or potentially harmful the technology, moreover, the greater the perceived challenge in coming to terms with the ethical, legal, and societal impacts (ELSI) every such technological innovation is thought to have. Hence the subtitle, "Confronting Disruptive Innovation," and the main title (which encompasses the aim of this book): the effort to identify, enumerate, and constructively address the problems of *adequate governance* for the development, deployment, and eventual uses of exotic military technologies that have recently been introduced in military practice or that will be available for deployment and military use in the very near future.

Proposals for modifications in governance closely track the anxieties of many critics of these technologies regarding the likelihood that the technologies themselves will proliferate, or prove destructive in unanticipated ways, and might partially or wholly escape regulation under current law, treaties, and regulatory regimes. In addition to such concerns in domestic, and especially in international law (specifically international humanitarian law (ILH), or the law of armed conflict (LOAC)), I address ethical norms in the professions involved in the design and eventual use of specific technologies, principally involving the *professional norms of practice* in engineering in the defense industries, the military, and, in at least one instance, biomedical research and health care practice. All these sectors impose moral obligations on their members to avoid *reckless endangerment*, let alone *criminal negligence* or wanton disregard for human welfare in the course of their practice. Thus, in addition to exploring the application of existing legal regimes and moral norms in the international community, I examine how members of these multinational professions might develop or improve the voluntary constraints on forms of malfeasance that are enshrined in the history and best practices of those professions.

DOI: 10.4324/9781003273912-1

The gist of much of this book is that military technologies (from weapons, communications, logistics, and surveillance/reconnaissance to human enhancement) that seemed exotic and futuristic even a few years ago have rapidly become commonplace. The proliferation of such exotic innovations in warfare has proceeded apace. Lethal weapons systems (LAWS), for example, have become ever more precise, sophisticated, autonomous, intelligent, affordable, and unfortunately available to an ever-widening array of combatants (both legitimate and illegitimate) throughout the world.[1] This leads many experts in military technology and international relations to conclude that access to the means of warfare, and accordingly, the resort to lethal force as a means of conflict resolution, will continue to increase.

We therefore begin our summative evaluation with an overview of recent transformations in international conflict principally since the turn of the twenty-first century, including increasing reliance upon remotely piloted or increasingly autonomous weapons systems (AWS) and cyberattacks (state-sponsored hacktivism) that are fundamentally changing the way nations and allies approach the use of hard and soft power in international relations. These emerging military technologies challenge (and in extreme cases threaten to obviate altogether) conventional moral and legal thinking, ranging from the application of classical just war theory (JWT) to the perceived limitations of current international humanitarian law. Such widespread anxieties have in turn prompted profound concern and spirited multilateral discussions of possible revisions in the understanding and application of specific norms and principles enshrined in both that might prove necessary to address the perceived deficiencies in each.

A principal objective of this book, accordingly, is to examine what has been done, what is being proposed, and the prospects for new international agreements or other forms of governance to address these concerns. I propose specifically to examine some possible alternatives to formal agreement and legislation that might prove more feasible to pursue.

Intelligence and Autonomy in (War) Machines

Colleagues drawn from NATO and the European Union (EU) called to work on these various problems at the Peace Research Institute in Oslo (with whom I have specifically collaborated on writing this book) collectively designate the objects of our concern as war machines. The title of their research project is "Warring with Machines," although I think a more accurate and descriptive title would be something awkward but somewhat more accurate: legal and ethical issues *arising in the use of artificial intelligence* to enhance the range and performance of war machines. *Machines* itself is somewhat archaic as a description of weapons systems (like drones or robot swarms) or complex operational systems (like command-and-control centers, networked computers, global positioning satellites, or strategic planning centers). But that is the general idea.

College students and the wider public also number among the audience for this book. Without wanting to seem in the least condescending, therefore, I suggest we begin with a simple example into which we can then gradually introduce relevant technological complexities. This is a common gambit for problem analysis in my own discipline of analytic philosophy (dating at least back to the mathematician Descartes). This strategy should help us to both identify and address the resulting moral and legal issues, and it should also show how even the most technically advanced subject matter experts can inadvertently fall into disagreement and confusion regarding the most fundamental concepts in this important discussion. Ludwig Wittgenstein termed this the "bewitchment" of language, and he believed it to be an almost universal affliction that lay at the heart of most of our most urgent and seemingly intractable conceptual conundrums, certainly to include the dilemmas we examine in this book.

Like a surprisingly large percentage of the global population at present, I own a Roomba. Mine is an early model of the robot carpet sweeper first introduced by iRobot in Massachusetts over a decade ago. My wife and I love it very much. We have named it Alfred, after Batman's (Bruce Wayne's) butler. "Don't you worry, sir! I'll just tiddle up a bit in here and be on my way. I'm sorry, madam. The Batman is unavailable. You will have to make do with me!"

My Roomba is autonomous, *in a machine sense* (although *not*, as we shall learn, in a moral or legal sense). Importantly, my early model is *not intelligent*, even in a machine sense. We will clarify these distinctions in a moment.

Alfred is autonomous in that it can perform its assigned task largely on its own, without continuous human oversight or supervision. But it is entirely restricted to performing *one general kind* of activity, namely vacuuming a floor. It was not programmed to perform any additional, similar tasks (such as washing or waxing the floor, let alone blowing leaves off the front porch). It does not have the physical capacities or onboard equipment for these additional (albeit similar) kinds of tasks. It would have likely proved prohibitively expensive to design and build this particular household device in such a manner. Hence, there was no call to design more generalized algorithms or install more complex software to handle additional tasks of this sort. Instead, we simply design additional, similar machines to perform one or two of these similar additional tasks at a similar price.

But that was a design choice, driven largely by some engineer's intention: in this instance, to design a commercial robotic device that would be able to perform a well-defined, repetitive household chore with a degree of efficiency and satisfaction roughly equivalent to a human agent, at a price within range of the average middle-class household. It is especially noteworthy that Alfred can substitute his efforts in place of mine to clean the living room carpet. *But he does not go about it at all as I would*. I start at one end of the room and more or less work systematically toward the other end. Alfred travels in straight lines, until he bounces off furniture, changes direction, sometimes spins in circles. In this manner, he ends up crisscrossing his assigned accessible vacuum area seemingly at random. But in the end, he can vacuum a room in about the same time it would take for me to do it and do about as good a job. (We both miss spots, occasionally.)

This principle of machine behavior is important to bear in mind when discussing varying definitions and concepts of machine intelligence and autonomy. Machines can perform some of the same tasks that human agents perform. *But they do not always go about them in the same way.* Throughout this book this will be the case, whether we are describing the machine as acting or thinking (learning, innovating, and reasoning).

Returning to our example, Alfred can perform remarkable feats within the narrowly prescribed boundaries of his design framework. He can redirect his activity to avoid obstacles in his path and he can even sense stair steps or ledges over which he might fall and avoid those as well. He can be set like an alarm clock to vacuum his designated floor space periodically and return to his charging station while I am away at work. According to his manufacturers, he even can learn or familiarize himself with his customary environment when deployed repeatedly over several times within the same workspace. That is to say, he can *optimize* his efficiency (to a very limited degree) and thereby reduce the runtime required for him to clean my carpet.

Unlike Batman himself, however, Alfred cannot overcome every obstacle or respond to every random new challenge he encounters. If he swallows a stray sock or gobbles up a random pair of wired smartphone earbuds accidentally dropped behind a desk, his controlling software will pause or shut down his operation to avoid damaging his hardware and he will emit a mournful signal to indicate he is stuck and requires human intervention. Because he sometimes requires human oversight or operational intervention in certain circumstances, we would be more accurate in describing his operation as semiautonomous, in that a human being is deliberately included in principle on (but not necessarily in) the machine's normal operational cycle. This is often referred to (in a politically incorrect fashion) as having a man on the loop.

What about *agency*? Alfred is certainly an agent, in a limited sense. If I come home and wonder who vacuumed the carpet, for example, it is perfectly reasonable to say that Alfred did it. My wife gives him a lot of credit: "Honey, I love you, but I think I love Alfred even more! There is nothing like a man with a vacuum." She ignores my snarky reply under my breath, "how about a man who *is* a vacuum!!" The tables change, however, if I also notice that a small vase on the coffee table has been knocked over. It is perfectly reasonable to conclude that Alfred did that as well. This surmise is not beyond reasonable doubt. It could be instead that a large truck rumbled by the house and caused the table to shake. I observe Alfred's pattern of tracks on the carpet, however, and notice one path led him to bump into the coffee table at full tilt and change direction. This more than likely *caused* the vase to fall over.

Even with so simple an example and owing in part to the human propensity to use metaphorical or anthropomorphic language to describe and order our physical environment, it is extraordinary how quickly we can get confused and wrapped around the axle (or bewitched) in sorting out the factual from the fanciful. Strictly speaking, it is nonsensical for my wife to praise the robot for his (its) good work.

(Of course, it is not the least inappropriate for me to blame him (it) for knocking over the vase!) These attributions are merely an amusing sort of anthropomorphism that human beings engage in virtually all the time, attributing human traits like *purpose* and *intentionality* to their machines. Consider how often readers of this book plead with their cars not to run out of fuel before reaching the next gas station or charging station or kick and curse the inanimate dysfunctional drink machine that accepts their payment but jams when attempting to dispense the selected beverage. This routine boilerplate for comedians is all harmless, perhaps even psychologically comforting, so long as we don't allow ourselves to become too taken in or confused by it.

Should such confusion begin to set in, colleagues in law and philosophy will come to our rescue, both linguistically and conceptually (which is likely why the rest of us tolerate having them around). They will perhaps chuckle in patronizing amusement at our anthropomorphisms. They will go on to describe the robot in these instances as an agent of a very specific kind: his behavior has brought about, or *caused*, the carpet to be cleaned and the vase to be knocked over. The nature of his agency is extremely limited: *purely causal* (cause and effect). We would accurately ascribe the cause (or, more precisely, *proximate* cause, lest we forget the contributions of builder, designer, and programmer) of these events or states of affairs to the robot: it brought them about.

But importantly, we would not praise the robot for its work. After all, it could not do otherwise than that for which it was designed and programmed. It could do only an unsatisfactory job of its task if its design were flawed in certain respects, or if some of its components were wearing out or otherwise failing to function properly. Likewise (and perhaps more importantly for our deliberations regarding war machines in this book), we could not blame or otherwise hold the robot legally or morally *culpable* for knocking over the vase. Likewise, it would be absurd to prescribe punishment or demand restitution from Alfred if the vase were damaged. If restitution were required (and merited), we would seek redress from the manufacturer (presumably for flaws or weaknesses in design or performance). Thus, while a robot can be a *causal* agent, it cannot be meaningfully said to be a *legal or moral* agent, *even though it is autonomous* (i.e., able to act on its own, without immediate or continual supervision).

From this admittedly frivolous example, accordingly, we learn that the term *robot* (originally derived from a Czech word denoting a servant or slave) designates a machine that can perform one or more specific tasks under its own power, so that it can substitute its efforts for those of a human agent in performing the task(s) in question. The robot can thus *relieve* a human of the performance of the task, as when robots fill in for factory workers on an assembly line – but the robot might not necessarily *replace* the human agent entirely (who may be reassigned to oversee the robot's performance, or even operate or control the robot at a distance).

The advantage of the latter arrangement is something that, in military settings, is termed *force multiplication* – reconfiguring or supplementing a customary arrangement of agents to derive greater scope or efficiency of activity. Adding robots into the factory workforce mix relieves humans of monotonous, repetitive, laborious, and sometimes even dangerous work without the disadvantage of getting tired or bored, or otherwise failing to maintain their focus on their primary tasks, thereby increasing production efficiency and/or lowering the costs of production. An *autonomous* robot in principle can accomplish the same task or tasks without constant, immediate, or ongoing human control. The human operator of a *semiautonomous* robot (as in the factory), however, will retain the ability to monitor, supervise, and occasionally intervene in the robot's functioning. As we noted earlier, that provision is sometimes referred to as retaining a "man on the loop." Most present-day industrial and manufacturing systems that are automated and employ robots retain some degree of this level of control. By way of contrast, a *remotely operated* system (such as a hobbyist's or firefighter's observational drone) requires a human operator to constantly control (as well as oversee) the safe and proper operation of this aerial robotic device, which therefore is said to require a man *in* the loop.

A *fully autonomous* robot does not require such constant supervision or routine intervention but can carry out its assigned range of tasks on its own. A human operator or operators may still *observe* that operation and may retain the ability to intervene in the ongoing performance of the robot or system of robots, but such observation is *not entirely necessary or integral* to the functioning or performance of the robot itself. Once set in motion or launched (so to speak), the robot can, in principle, carry out its tasks or fulfill its designated mission without future intervention by human operators. Importantly, however, *machine autonomy does not encompass an ability to modify or change the task or mission*: that is, the robot cannot decide suddenly to go on strike or stop operating in quest of better working conditions. It (or they) likewise cannot decide to stop vacuuming the carpet, or manufacturing automobiles, and turn instead to providing me with home surveillance and security, let alone start manufacturing planes or tanks. Such a change in function and mission would require redesigning, retooling, and reprogramming the machine, at minimum. The autonomous robot, that is to say, is not (or need not be) intelligent in any normal use of that term or concept. Instead, these are among the characteristics of intelligent human autonomy, or moral autonomy, which few engineers or artificial intelligence (AI) researchers knowingly seek to emulate in machine behavior (even if there is occasionally some confusion on this point).

As we move robots gradually from homes and factories into military operations, including combat, we can see some distinct advantages to be gained from the use or integration of such machines. Many concerned critics of military operations, likewise, will notice some important gaps or weaknesses or potential pitfalls in this arrangement, especially when the machines become more numerous, or more autonomous, let alone if they should be afforded some kind of *machine intelligence* that would encompass the capacities to reason, deliberate, learn on the job, or even abandon that job to take up new and unrelated tasks.

Autonomy itself comes in degrees: from remote human control (as in early Predator drones, initially designated remotely piloted vehicles (RPVs) or uncrewed/uninhabited aerial vehicles (UAVs)), to semiautonomous operation for such systems (eliminating the human operator *in* the loop, while retaining supervisory control *on* the loop), to fully autonomous systems (launch and forget, as military personnel might say). One might argue that cruise missiles and precision-guided torpedoes are examples of the latter, but that is not strictly the case. Their targets have been preselected, and their mission (which they cannot modify by themselves) has likewise been thoroughly prescribed in advance. They may (as a built-in precaution) be enabled to abort their mission and return to their launch site (or self-destruct) if onboard sensors determine there is something wrong or out of place in the battlespace. But they cannot decide that their submarine captain or battalion commander is a sonnuvah bitch and frag him or her (shoot to kill), as an angry or frustrated human combatant might. They are therefore lethally armed autonomous weapons systems (LAWS), but importantly, not *fully* autonomous (at least in the sense feared), and neither are they intelligent (although possessing sophisticated, environmentally sensitive operating and control systems, including programs that might improve or optimize their performance or protect innocents from inadvertent harm).

These are among the factors that lead us to dismiss the autonomous lethal weapon itself from any liability if it should nonetheless strike a hospital or a nursing home. It is individual human members of the operational structure or chain of command who, without confusion, are held responsible for these results. If the cause of the tragedy is random or accidental, then blame is affixed, and restitution must be made to the victims (and some kind of penalty for incompetence or malfeasance may be levied). If the cause instead stems from operator errors, then an inquiry must be made and blame affixed based upon whether the use of the weapon was intentional or unintentional and whether the operational error stemmed from mechanical malfunction, careless or negligent use or operation, or instead from deliberate and malevolent intent resulting in illegal military actions. The last is what determines the tragedy to have been a war crime.

Acronyms are rapidly proliferating, and there are already conceptual difficulties inherent in this elementary account. As the last examples illustrate, even more difficulties are introduced when the autonomous systems are lethally armed killer robots, in contrast to those with missions like ISR (intelligence-gathering, surveillance, or reconnaissance). Once again, however, note that in none of the descriptions offered earlier is anything said about intelligence. None of the robots or automated systems thus far described (whether a human is in, on, or outside the control loop) is intelligent. None of these systems, under the foregoing descriptions, has been augmented or enhanced in their performance or abilities with artificial intelligence. None are involved in making choices or decisions (in the customary understanding of such terms), nor do they have the capability to alter or change their designated tasks or abort their mission altogether on their own. At the very most, such options are alternatives on a predetermined and programmed flow chart or decision tree governing responses by the system to their prevailing operating environment.

It is somewhere around this juncture that discussions of these machine capabilities, especially among individuals from different disciplines, professions, or operational environments, can go quickly off the rails (bewitchment again). So once more: is a cruise missile a fully autonomous robot under this description? How about that precision-guided torpedo? Some military personnel specializing in mine warfare even argue that mines (especially so-called smart mines) are autonomous robots under this account (raising the question of whether a system must also include capacity for locomotion or movement to qualify as a robot). Numerous intriguing and even amusing conundrums like this are recounted by one of the pioneers in the field: Peter Warren Singer, in his pathbreaking book, *Wired for War* (2009). And we have not even begun to explore the supposed ethical and legal issues that might be generated in the development and use of such systems.

Outline of the Presentation

I propose to undertake the latter task in a series of steps in the following chapters. The first and second chapters focus largely upon the extensive (and thus far fruitless) debate since the turn of the twenty-first century on remotely piloted and semiautonomous robotic weapons systems, examining the prospects for marrying capacities for increased *machine autonomy* with lethal armaments for defensive purposes. In these chapters, I focus on engineering design and use of autonomous systems, examining the reliability, safety, and proliferation of several remotely operated systems that have been deployed during this period. I will examine the moral concerns, as well as the status of ongoing discussions and negotiations in international law, attending these technological innovations. Apart from an occasional allusion to the more recent controversies over the use of artificial intelligence to augment the capacities of automated systems, I deliberately defer the AI controversy to later chapters.

In response to the dilemmas of adequate governance and arms control these innovations confront us with, I then revise a proposal that I originally put forward in a law review article in 2014[2] to direct efforts aimed at reform in governance more directly toward encouraging voluntary compliance within the professional engineering communities involved in LAWS research and development. This very specific and concrete code of ethical precepts (defining both prohibited practices and standards of best practice) would serve to govern responsible research, development, and military use of autonomous systems, including those that might be lethally armed. Specific precepts in this professional code of conduct are aimed at encouraging greater attention to *due care* and warning against *reckless endangerment* and possibly even *de facto* criminal *negligence* in calculating the likelihood of unintended uses and harms of their research products. By and large, this code is voluntary, although I proposed that it be imposed as a requirement in the process of awarding research funding and government defense contracting, as a condition of strict liability for awarding any future weapons grants and contracts. It could be suitably refined and enacted more or less immediately by engineers, defense industries, and military end users, in contrast to the present years-long debate within the United Nations Convention on Certain Conventional Weapons (CCW) over outlawing all development and use of lethal autonomous weapons systems. I conclude by describing how many of these precepts have since been adapted by several engineering professional organizations either as good practices or as criteria for qualifying specific private defense industries for recognition and awards for achieving excellence in practice.[3]

Chapter 4, When Robots Rule the Waves, introduces a far less familiar extension of this discussion, moving from land-based to maritime conflict. Based upon a report originally undertaken in 2015 with my colleague at Monash University, Robert Sparrow, for the United Nations Agency for Disarmament Research (UNADIR), this chapter discusses a wide range of maritime and submersible robotics systems, many of which remained largely unfamiliar to both critics of military technology and the wider public (including delegates to the CCW) until quite recently. Even though such systems are far less discussed and studied than, for example, unpiloted aerial systems (drones) and ground-based systems, remotely operated maritime systems are actually far more numerous and far more likely to be used routinely in the near future, especially in any emergent conflicts with China. This chapter will explain why that is.

Chapters 5 and 6 take up the recent and contentious AI controversy, describing the increasing extent to which advanced, sophisticated forms of AI are being integrated within the designs of weapons and systems (including cybersecurity systems) to enhance their performance capabilities. Chapter 5 examines the impact of AI augmentation on military robotics and military strategy primarily in conventional military operations. Chapter 6 zeros in on the increasing reliance of AI in both defensive and offensive cyber conflict. These are the main focus of the Peace Research Institute in Oslo (PRIO) project described as the inspiration for this book and represents a summary of the initial results of that collaboration.

Chinese (PRC) President Xi Jinping, for example, predicted ominously in 2018 that the nation that first masters the full development and applications of AI will eventually lead the world in industrial and technological development, as well as in the worldwide projection of military power. But at what costs, and with what attendant risks to privacy, security, personal freedom, and social welfare will such mastery be realized? Innovations and enhancements from this sector pose risks from negligent or wholly unintentional consequences arising from the increased use of AI in everything from commercial and military robotics and enhanced cybersecurity to vastly upgraded capacities for strategic and economic planning. This chapter accordingly introduces and explains different forms of AI and their current and proposed uses, including both modular (narrow) and general (strong) AI (and recent proposals for limiting their uses to so-called responsible or explainable AI), principally in developing wholly autonomous weapons systems and proactive cyber defenses, exploring ethical dilemmas and requisite legal reforms likely to arise in these applications.

From the relatively familiar domains of armed conflict on land, as well as in the sea and air, we then pivot to prospects for governance in the so-called fifth domain of conflict in cyberspace. Rather than inquiring further into warfare *per se*, Chapters 7 and 8 pose the question of whether peace and stability will ever prove feasible in the cyber domain. I trace the vector of norms of responsible state behavior (originally tracked from Estonia to Stuxnet in 2015)[4] to recent cyber operations like SolarWinds, WannaCry, NotPetya, Cozy Bear and Holiday Bear, with particular focus on the attack on Israel's water desalination and purification systems allegedly undertaken by Iranian cyber operators in late 2019. The even more recent ransomware attacks by Russian-based criminal organizations against Colonial Pipeline and JB Meats are also among the cases considered.

Tragically, this work requires updates literally by the hour as this book goes to press in the midst of the Russian military invasion of Ukraine, which was preceded by some of these aforementioned massive cyberattacks. Although the Ukrainian all-volunteer IT Army is proving capable of giving at least as good as they get when warding off Russian-based cyber intrusions, these developments overall suggest a regrettable degradation or devolution in what otherwise and earlier seemed the moderately hopeful evolution of behavior among cyber adversaries toward greater target and victim discrimination and toward an emerging principle of proportionality that appeared to have guided adversaries away from destructive and indiscriminate physical effects-based tactics in cyber conflict of the sort that threatened the public a decade ago. The new episodes erode that hope and display once again a willingness to attack any target and inflict a degree of suffering and harm altogether incommensurate to any specific goals motivating the attack.

All this leads in Chapter 8 to pose the question of whether peace of some form is even possible in the cyber domain. Yet – in an intriguing echo of philosopher Immanuel Kant's celebrated "race of devils" – even the criminal organizations involved in the Colonial Pipeline attacks subsequently suggested that their own activities might well have crossed a line of proportionality and that in the future, a norm should be followed that would place off-limits any further ransomware attacks on hospitals and medical facilities. Where do we stand, what may we hope for, and what needs to be done specifically to move us toward that elusive goal?

Chapter 9 then examines whether forms of cyber surveillance (generally classified as unprovoked intrusions), as well as active defense tactics like hacking back, might in some instances qualify as legitimate forms of preventive self-defense. These complex subjects initially require a short review of the highly controversial topic of preventive self-defense, initially raised at the beginning of the present century regarding forms of conventional and hybrid warfare (such as the Iraq war) ostensibly intended to deter terrorist operations or topple hostile regimes supportive of terrorism. My purpose in this chapter is subsequently to inquire whether big data analysis and surveillance in the grey zone between low-intensity conflict (e.g., espionage) and genuine warfare might now properly be seen as this sort of activity rather than merely as an effort at domestic espionage or political oppression of its own citizens by powerful governments. The key to legal permissibility and moral justification of such preventive activities lies in the intent, and even responsibility, to *protect* rather than surveil on the part of agencies like the U.S. National Security Agency (NSA).

I recognize that this is a provocative and contentious proposal. The distinction between political oppression and public protection, and the ultimate moral justification for the latter policy, I argue, depends further upon obtaining the *informed consent* of those protected through a greater degree of program transparency, accountability, and adversarial review and oversight than has heretofore been customary among intelligence agencies. This chapter recognizes the gravity of the cyberattacks detailed in the previous chapters as themselves warranting a robust and vigorously proactive policy of self-defense against them. This continues and develops my earlier position in defense of government signal intelligence agencies against the still-unsubstantiated charges of Edward Snowden in 2013, who failed to recognize the distinction between these very different kinds of activities and charged (mistakenly, I believe) that the pursuit of such a policy *necessarily* results in massive and unwarranted surveillance by government agencies of private citizens utterly without their knowledge or consent. Whatever a gullible, hysterical, and conspiracy-prone public is willing to believe, there is, I conclude, an enormous difference between surveillance conducted by the *Stasi* in East Germany (or by domestic security officials in the PRC or the Russian Federation at present) and the efforts aimed at public security undertaken by NSA and the U.S. Cyber Command.[5] It is vital to acknowledge these differences so as to establish appropriate (rather than hysterical or misguided) constraints and oversight for the latter, legitimate kinds of security activities.

Every single development or advancement covered in each of the preceding chapters requires the concerted effort of scientists and engineers (including aerospace and biomedical engineers) working in the defense sector. The innovations we have examined, for good or ill, are impossible without the willing participation of such experts, whether working directly for national governments, their militaries, or private defense contractors. *Are there relevant legal boundaries, or guiding ethical precepts, for responsible and humane technological innovation?* These are questions I have been repeatedly asked since the turn of the twenty-first century by such individuals, as well as by students (especially at military academies) preparing for careers in defense engineering and military operations. The questions betray a healthy shared anxiety among many of these individuals who genuinely desire to assure themselves that their chosen activities are morally justifiable and specifically do not violate the extant provisions of international law or otherwise represent reckless or irresponsibly risky behavior.

My concluding chapter begins with a project site visit with the CEO and chief engineers of a major international weapons manufacturer that manufactures everything from ordnance for the F-35 to shoulder-fired recoilless anti-tank weapons for the Ukrainian Army. Those discussions reveal the depth of ethical literacy and insight among defense engineers anxious about introducing AI and increasing autonomy into their weapons systems and frustrated by the lack of moral clarity and guidance currently available to them in international law. This permits us to revisit my own earlier analysis of these problems and presents a summary of my own findings, accompanied by comprehensive overview of the moral norms embodied within IHL and LOAC. Taken together, we use these findings to review voluntary compliance or "soft-law" provisions to revise the understanding and applicability of these moral and legal norms to meet the novel challenges posed for both by the foregoing exotic and disruptive contemporary situations of armed conflict and its physical and political effects-based equivalents.

The included appendix consists of the transcript of testimony presented by the author to a select *ad hoc* committee convened by the National Academy of Sciences (USA) in response to a request from the U.S. Defense Advanced Research Projects Agency (DARPA) to evaluate the "Ethical and Societal Implications of Advances in Militarily Significant Technologies that are Rapidly Changing and Increasingly Globally Accessible." The testimony was delivered at the inaugural meeting of the committee on 31 August 2011 at the NAS Beckman Center on the campus of the University of California at Irvine.

Notes

1 See, for example, Paul Scharre, *An Army of None: Autonomous Weapons and the Future of War* (New York: Norton & Co., 2018); Audrey Kurth Cronin, *Power to the People: How Open Technological Innovation Is Arming Tomorrow's Terrorists* (New York: Oxford University Press, 2019).
2 George R. Lucas, Jr., "Automated Warfare," *Stanford Law and Policy Review* 25 (2) (2014): 317–339.
3 See the current recommendations for achieving "B Corporation" certification for best practices in defense-sector engineering: "As for-profit companies that meet the most rigorous standards of overall social and environmental performance, accountability, and transparency, Certified B Corporations are leaders in the movement to use business as a force for good." My legal and ethical precepts governing weapons engineering research, development, and marketing are cited in B Labs July 2020 article, "Engineering Consulting Companies with Clients in the Defense Sector," https://assets.ctfassets.net/l57 5jm7617lt/17ibvcf5c1kzYqXby67SCO/642ddb0056f6f7956f5b4256143beb48/B_ Lab_Engineering_Services_Defense_Controversial_Industry_Jul_2020.pdf [accessed 24 March 2022]. For more information on B Lab Global and B Corporation certification generally, see: www.bcorporation.net/en-us/movement/global-network.
4 See George R. Lucas, *Ethics and Cyber Warfare* (New York: Oxford University Press, 2017): 109–128.
5 George R. Lucas, "NSA Management Directive #424," *Ethics & International Affairs* 28 (1): 29–38. Peter Lee, "Ethics of Military Cyber Surveillance," in *Cyber Warfare Ethics*, eds. Michael Skerker and David Whetham (Hampshire, UK: Howgate Publishing Ltd., 2022): 110–128.

References

Cronin, Audrey Kurth. *Power to the People: How Open Technological Innovation Is Arming Tomorrow's Terrorists* (New York: Oxford University Press, 2019).

Lee, Peter. "Ethics of Military Cyber Surveillance," in *Cyber Warfare Ethics*, eds. Michael Skerker and David Whetham (Hampshire, UK: Howgate Publishing Ltd., 2022): 110–128.

Lucas, George R. Jr. "Automated Warfare," *Stanford Law and Policy Review* 25 (2) (2014): 317–339.

Lucas, George R. Jr. "NSA Management Directive #424," *Ethics & International Affairs* 28 (1) (2014): 29–38.

Lucas, George R. Jr. *Ethics and Cyber Warfare* (New York: Oxford University Press, 2017): 109–128.

Lucas, George R. Jr. "Engineering Consulting Companies With Clients in the Defense Sector," https://assets.ctfassets.net/l575jm7617lt/17ibvcf5c1kzYqXby67SCO/642ddb0056f6f7956f5b4256143beb48/B_Lab_Engineering_Services_Defense_Controversial_Industry_Jul_2020.pdf [accessed 24 March 2022]. For more information on B Lab Global and B Corporation certification generally, see: www.bcorporation.net/en-us/movement/global-network.

Scharre, Paul. *Army of None: Autonomous Weapons and the Future of War* (New York: Norton & Co., 2018).

Singer, Peter Warren. *Wired for War* (New York: Penguin, 2009).

1

POSTMODERN WARFARE

This examination is conducted against a wider background that Italian novelist and semiotician Umberto Eco described (during the first Gulf War in Kuwait) as "postmodern warfare."[1] In my own conception, "postmodern warfare" encompasses a wide range of novel and unanticipated developments in the evolution of combat and armed conflict: initially, it referred to the rise to prominence of so-called irregular warfare, asymmetric and riskless war, fourth-generation war, and hybrid or unconventional war (including humanitarian interventions, counterinsurgency, and peace-keeping and stability operations, such as the recently abandoned Afghanistan campaign). Other, more recent terms or acronyms for this evolution include the U.S. Department of Defense's "third offset" (referring primarily to technological and tactical innovations) and "grey-zone" warfare (a generic covering term for all the varieties of anomalous low-intensity conflict that do not quite rise to the level of conventional kinetic war). These terms sometimes overlap or supplant earlier terminology. All are meant to include the changing character of warfare, including increasing reliance on

- *robotics* and remotely operated aerial and ground vehicles, to which I will add attention in this book to autonomous maritime *vessels* and *weapons* systems, all of which categories include autonomous (AWS) and lethally armed autonomous weapons systems (LAWS);
- nanotechnology, genetic engineering, and other biological and psychological means to *augment the capabilities* of human combatants (*warrior enhancement*);
- advances in *artificial intelligence* for the management and ever-more-autonomous operation of all such systems; and, of course,
- cyber weapons, *cyber conflict* (including the exponential growth of capabilities in cyber espionage), and the consequent need for improved cybersecurity.

DOI: 10.4324/9781003273912-2

This list is hardly exhaustive, but it includes several of the topics treated specifically in this book. The difficult feature in attempting to identify, classify, and evaluate the ever-expanding military uses of these technologies is that the technologies themselves continue to evolve and proliferate rapidly while the terminology and acronyms used by defense analysts to keep track of these various evolutions and transformations in tactics and strategy are in a state of constant flux. In addition, they are not neatly bounded or categorized, but spill over into one another in mutually enhancing fashion. Cyber operations pervade all other four domains of warfare: air, space, land, and maritime. So do developments in artificial intelligence (AI), affording all sorts of innovations and improvements of scale and performance of objects and operations in all five domains of conflict.

Alternatively, we could approach the concept of postmodern war by attempting to assess the evolution of military technology in terms that critics, especially, frequently describe as its *dehumanizing, devalorizing, and deskilling* effects on human combatants.[2] The growing dependency of human beings on their technological creations unquestionably ends up making *greater use* of *fewer* humans in the battlespace, dramatically altering the force mix of weapons systems and human combatants that we do ultimately use.

In this vein, we should attend to what we might call the *ontological* as well as the ethical dimensions of all these innovations, that is, the ways these technologies effectively transform the material and physical characteristics of human beings engaging in combat.[3] They do so, for example, by reducing fatigue and obviating the need for sleep, mediating fear and enhancing courage, not to mention imparting immediate language competency or enabling various physical enhancements (strength, resilience) through promising brain implants.[4] Certainly, from the standpoint of ethics, we are entitled to wonder whether such ontological transformations of combatants are necessarily or unqualifiedly an improvement for those individual combatants, let alone for the militaries and societies of which they remain a vital part.

We might also examine the increasing reliance on additional, nonmilitary personnel in the battlespace: for example, private military and security contractors, civilian engineers from the defense industries (used as on-site consultants in the proper use and maintenance of their weapons systems), or the programs begun in Iraq and Afghanistan to embed anthropologists and other social scientists within brigade combat and reconstruction teams to provide the cultural and regional knowledge needed to successfully navigate the "human terrain" (presumably while our robotic creations handle the geographical terrain).

Robots and remotely operated air vehicles, riskless war, and (somewhat ironically) the increased reliance upon academics and scholars providing cultural knowledge and insight into the human terrain, alongside the geographical terrain, are all part of this emerging picture. The first Gulf War made increasing use of air power, precision-guided munitions, computer-coordination, and real-time aerial surveillance and battlefield intelligence (net-centric warfare). These transformations in tactics allowed the U.S.-led United Nations coalition forces to demolish their opponent's enormous conventional battlefield capabilities in a relatively short time and with minimal friendly force or noncombatant casualties. That unanticipated, massive combat success marked a first phase in this overall technological evolution that we have termed postmodern warfare. It led, in turn, to the subsequent preponderance of irregular, asymmetric, and hybrid warfare during the ensuing two decades because, in essence, never again would an adversary directly attempt to engage the conventional might of the United States and its allies, as Saddam Hussein had dared to do.

The First Gulf War also inaugurated a dramatic increase in the use of private military contractors (PMCs) as yet another feature of contemporary irregular warfare. Peter W. Singer wrote his first blockbuster book on this phenomenon of corporate warriors.[5] Their use in allied warfare ever since turned out to be troubling for the same reasons that a greater recent reliance on robotics is problematic: both of these developments invoke the *threshold problem*, the *accountability problem*, and the *discrimination/proportionality problem*. All three of these, in turn, contribute to desensitizing the wider public to the true costs of war. That is,

- the reliance on either or both kinds of combatants threaten to make the resort to armed conflict easier (lower the *threshold*) from a domestic political point of view;
- it is difficult to hold either kind of entity fully or meaningfully *accountable* under existing legal regimes for the injury or death they may inflict; and
- in the view of critics of these developments, neither human contractors nor lethally armed machines can necessarily be relied upon to exercise *restraint* in their use of force or *discriminate* between enemy combatants and noncombatants caught in the crossfire.[6]

To be sure, all technology ultimately has this effect of making human beings of all sorts ever more reliant on their creations – a principle of which we are reminded every time the Internet goes down or our mobile phone battery dies.

At the same time, however, we must attempt to remain cautious about overdramatizing the nature and scope of this technological transformation and dependence. Futurists and defense engineers sometimes seem to enjoy hyperinflating their largely undocumented claims regarding the future of technology, while opponents, fearful of these developments, often exaggerate the risk. We can at least sort out these competing anxieties a bit by contrasting the changing historical and technological impact of weapons *on the warfighter himself* over millennia (from catapult and crossbow, say, to machine guns and aerial war), as distinguished from the different impact of military technologies at present that promise instead to *replace* the warfighter altogether. That, in turn, contributes to the aforementioned devalorizing of war, or perhaps to the casual ease with which we engage in it. This kind of *moral distancing* or numbing of humane sensibilities concerning the serious and inevitably tragic dimensions of warfare is additional feature of postmodern war, first described by Canadian journalist Michael Ignatieff following the Kosovo air war.[7]

Such features of postmodern war are perhaps nowhere better illustrated than in the prospects for cyber war. In the space of the past two decades we have moved, incredibly, from an almost exclusive focus on cyber*crime* and individual cyber *vandalism* (in which we or our immediate family and friends might be victimized in a limited but personally painful fashion), through apathy and ignorance about the larger, systemic warfare prospects and finally to a concern approaching acute (even hysterical) anxiety about the increasingly destructive prospects for cyber warfare and cyberterrorism.[8] Here it is useful to draw some interesting *parallels*, as well as make some unique *distinctions*, between the ethical and legal questions raised by cyber war, as compared to those attending these other military technologies. First, the thread of concern running through all of these discussions has been the threshold question: will the technology in question, including resort to cyber war in this case, lower the threshold for resorting to war of any sort, traditionally consigned to being the last (rather than the earliest) resort to conflict resolution with adversaries or competitors? Any technology, weapon, or tactic that makes it inherently easier to resort to destructive uses of force to resolve disputes automatically constitutes a ground for concern on this criterion. Using robots cuts down on human casualties and costs (at least for the side that employs them); cyber war is "virtual" war, and more like a game than reality, at least until your own financial or civil infrastructure is shut down. In both instances, therefore, we might more readily resort to war using these technologies when we should instead refrain. Second, we must confront the question that moral philosophers call *jus in bello* (morally permissible conduct during armed conflict) and that lawyers term the "law of armed conflict" (LOAC). Will the technology in question present increased risks of harm to civilians or otherwise threaten disproportionate destruction and collateral damage (unintended harm to themselves or their property and civil institutions) in war? Is the very development of the technology itself a violation of international humanitarian law?

With lethally armed autonomous robots (LAWS), for example, the initial concern was with what Robert Sparrow termed "an accountability gap," consisting of a potential lack of meaningful accountability for the actions and errors inevitably accompanying ever-greater reliance on such weapons systems.[9] Strictly speaking, one is prohibited under existing international law from proposing or developing any weapons system for whose use (or misuse) military personnel cannot be held meaningfully accountable under the laws of armed conflict.

With cyber warfare, the principal LOAC concern has been slightly different in focusing primarily on the indiscriminate nature of cyber weapons and tactics that are sometimes proposed. Computer scientist and cyber weapons design expert Professor Neil Rowe, of the U.S. Naval Postgraduate School (Monterey, Calif.), for example, has published several papers raising an alarm that the weapons and tactics frequently envisioned in a cyber war are aimed at civilians, and their use would likely cause widespread destruction of lives and property and would otherwise inflict surprisingly massive and terrible suffering among the civilian population of the target state.[10]

Such cyber strategy is inherently a violation of LOAC. As the moral philosopher and cyber expert Randall Dipert (University of Buffalo) also observed, no intentional targeting of civilians or civilian infrastructure is permissible under international law (*distinction*, or the principle of discrimination), and in targeting legitimate military or dual-use targets, *due care* is required to be taken to avoid collateral damage to such persons and property (the doctrine of double effect). Moreover, any such collateral damage that inadvertently occurs must be found *proportional* to the strategic importance of the overall target.[11]

Bearing in mind that we are never told how exactly to perform this rather amazing calculus, it remains the case that Prof. Rowe's objections seem to have validity, in that purposive targeting of civilians, civilian property (e.g., bank and investment accounts), or infrastructure (e.g., electrical power grids, hydroelectric dams, or water purification and supply facilities) is a common feature (though by no means an exclusive focus) of the tactics of cyber warfare. This, in turn, raises a couple of interesting points that tend in different analytical directions.

First, roboticists are part of the overall defense industry research and development (R&D) structure that reports finally to the military, delivering hard platforms and kinetic weapons, even when these are governed by computers and software. The operational or combat commands are the customers, and those customers think instinctively like warriors: their job (as they sometimes quip) is to "kill people and break things" until ordered to cease, but they operate within known constraints of the law regarding whom to kill and what to break and when to stop.

By contrast, cyber warfare experts deal almost exclusively in software: their weapons are virtual rather than kinetic (although some can be made to do substantial physical damage in the real world). Theft of data, denial of access, and, most of all, deception and psych-ops to sow confusion and demoralization – all these are *tools of the intelligence community rather than the combat warrior.* By custom and conventional practice, intelligence gathering, espionage, and even covert operations are not bound so rigidly or governed or constrained strictly by LOAC (since these low-intensity conflicts do not constitute armed conflict under the law). In any case, targeting civilians for information, for access to data, or to sow confusion or cause deception is simply standard practice. This difference in the moral and legal background assumptions of the two distinct communities helps, I think, account for why cyber war strategists have been more ready to aim their weapons at civilian targets than have their counterparts in conventional military kinetic combat.

That brings me to the *second* observation, which goes in the opposite direction: notwithstanding the very real physical damage and genuine suffering that denial of access or theft can bring to the target victims, there is a background assumption that most of such destruction or suffering is virtual rather than real and can even be readily reversed.

Rowe, for example, acknowledges this in his analysis, and he even cautiously commends some cyber tactics as morally (and legally) superior to conventional, kinetic counterparts because the *damage is momentary, easily contained, and easily reversed*. One can, for example, restore electrical power or access to financial accounts by supplying the code or password upon resolution of the conflict far more easily than one can physically rebuild the banks, dams, or power plants destroyed in a conventional attack, as witnessed in the aftermath of NATO bombing in Kosovo, and currently in Kyiv. Thus we have a cyber counterpart to roboticist Ron Arkin's advocacy of the morality of robotic warriors, to the effect that cyberattacks could prove to be more discriminate, more proportional, and thus more in compliance with the statutes of LOAC and the moral principles of *jus in bello* than any conventional alternative.

With all this in mind, what might constitute important red flags or precautionary observations concerning cyber weapons and cyber strategy and tactics? First, when all is said and done, it appears that the most threatened targets are financial institutions and systems and commercial or industrial sabotage. Sophisticated air-gapped and software-encrypted military targets, while clearly vulnerable, require a great deal more skill and ingenuity to crack. For that reason, despite the legitimate concerns that Aegis systems, battlefield robots, or satellite "blue force" command and control are vulnerable to enemy attack, the far more likely targets are (as we have seen) Google, Facebook, Wells Fargo and Bank of America, and Pacific Gas & Electric (PG&E).

Second, despite a great deal of sustained public hysteria on this point, the threat of small-group, nonstate cyberterrorism still remains remote, largely hypothetical, and somewhat exaggerated.

We have no concrete evidence that *nonstate* cyberterrorism has even been attempted, let alone succeeded. Instead, truly damaging cyberattacks listed and updated by, for example, the Center for Strategic and International Studies[12] and sometimes classified as terrorist attacks have all in fact been carried out by nation-states while smaller attacks of the theft-and-nuisance variety were undertaken by criminals and vandals. Gabriel Weiman writes

> [I]t is important to remember one simple statistic: so far, there has been no recorded instance of a terrorist cyberattack on U.S. public facilities, transportation systems, nuclear power plants, power grids, or other key components of the national infrastructure. Cyberattacks are common, but they have not been conducted by terrorists and they have not sought to inflict the kind of damage that would qualify them as cyberterrorism.[13]

That, in turn, is because, despite our glorification of the individual teenage "hacker" and the estimates of the damage (I would call it vandalism) such an individual might wreak random havoc or even clever crime is not quite the same as massive, coordinated cyberattacks on key institutions and infrastructure, of the sorts launched in Georgia and Estonia, or more recently in Israel, Saudi Arabia, and Ukraine, for example. Computer science experts have heretofore largely maintained that the development of cyber weapons and tactics capable of such massive, coordinated strikes requires an enormous array of technical expertise and expenditure of time and resources, well beyond even the most bankrolled and coordinated nonstate group to muster.

In addition, the use of such weapons is most often a one-off affair: once deployed, the weapon or tactic is subsequently ineffective because it is quickly recognized and countered by the victims. So the R&D must be constant and ongoing. In sum, despite the advent of irregular war and diffusion of state involvement in other respects, in this area of cyber war, the principal actors are, of necessity, once again, nation-states with vast technical and financial resources.[14]

The good news is that this renders cyber war, after all, more amenable to governance. There are broad common interests among adversaries, as during the Cold War, not to be wrongly accused of having launched an attack or having cyber hostilities attributed to them, let alone directed in reprisal against them. Such common interests could lead to the recognition and banning of the most destructive and indiscriminate weapons (e.g., uncontrollable viruses whose release and spread would ultimately be in no one's interest). It might lead to adoption of treaties mandating forms of attribution to otherwise legitimate cyber weapons and tactics, so as to obviate mistaken attribution that might lead to reprisal. And it may well mean that the new era of cyber war may be more one of proliferation of virtual strategies, counterstrategies, parry-and-thrust, and security upgrades rather than full-scale destructive war.

Notes

1 Umberto Eco, "Reflections on War," *La Rivista dei libri* (1 April 1991); reprinted in Umberto Eco, *Five Moral Pieces*, trans. Alastair McEwen (New York: Harcourt, 1997): 1–17.

2 Shannon Vallor, *Technology and the Virtues* (Oxford: Oxford University Press, 2017).

3 *Ontology* (as first defined by Aristotle) is one of two branches of metaphysics that deals specifically with "Being" or existence, *per se*, along with examination of the various types of beings or "entities" that we encounter in the cosmos.

4 At the 2022 McCain Conference at the U.S. Naval Academy, DARPA and IEEE neuroscientist James Giordano (Georgetown University) offered a provocative prospective on the use of brain–computer interfaces (BCIs) in military medicine and weapons technology. See, for example, James Giordano, et al., "Redefining Neuroweapons: Emerging Capabilities in Neuroscience and Neurotechnology," *PRISM* 8 (3) (2019); "Emerging Technologies for Disruptive Effects in Non-kinetic Engagements," *HDIAC Currents* 6 (2) (2019): 49–54.

5 Peter W. Singer, *Corporate Warriors* (Ithaca, NY: Cornell University Press, 2003).

6 As in the case of Blackwater military contractors later indicted for killing Iraqi civilians in Nisour Square, Baghdad (September 2007).

7 Michael Ignatieff, *Virtual War: Kosovo and Beyond* (New York: Basic Books, 2000).

8 Richard A. Clarke and Robert K. Knake, *Cyber War: The Next Threat to National Security and What to Do About It* (New York: HarperCollins, 2010). Joel Brenner, *America the Vulnerable: Inside the New Threat Matrix of Digital Espionage, Crime, and Warfare* (New York: Penguin, 2011).

9 Robert Sparrow, "Killer Robots," *Journal of Applied Philosophy* 24 (1) (2007): 62–77.

10 Neil C. Rowe, "War Crimes From Cyber Weapons," *Journal of Information Warfare* 6 (3) (2007): 15–25. "The Ethics of Cyber War Attacks," in *Cyber War and Cyber Terrorism*,

eds. Lech J. Janczewski and Edward M. Colarik (Hershey, PA: Information Science Reference, 2008): 105–111.

11 Randall R. Dipert, "The Ethics of Cyber Warfare," *Journal of Military Ethics* 9 (4) (2010): 384–410; "Other Than Internet Warfare: Challenges for Ethics, Law and Policy," *Journal of Military Ethics* 12 (1) (2013): 34–53; "The Essential Features for an Ontology for Cyberwarfare," *Conflict and Cooperation in Cyberspace*, eds. Panayotis A. Yannakogeorgos and Adam B. Lowther (Boca Raton, FL: CRC Press/Taylor and Francis Publishers, 2013).

12 www.csis.org/programs/strategic-technologies-program/significant-cyber-incidents [accessed 12 May 2022].

13 Gabriel Weiman, "Cyberterrorism: How Real Is the Threat?" *Special Report 119: United States Institute of Peace* (December 2004): 8. This observation remains true to this day (1 June 2022).

14 For a current update, see Marina Cortés, "Cyberterrorism in the West Now," *Talking About Terrorism* (blog), 2020, www.talkingaboutterrorism.com/post/cyberterrorism-in-the-west-now [accessed 18 April 2022].

References

Brenner, Joel. *America the Vulnerable: Inside the new Threat Matrix of Digital Espionage, Crime, and Warfare* (New York: Penguin, 2011).

Center for Strategic and International Studies. "Significant Cyber Incidents," www.csis.org/programs/strategic-technologies-program/significant-cyber-incidents [accessed 17 May 2022].

Clarke, Richard A.; Knake, Robert K. *Cyber War: The Next Threat to National Security and What to Do About It* (New York: HarperCollins, 2010).

Cortés, Marina. "Cyberterrorism in the West Now," *Talking about Terrorism* (blog), 2020, www.talkingaboutterrorism.com/post/cyberterrorism-in-the-west-now [accessed 18 April 2022].

DeFranco, Joseph; DiEuliis, Diane; Bremseth, L.R.; Snow, J.J.; Giordano, James. "Emerging Technologies for Disruptive Effects in Non-kinetic Engagements," *HDIAC Currents* 6 (2) (2019): 49–54.

DeFranco, Joseph; DiEuliis, Diane; Giordano, James. "Redefining Neuroweapons: Emerging Capabilities in Neuroscience and Neurotechnology," *PRISM* 8 (3) (2019).

Dipert, Randall R. "The Ethics of Cyber Warfare," *Journal of Military Ethics* 9 (4) (2010): 384–410.

Dipert, Randall R. "The Essential Features for an Ontology for Cyberwarfare," in *Conflict and Cooperation in Cyberspace*, eds. Panayotis A. Yannakogeorgos and Adam B. Lowther (Boca Raton, FL: CRC Press, 2013): 33–47.

Dipert, Randall R. "Other Than Internet Warfare: Challenges for Ethics, Law and Policy," *Journal of Military Ethics* 12 (1) (2013): 34–53.

Eco, Umberto. "Reflections on War," *La Rivista dei libri* (1 April 1991); reprinted in Umberto Eco, *Five Moral Pieces*, Trans. Alastair McEwen (New York: Harcourt, 1997): 1–17.

Giordano, James, et al. "Redefining Neuroweapons: Emerging Capabilities in Neuroscience and Neurotechnology," *PRISM* 8 (3) (2020): 48–63.

Giordano, James, et al. "Emerging Technologies for Disruptive Effects in Non-kinetic Engagements," *HDIAC Currents* 6 (2) (2019): 49–54.

Ignatieff, Michael. *Virtual War: Kosovo and beyond* (New York: Basic Books, 2000).

Rowe, Neil C. "War Crimes From Cyber Weapons," *Journal of Information Warfare* 6 (3) (2007): 15–25.

Rowe, Neil C. "The Ethics of Cyber War Attacks," in *Cyber War and Cyber Terrorism*, eds. Lech J. Janczewski and Edward M. Colarik (Hershey, PA: Information Science Reference, 2008): 10–111.

Singer, Peter W. *Corporate Warriors* (Ithaca, NY: Cornell University Press, 2003).

Sparrow, Robert. "Killer Robots," *Journal of Applied Philosophy* 24 (1) (2007): 62–77.

Vallor, Shannon. *Technology and the Virtues* (Oxford: Oxford University Press, 2017).

Weiman, Gabriel. "Cyberterrorism: How Real Is the Threat?" *Special Report 119: United States Institute of Peace* (December 2004): 8.

2

LAWS FOR LAWS

This chapter embarks on a summative assessment of the legal and moral challenges of emerging military technology with a recap and reflections on the disappointments suffered and the lessons learned during the debate over the status and future of lethal autonomous weapons systems (LAWS).

In one sense that controversy is easy to characterize. Defenders of LAWS believed that machines could prove more reliable, less destructive, and *more humane* than human combatants and reduce casualties in the process. Opponents have never wavered in their belief, by contrast, that LAWS are inherently immoral and should be declared illegal.

The reasons for holding the second view in opposition to LAWS vary, as do proposed remedies. The manufacture and use of LAWS ought to be banned outright, included alongside other banned weapons of war (like poison gas, land mines, and expanding ordnance) that are *male in se.*[1] Failing this, they should at least be strictly regulated. LAWS can be very inexpensive and expendable, and so they threaten to proliferate as weapons of choice among militaries throughout the world, making war itself easier to declare and fight. Finally, autonomous machines empowered to target and kill human beings entirely without human operators or any other variety of *meaningful human control* constitute an affront to human dignity.

If there was anything shared among these otherwise opposing viewpoints, it was perhaps the conviction that military engineers and defense industries ought not to be left entirely on their own recognizance nor should they be permitted to increase the world's robot armies without limit or oversight. As with other ominous lethal weapons (e.g., nuclear weapons) there should be some provision for arms control.[2]

All this will likely be familiar to some degree to readers of this book. What proves discouraging is that, after nearly 20 years of intense debate and numerous regulatory proposals, little if anything has actually been achieved. One might in utter despair compare this situation with the Western allied withdrawal from

DOI: 10.4324/9781003273912-3

Afghanistan in 2021: after two decades, all involved found themselves right back where they had started, really no better off than before, despite intense efforts and grave sacrifices by all concerned. Just as discouraging, the unchecked growth and development of these war machines has itself continued unabated. Despite years of conferences, seemingly endless hearings by the Convention on Certain Conventional Weapons (CCW) and International Committee of the Red Cross (ICRC) in Geneva and throughout the world, and despite resulting proposals for regulation, good governance, and prudent restraint,[3] the engineering and development of these artifacts has continued undeterred, as relentlessly as Russian military forces initially marched into Ukraine in early 2022 despite all diplomatic attempts to dissuade them.

How did we reach such a demoralizing impasse? How, if at all, should we proceed on all fronts, and with what goals, in light of such discouraging results? Perhaps, an assessment of some of the lessons learned during the varied campaigns and experiences over the years can enlighten us on a more promising way forward.

Ethics and Remotely Operated Systems

A view prevalent early on, and largely unquestioned until quite recently among defense industry engineers and U.S. Department of Defense (DoD) policymakers was that (in their earliest *nonautonomous* status at least) *remotely operated systems raised no genuinely new legal or moral questions.* They merely placed the "pilot" (operator) at a safe distance from the mission, which was otherwise unchanged. Hence, the initial public expressions of concern over the development and deployment of these new systems were misplaced.

That position was frequently reinforced by an accompanying prejudice that the ethicists and international lawyers who were the principal critics of drone warfare (and of military uses of emerging technologies in general) seemed to the defenders of LAWS to be merely ignorant obstructionists with little comprehension of what they were condemning. Indeed, all too often it seems that scientists, engineers, warfighters, and defense industrialists regard ethicists as scientifically illiterate, naysaying, fear-mongering Luddites perversely determined to disrupt those (like themselves) who are simply trying to defend the nation and sustain the rule of law in international relations.

It goes without saying, of course, that the most ardent critics of drone warfare could hardly agree. Here again, however, we need to untangle the considerable conceptual confusion that plagued the drone debate almost from its inception. For example, there was arguably some measure of truth to the defense engineers' initial claim, at least when applied *strictly* to "remotely piloted" systems (RPVs). Surely, the mere technological capacity to place the pilot at a distance (even a distance of some 7,000+ miles!) did not itself abruptly cause an otherwise legally permissible and morally justifiable combat mission to be transformed into something illegal or immoral. After all, adversaries operating within the constraints of the law of armed conflict (LOAC) routinely launched heavy artillery strikes or aerial bombing missions at their adversaries from considerable distances, as in the Kosovo conflict. These were mostly deemed permissible or justifiable, *provided* due care had been exercised to avoid mistakenly targeting and damaging civilians and civilian objects or increasing the probability of such collateral damage on account of the distance from which the attack was carried out.[4] The use of an RPV in lieu of these other means of attack does not by itself change that legal or moral calculus. Defenders of drone warfare even claimed that using drones *improves* this calculus and can actually lessen targeting errors or collateral damage. (We will postpone consideration of that argument for the moment.)

Plenty of technology-driven moral and legal issues remained, however, even in this limited case. RPVs, for example, increasingly rendered it feasible to conceive and carry out missions whose objectives would otherwise prove exceptionally risky, dangerous, and difficult (if not impossible) to undertake from a logistical standpoint. Hence, the criticisms of drone warfare in the literature (as well as in this book) mirrored the concerns raised by this dramatic expansion of mission feasibility, to include an increase in the capacity to undertake or inflict

- assassination or "targeted killing," especially across or within the sovereign borders of nations with whom we are not formally at war;
- collateral damage to innocents and their property; and thereby
- magnify the probability for errors in targeting judgment (i.e., mistakes) that would not otherwise be made (since many of the missions in question would not otherwise be undertaken); and
- perhaps most troublingly, increase the opportunities and incidents of use of deadly force in a military context by nonmilitary personnel (such as civilian intelligence operatives or private security contractors).

Such aspects of drone warfare are disconcerting on many levels but especially when the first kind of mission involves what the United Nations classifies as "extra-judicial killing," namely, the summary execution, without any form of legal due process, of individual citizens of member states not formally indicted for specific crimes but alleged by agents of their own government to have been engaged in unlawful activities beyond that government's own jurisdiction. The heated dispute between proponents and opponents of drone warfare for the most part boiled down to these issues rather than to some inherent moral defect in the drones themselves.

Regarding the other items on this list, anomalous and morally murky activities like targeted assassinations often occur during the conduct by states of espionage and covert actions. It seemed valid, however, to worry that *drone technology (RPVs) by itself substantially magnified the prospects* for engaging in such missions. In fact, this odd kind of escalation of morally problematic activities that are only just barely within the permissible boundaries of international law constituted a striking new systemic feature of unconventional or irregular warfare.[5] First, confronted with the overwhelming conventional military forces of states, their adversaries and insurgent interest groups sought to offset the radical asymmetries that normally favored conventional militaries. They did so by disrupting social systems and attacking the weak links in their enemies' logistical supply chains through the use (for example) of suicide bombers and improvised explosive devices (IEDs) that threw conventional military forces seriously off balance. Subsequently, a new technology (like drones), initially possessed exclusively by the conventional state forces in the conflict, quickly became the optimal response for those forces. Drone attacks by conventional militaries proved to be *systemic* in precisely the same sense as had insurgents' IEDs and suicide bombers: both kinds of attacks disrupted the adversary's command structure, relentlessly hunted adversaries out from where they live and hide, and demoralized partisans on both sides, hopefully resulting in the successful side breaking the will or ability of their adversaries to fight. The host of legal and ethical questions and conundrums described and evaluated in other literature on this topic arose from this *relentless tactical arms race* – this perennial systemic disruption between political adversaries, or between security forces representing the rule of law, and international criminals intent on circumventing that rule.

Increasing Degrees of Autonomy

In what way, if at all, was that initial debate over ethics and law significantly altered or transformed by rendering the robotic or remotely operated systems technology *autonomous* in one or more of the ways described in the Preface and Introduction: self-governed and self-directed, requiring little or no human oversight, once those weapons were enabled and launched?

Paradoxically, if we are concerned about nonmilitary personnel operating military assets and undertaking inherently military operations, then the advent of machine autonomy could be said from a legalist viewpoint to transform that debate – albeit in a strange fashion. Strictly speaking, when launching truly autonomous aerial weapons it ceases to be nonuniformed personnel *directly* engaging in military operations. At most, their involvement is indirect. The combat missions are *being undertaken* solely by machines (presumably with military authorization and oversight). This weird result turns the accountability gap entirely on its head. Defenders of the practices that Sparrow and Noel Sharkey, for example, first criticized could now plausibly claim (using Sparrow's own logic, albeit disingenuously) that nonmilitary personnel were no longer directly engaged in questionable combat actions like extrajudicial killing of adversaries or rogue U.S. citizens.[6] *Only machines* (and not persons) would henceforth be undertaking the activities in question. In short, we can make many of the moral and legal anxieties raised by the policies and practices considered elsewhere in this volume *simply disappear* merely by redefining the activities in question as involving machine behavior exclusively and hence, immune from the charges leveled against earlier, remotely piloted missions conducted by nonmilitary personnel (CIA agents or private military contractors).

This rather odd line of argument regarding autonomy closely resembles the more familiar denial of responsibility by military and defense engineers and others involved in the research, development, manufacture, and ultimately deployment of any new weapons technology during wartime. In that instance, the arguments rest on the claim that a nation's defense industries – as well as its scientists, engineers, and privately contracted personnel – are to a large extent *servants* of the policy decisions of the ruling government. It is *the government and its political leadership*, and not its defense industries, scientists, or contractors, that determines whether and how to prosecute its military conflicts and, accordingly, whether to use military or nonmilitary means and personnel to do so.

Indeed, senior-level managers and directors of private military contractor and defense contracting firms are often eager to emphasize the point that their efforts contribute to the defense of the State and that their industries and organizations exist solely to support the requirements of the State in carrying out this inherently governmental responsibility. But this attempt to evade any liability amounts to equating their behavior with the morally neutral behavior of machines rather than of morally autonomous human beings. That defense, similar to attempts to exempt individual combatants for any moral liability for their legally permissible actions in war, is a recurrent and troubling theme in the history of this drone discussion. The sleight of hand evident here aims to lodge overall liability for inherently governmental functions to military personnel or political leaders. When we consider that many leading military and political decision-makers (or their most trusted colleagues and associates) often leave government service to work for the defense industries or for private military contractors, and vice versa, however, boundaries between what or who is military or nonmilitary, private or inherently governmental, turn out to be fluid and extremely porous.[7]

Even beyond these potential conflicts of interest, however, the public–private division of authority does not specifically excuse defense industries or their employees for performing merely as mindless (let alone narrowly self-interested) technocrats. CEOs, as well as essential scientists, engineers, and employees of such industries, are also citizens of the State, who should be concerned to avoid increasing either the risk or the incidence of war through their efforts (even if they claim their efforts otherwise intend to lessen war's most destructive effects). Their dual responsibilities as citizens as well as subject-matter experts in military technology might be said to run parallel to those of military personnel themselves to offer faithful advice, grounded in their professional experience, on the prospects and problems inherent in political policies regarding preparation for or engagement in military conflict. Peter W. Singer, in particular, strongly maintains that scientists, engineers, and captains of industry engaged in the development and manufacture of military robots and remotely operated systems generally must take upon themselves much more explicitly the responsibility for ensuring their wise and lawful use.[8] His important observation on professional ethics in the context of defense engineering may offer a promising way forward in the midst of this impasse, and we will take it up again at the conclusion of this chapter.

From yet another vantage point, it remained a well-recognized problem in robotics and remotely operated systems research that the most substantial dividends from automating certain features of the battlefield would come from what is termed force multiplication. On the one hand, it has long been the case that a single Predator or Reaper, remotely piloted by one or more human operators, considerably magnifies the ability of military forces engaged in justified missions to accomplish those missions with greater success, precision, and reduction of risk of harm to innocents than their crewed counterparts. This is an important dimension of what defense ethicist Bradley J. Strawser defined as the principle of unnecessary risk (PUR) in undertaking otherwise justified security operations.[9] Adding the ability for a single remote pilot to operate several of these platforms simultaneously, however, would considerably amplify mission capability without a corresponding increase in scarce and expensive (and nonexpendable) human personnel. Thus, the pursuit of force multiplication through systems engineering modifications or technological enhancement of existing military weapons systems was an additional logical implication of that principle.

Meaningful Human Control[10]

In principle, the objective of force multiplication with respect to military robotics could be achieved in either of the following two ways.

- By improving the human–automation interface (e.g., by cleaning up the earliest messy and cluttered Predator control stations and replacing them with vastly simplified and more effective operational hardware); or
- By endowing each remotely operated platform with *enhanced autonomy* and independence of operation.

The first of these alternative strategies proved to be relatively straightforward: placing an ever-greater number of remotely operated systems under a decreasing number of human operators can be largely achieved through the application of thoroughly conventional engineering ingenuity.[11] Four or five computer terminals (and their corresponding keyboards and mice), for example, were initially required to operate a Predator drone, with at least an equal number of personnel. Subsequently, as few as two operators occupying a neatly designed modular control station replaced this clumsy arrangement.[12] Significantly, this path of engineering modification in the pursuit of force multiplication does not by itself invoke any new ethical or legal challenges beyond those already considered in the preceding overview. That is, if it had otherwise been deemed ethical as well as legally permissible within the framework of international humanitarian law (IHL) for a *team of operators* to conduct a remote strike against a Taliban or al-Qaeda stronghold during the Afghanistan campaign, that status did not change if we subsequently replaced the four or five remotely located operators with *a single operator* employing more efficient command and control technology (unless doing so was shown to increase the probability of targeting error or collateral damage).

Far more appealing to engineers and many policy analysts, however, is the force multiplier dividend attained by *dispensing altogether* with the human operator, whether in or merely on the loop (exercising merely supervisory or executive oversight). The appeal is many faceted, from the straightforward projected cost savings anticipated by acquisitions and supply officers to the improvements in latency (i.e., signal and reaction time), targeting, and overall mission effectiveness imagined by remotely operated systems operators and commanders in the field. Computer scientists and artificial intelligence (AI) researchers were eager to take on such an interesting and engaging challenge.

But to concerned critics, such as Sparrow, Sharkey, and Singer (or the father of American robotics, George Bekey), this *relentless drive toward machine autonomy* constituted the source of the most problematic moral and legal conundrums.[13] The seemingly unreflective eagerness of scientists, engineers, and military and political leaders to move ahead with the development of autonomous weapons systems, notwithstanding these objections and concerns of critics, constituted an attitude toward public welfare and the substantial risk of unintended consequences that is still characterized by these same critics as ranging from reckless endangerment to outright criminal negligence. (We will shortly encounter the same tendencies at work in the rapid advancement and myriad applications of AI.)

To make matters even worse, much of this dispute between proponents and critics over the relinquishing of all meaningful human control through enhanced machine autonomy was likewise mired in a nearly hopeless muddle of conceptual confusion and linguistic equivocation. Proponents of increased machine autonomy, for their part, insisted on complicating their defense of autonomous machine performance by invoking provocative concepts like machine "morality," or by describing a quest to design some sort of "ethical governor" that, even if wholly divorced from direct control of human operators, would be able to regulate and constrain the behavior of lethally armed autonomous robots.[14] These enthusiastic advocates frequently betrayed a fundamental lack of understanding of both ethics and moral reasoning, mistakenly ascribing to future autonomous combat weapon systems the ability to make moral decisions and judgments (even when, as it turns out, no such capacities are required to ensure that machine behavior *complies* with international humanitarian law). They naively reduced their accounts of complex human emotions (guilt, for example) to behavioral feedback and modification systems that could be modeled and coded to enable machine learning in such a manner that (they claimed) lethally armed, autonomous military robots would one day prove more ethical and even more humane than their human counterparts. (We will explore the technical details and feasibility of their proposals in greater detail in Chapter 3.)

For the moment, suffice it to observe that, far from describing realistically achievable or even necessary characteristics of machine behavior, such claims seem merely to betray a wholesale lack of familiarity with the features or requirements of morality itself.[15] It is oxymoronic, for example, to describe machine behavior as "humane," let alone as "more humane" than a human. It is rather the legal requirements of the law of armed conflict that deliberately embody what lawyers and scholars describe as "the principle of humanity," one of the five cardinal principles underlying the collective statutes of international law.[16] We require that human combatants behave humanely at very minimum by complying with these restrictions when engaged in armed conflict, whether or not they actually understand or agree with the specific legislation embodied in their rules of engagement. We recognize, however, that compliance would improve considerably on the part of human combatants – that is, they will behave even more humanely – if the military personnel involved base their compliance on fundamental understanding and respect for the moral norms embodied in those laws, rather than uncomprehending, bewildered, or even resentful attitudes regarding these restraints imposed by law on their individual conduct in combat.

Obviously, because machines lack self-consciousness and free will, let alone other competing interests or emotions, none of these considerations apply to machine behavior. The straightforward description of the moral conundrum surrounding LAWS, in contrast to humans, is simply whether such systems can be *designed to comply reliably* with these constraints (failing which, their deployment or use becomes a violation of IHL).[17] There is no meaningful way a machine could behave more or less humanely in doing so. At most, we could inquire how reliably they could comply with IHL (and whether their degree of compliance could equal or surpass some baseline established by human behavior under the same circumstances). That human behavioral norm (which is not perfect) establishes a baseline from which the reliability of machine behavior might be determined. The claim would be that, under such comparable conditions, machines would comply with IHL restraints as or more reliably than their human counterparts do. That, most likely, is what engineers meant at the time by claiming an autonomous weapons system might prove to be more humane than humans during combat. From the proponents' perspective in the LAWS debate, this continues to constitute a sufficiently challenging goal for machine reliability without dragging in superfluous and ultimately meaningless considerations of additional prospects for machine "emotions" and machine "morality."

Relinquishing Meaningful Human Control

Critics for their part were often equally and needlessly provocative about the prospects for relinquishing meaningful human control over LAWS. Some literally ranted in a phantasmagorial fashion about the prospects of killer robots running amok[18] while others complained about the threat to human dignity and moral inappropriateness of machines making decisions to kill humans.[19] The most substantive of these objections was the possible lack of meaningful accountability for the resulting war crimes that might be committed by LAWS.[20] Some critics appeared to envision cyborgs (like the Terminator), or the infamous intelligent computer, HAL (from Arthur C. Clarke's science fiction novel *2001: A Space Odyssey*) in command on the bridge of a nuclear submarine, or R2D2 and C3PO, presumably abandoned after the coalition withdrawal but still fully weaponized and roaming the mountains of southern Afghanistan, woefully unable to distinguish (absent human supervision) between an enemy insurgent and a local shepherd.

In light of some of the baseline conceptual and linguistic distinctions made at the beginning of this book, however, we now quickly see that such extreme scenarios were, frankly, preposterous. The prospects for machine autonomy, even when enhanced with AI and conjoined with lethal force (see Chapter 5), represent something far different from what either critics or proponents described or imagined, and it poses its own unique ethical and legal challenges for engineering and industry. Nothing so fanciful or technologically infeasible as the outlandish scenarios outlined earlier need ever be envisioned. Machines need not be ethical or thought of as engaging in anything like human moral deliberation (let alone impugning human dignity by attempting to "make" life or death decisions on their own).

Respect for human dignity amid the decided indignity and inhumanity of armed conflict requires that targeting, wounding, or killing an adversary by whatever method not inflict unnecessary injury or superfluous suffering. Precision-guided weapons (bombs) raining down on targets from a height of 30,000 feet, as in the Kosovo conflict, are nevertheless likely to cause such foreseeable injury and death, even absent a deliberate intent to do so. The same is true for other weapons, whether crewed or remotely operated, semiautonomous or fully autonomous. Their degree of autonomy and human supervision at the moment of impact is hardly relevant to any considerations of human dignity.[21]

Strictly speaking, machines simply cannot commit war crimes because they lack intentionality or self-motivation and are utterly devoid of the interests (or emotions) required as ingredients for criminal culpability. Their designers and end users, however, conceivably can commit such crimes by designing or deploying them recklessly, thoughtlessly, or otherwise irresponsibly. Ethics and accountability under international law, however, remain invariant throughout and wholly within the purview of human experience.[22]

Once again, the autonomy requisite for moral decision-making by human agents is something quite distinct from machine autonomy. The latter, as we have seen, merely involves remotely operated systems performing in complex environments without the need for continuous human oversight. In the latter, purely mechanical sense of "autonomy," a Patriot cruise missile and my iRobot Roomba vacuum cleaner were both correctly described as autonomous, in that they could perform their assigned missions, including encountering and responding to obstacles, problems, and unforeseen circumstances without routine human oversight. For his part, Noel Sharkey describes five levels of autonomy, the greatest degree being the fifth, in which the machine operates and selects and strikes targets without further human intervention. But note that even this does not require or entail an AI system so complex as to be subject to emergent or unpredictable behavior. The intelligent system at this highest level still can only malfunction or make mistakes, not govern its own behavior in the relevant sense. Targets are selected from a predetermined range, such as knowledge that enemy ships are operating within some designated region, with the weapon capable of selecting final targets based on determining their precise location, with proper identification. Such a system may also reject a target or cancel its operation if the target recognition software disqualifies permissibility of firing.[23]

The essential difference is this: the missile does not (nor can it) unilaterally change its mission en route, or reprogram its targeting objectives, let alone does it raise "moral objections" about the appropriateness of the targets selected for it. The latter would be the hallmarks of moral autonomy, and they are obviously (and likely forever) outside the realm of machine behavior. Likewise, I would not wish to have my Roomba lethally armed in a security or surveillance capacity or have it "decide" whether it is necessary or appropriate to shoot an intruder who is breaking into my home. If I did manage to modify the robot myself so that it did shoot an intruder, then under almost all regimes of domestic law *I myself* would be legally liable for the death or injury inflicted (and certainly not the machine!). Armed conflict in the international arena is, in that respect, no different regarding liability and legal accountability.

In public discussions and online forums, viewers are occasionally treated to the hypothetical specter of a hunter–killer missile as a prime example of the kind of monstrosity ultimately feared by opponents of autonomous weapons. Such a weapon, however, does not (yet) exist. At the moment, such weapons remain entirely a figment of video game imagination. Moreover, any real-world prototype of such a device would have to be specifically instructed (programmed) by a human engineer or operator concerning whom or what to kill and when to refrain. Those human agents, rather than the missile, would be both legally and morally accountable for its resulting actions. In fact, if one takes the trouble to track down references to real-world prototypes of autonomous war machines, one discovers that the references are to drones (like the MQ-9A Reaper or the Sea Guardian) rather than missiles. Despite sometimes carrying the ominous moniker of fully autonomous hunter–killers, these advanced drones are at all times fully under the supervision of human operators who make, and are legally and morally responsible for, all targeting decisions.[24] Whence meaningful human control over them is always maintained, with full accountability and liability for their actions resting firmly with human agents.

Reviewing all this, one wonders how such far-fetched discussions and fears ever gained credence. In general, with a few exceptions, we neither require nor desire our autonomous machines be equipped to make the kinds of moral judgments about killing that critics fear and decry. Even when we turn (in Chapter 5) to the discussion of adding modular (or "weak") AI to enhance a robot's autonomous operation, we will quickly conclude that this enhanced capacity will never amount to an attempt to equip autonomous machines with the capacity for ethical deliberation or moral agency nor will it ever conceivably exempt them from some form of meaningful human control. The problems that should be highlighted instead (as security and technology expert Audrey Cronin warns) are the widespread proliferation, affordability, and relative ease of use of such weapons of destruction, placing them far too readily in the hands of human agents who are not likely to worry in the least about liability, accountability, or meaningful human control.[25]

One possible exception to this general conclusion, however, is the use of "single-state, mission oriented" *robot sentries* in a bounded or highly scripted environment. Lethally armed sentry robots, for example, are used in Israel and South Korea exclusively along hostile borders or in the demilitarized zone between North and South Korea. To be clear: they don't hunt, but they do patrol, and they do shoot to kill. But they do not themselves select their targets. They are programmed to attack wherever targets are self-selected by intruding into a prohibited space. The U.S. Navy similarly employs armed autonomous robot sentries to protect what is termed the "no-go zone" around a Naval flotilla, in which ample warning is given, and all attempts are made to dissuade violation of the boundaries or prohibited zone before opening fire on violators. None of these examples entails having an autonomous machine ever "deciding" by itself whether to kill a human being. Instead, in all these exceptional instances, the autonomous and lethally armed weapons and their actions fully reflect human intentionality and serve only the explicit purposes for which human agents are finally and solely morally responsible and over which full human control is ultimately retained.

Assessing Robot Performance in Combat

Unfortunately, when combined with unrestrained anthropomorphism and science fiction fantasy, the rhetoric of ethics and law itself is not always a useful analytical tool in these discussions. Invariably in these contexts, moral and legal concepts are widely misunderstood, misinterpreted, and inappropriately applied to imaginary circumstances and scenarios by participants from both sides in this debate. Robots, regardless of design or capacity, could never themselves select targets or commit war crimes. Even fully autonomous systems have no intentionality or self-awareness. They do not *care* about their own survival or well-being. They have no interests. Importantly, they cannot get scared or get angry nor could they possible try to get even by seeking retaliation against enemies for harm done to themselves or their companions. All such actions arise from human emotions and intentions, which remain the sole source of activities classifiable as war crimes. Even fully autonomous weapons systems, by contrast, would do precisely and only what they were programmed or commanded to do, *unless they happen to malfunction*. The anthropomorphic, romantic nonsense attached to robotics in the popular mind by *Star Wars*, *Blade Runner* – elaborate video games – and other movie and science-fiction fantasies seriously compromises the ethical analysis of military uses of genuine, real-world military robots within the confines of international law. Robots that, by definition, cannot commit war crimes *per se*, but only malfunction or make mistakes, require a somewhat different metric for assessment than appeal to their alleged immorality or their threat to human dignity. Any commercial designer, manufacturer, or distributor will likely inform us that the relevant categories of assessment should instead be *safety*, *reliability*, and *risk*.

IHL, as we observed, currently bans the manufacture or use of weapons that are highly indiscriminate, needlessly dangerous, and destructive (disproportionate) or that inflict cruel and gratuitous injury and suffering. But what about weapons that are *unsafe*, or *unreliable* to deploy, or whose use entails undue *risk*? Combatants and their militaries often complain that there are plenty of "legal" weapons and systems that are nonetheless unsafe to use or whose use poses unacceptable risk. The Patriot antimissile system used in the first Gulf War, for example, was perfectly legal but exceedingly unreliable. So was one of the earliest land-based lethal autonomous robots, the Talon Sword. Both systems were marginally legal under current IHL statutes. Neither inflicted unusual suffering or superfluous injury. Instead, they tended to malfunction, and sometimes hit the wrong targets (not random civilians but their own operators!). The problems attending their use, however, seems dissimilar to currently prohibited means or methods of war (rape, poison gas, or the planting of land mines). So what is it, precisely, we are trying to identify, rectify, or else prohibit?

From an engineering standpoint, it would be utter madness to deliberately deploy a weapons system that is unreliable or defective or that killed the "wrong" people (let alone that killed innocent people) instead of destroying the legitimate enemy targets it was designed to attack. Accordingly, international legal restrictions might be amended or clarified ideally to also incorporate some of the distinctions found in domestic tort (personal injury) law, for example, regarding accountability for wrongful death and destruction. These include concepts such as due care and the absence of reckless endangerment or criminal negligence.[26] Deploying a patently unreliable system is surely reckless (and therefore morally culpable), and in extreme circumstances it might be found to be explicitly criminally negligent.[27] By contrast – and here is why such weapons should not simply be designated *male in se* – deploying an autonomous platform that has proved to be safe and reliable through rigorous testing under stringent conditions would, on the whole, constitute an acceptable, even a morally responsible action (particularly, if it could be definitively shown that the new system performed better than the weapons and personnel it replaced). If such an autonomous system malfunctioned (even as humans and their crewed systems sometimes make mistakes, hit the wrong targets, or inadvertently kill the wrong people), then the procedure in the machine case would parallel that of the human case in similar circumstances. An inquiry is held, and investigation into circumstances is conducted, and if no intentional wrongdoing or culpable error by manufacturers or operators is discerned, then well-intentioned governments and their militaries issue an apology and do their best to make restitution for the harm inflicted.[28]

This process is grounded, however, in the prior expectation of what Michael Walzer first termed "double intention" (in lieu of the more lenient criterion of double effect), in this instance, holding manufacturers and designers *strictly accountable* for exercising due care (as well as simply for not deliberately intending to do harm) in testing and ensuring the reliability and safety of their commercial and industrial products (for robots and drones, when all is said and done, are nothing more than that).[29] We would certainly define the engineering design specifications as *requiring that our autonomous machines perform as well as or better than human combatants under similar circumstances* in complying with the constraints of the law of armed conflict and the applicable rules of engagement for a given conflict.[30] If they can, and if they do achieve this benchmark engineering specification, then their use is morally justifiable. If they cannot, or if our designers and manufacturers have not taken due care to ensure that they can, then we have no business building or deploying them, and we (rather than the machines themselves) would be held criminally liable if we nevertheless did so.

Adopting this approach to assessing machine behavior instead of invoking ethics and morality would result in something legally akin to "strict liability" in domestic tort law. It is really just as simple as that. And like Aegis and Patriot missiles and other semiautonomous systems, this strict due care assessment would specifically require any war machine at minimum to incorporate a system of reliable target recognition and threat-level escalation, leading to a proportionate, discriminate, and, therefore, appropriate response in the use of deadly force.

All of that is quite enough of a technological challenge without muddying the waters with science fiction or with specious metaphysical worries about machines targeting and killing humans by themselves! We are not yet even remotely close to being able to have our machines engage in such activities, in any case, in terms of target recognition and discrimination software and hardware, for example. And the systems we do propose to build and deploy still have "autonomy" only in a very limited and highly scripted sense. Platforms such as Fire Scouts, Israeli-designed Harpies, and Korean border sentry robots are all designed to target adversarial threats reliably within extremely limited and very well-defined scenarios. In addition, these weapons systems usually focus on disarming a perceived threat or (as in the case of Harpies) disabling or confusing the target's weapons, radar, and command/control technology.[31] Such systems are designed to employ force in only very limited situations that leave little room for ambiguity or error. The mistakes that might nonetheless be made are regrettable, but they are usually not criminally negligent or culpable (as when a child strays into the DMZ, or a recreational boater foolishly transgresses the well-defined and well-publicized no-go zone around a Navy aircraft carrier).

Conclusion: Placing Greater Emphasis on Engineering Ethics

Whether or not we can devise algorithms for some sort of autonomous machine "morality" that reliably governs their behavior, it remains the case that the existence and increased reliance on ever-more-autonomous weapons systems and support machinery in the combat arena poses a range of moral and legal dilemmas and concerns that must be either solved or satisfied. Regardless of what specific avenues of research are finally pursued, for example, machines equipped with lethal force need to be designed to operate according to precise engineering specifications, including the specifications that their actions comply accurately and unerringly with current international law pertaining to distinction, proportionality, and the avoidance of needless suffering, as well as to the operant constraints of standing and specific rules of engagement. Such constraints are identical to those currently imposed upon human combatants in the field (often with less-than-perfect success).

Arkin, in particular (whose efforts in this field I greatly admire in other respects), has sometimes seemed needlessly provocative in citing the potential capacity for robots to behave "more ethically" or for autonomous, lethally armed platforms to be "more humane" than human combatants. This misused language enrages opponents and unnecessarily clouds the quest for reasonable consensus on the goals of good governance for emerging and technologically sophisticated weapons systems.

Autonomous military robots operating on land, in or beneath the sea, or in the air constitute a unique class of entity. Like our rifles, missiles, undersea torpedoes, and jet aircraft, we demand that our military robots be reliable and safe to operate (meaning that they won't malfunction and inadvertently destroy the operator or creator or wantonly destroy property or innocent human lives). Ever greater degrees of machine autonomy are desirable to increase the efficiency and force multiplier effects of using remotely operated systems in our overall force mix. But they cannot, nor, in the final analysis, do we need to have them, "behave ethically." That is certainly asking for much more than we can currently deliver and probably much more than we really require of them.

We wish, instead, for military robots to be safe and reliable in their functioning and to perform their assigned missions effectively, including following instructions that comply with the laws of armed conflict (just as human combatants do). Invoking "ethics" in lieu of strict compliance with the law (a far simpler domain of behavior to design) may simply serve to confuse or frustrate the proper objectives of robotics research.

If the proper engineering parameters and specifications for lethally armed autonomous systems are safety and reliability within defined limits of tolerable risk (as pertains to matters such as target recognition and threat-level escalation), then what is demanded of engineers, industrial designers and producers, and military end users of such potentially lethal and destructive weapons, in their turn, is both a personal and an overall organizational or corporate commitment to the exercise of due care and the strict avoidance of reckless, negligent, or criminally liable disregard for the possible risks of malfunctions, mistakes, or misuse. Those are entirely different matters from the spurious ethical concerns raised for or against lethally armed autonomous systems.

Such concerns are of paramount importance to efforts to increase the degree of autonomy, without loss of safety and reliability, in our remotely operated military platforms. In ISR missions, remotely operated systems should track and survey appropriate targets while avoiding doing any harm inadvertently to civilian bystanders or objects within the operational environment. We also want these systems to avoid surveillance (and violation of privacy) of inappropriate or impermissible targets. This is the very meaning of safety and reliability of operation and ensures that our increasing reliance on such systems conforms to the demands of ethics and the law. Success in this ethical dimension of robotics research is especially of importance to future DoD initiatives to combine the force multiplying effects of greater machine autonomy with lethal force. If responsibly and thoroughly undertaken, such research may lead to marked improvements in both the proportional and highly discriminate ability of the United States and allied militaries to project requisite force in conflict while greatly reducing collateral damage, thereby lessening the generalized destruction and the loss of life that otherwise routinely accompany armed conflict itself.

Although these alternative challenges are themselves extremely grave and very serious, they are nonetheless entirely encompassed within the existing governance framework for crewed weapons and systems.[32] Autonomous systems must likewise be designed within carefully defined limits of mechanical tolerance and risk and operated or deployed only for very specific, scripted missions (what computer scientists and systems engineers describe as "finite state" machines). In that capacity, lethal autonomous platforms are not required to "decide" or to "judge" anything: they merely execute assigned missions, recognize varying contexts, and respond as programmed for each contingency. In case of error or malfunction, the designer or end user is responsible, either criminally (for careless or willful misuse) or civilly (for restitution of harm inflicted or for damage done). Morality and legality (just as with crewed weapons systems currently employed in combat) are ultimately a property, and the responsibility, of the system as a whole, not solely its machine components. This presents a radically different and reassuringly more attainable operational goal than critics or proponents of machine autonomy currently envision.

Finally, let me return to the point initially raised regarding ethics and the engineering profession itself.

Earlier, I promised to return to Peter Singer's strong criticisms of what might be characterized as *ethical illiteracy* among engineers, whom he describes as uncomfortable with these questions and all too willing to proceed with their scientific and technological work while leaving the moral concerns to others outside their field.[33] This criticism is not entirely fair: in this chapter, we have considered the extensive contributions to moral debate and the framing of moral issues in military robotics made by a number of scientists and engineers in the field (e.g., Ron Arkin, John Canning, Noel Sharkey). Their work is every bit as significant, and perhaps more credible in their fields, than that undertaken by moral philosophers, lawyers, or experts in international relations. Moreover, many of the engineering contributions to the ethics of remotely operated and future autonomous systems is appropriately published in scientific and professional journals, such as the well-regarded *Proceedings of the IEEE.*

Singer is correct to complain, however, that despite these features of the moral debate, far too many practitioners in the field are simply unaware of, or unconcerned with, such matters. Far too many members of the engineering profession simply have not stayed current with the ongoing and published research undertaken by their colleagues. Arkin, as we observed, has at least taken these concerns seriously through attempts to develop methods for operationalizing what he terms "ethical governance" (i.e., legal compliance) for autonomous machine behavior.

Other research teams (e.g., Donald Brutzman et al.; see Chapter 3) are pursuing alternative, and occasionally less complex, methods of achieving the goal of satisfying the Arkin test.

Satisfying this test in some fashion, however, is not some sort of optional engineering design standard. Instead, the Arkin test poses a strict operational and design specification for future remotely operated systems armed with lethal force. Together, these efforts define a program of research involving alternative testable and falsifiable operational parameters designed to address this essential design specification for future autonomous systems. It therefore constitutes a serious lapse of professional ethics and must henceforth be recognized as professionally inexcusable for practitioners in the field of military robotics engineering to remain unaware of, unconcerned with, and uninvolved in this dimension of their scientific research. Deliberate and willful neglect of this essential dimension of the overall robotics engineering project constitutes what is known in law and morality as *culpable ignorance*. Practitioners guilty of it could henceforth find themselves morally culpable, and very possibly civilly or even criminally liable as well, simply for pursuing their current lines of research while ignoring this key engineering design specification.[34]

Notes

1 "Evil (or wrong) in themselves (inherently)" as opposed to wrong simply by virtue of having been prohibited by law. This designation applies to both means and methods of war that are gratuitous (like rape) or (like land mines or blinding lasers) prone to cause superfluous injury and needless suffering. An early proposal to assign LAWS to this IHL category can be found in Wendell Wallach, "Terminating the Terminator: What to Do about Autonomous Weapons," *Science Progress* (29 January 2013), http://scienceprogress.org/2013/01/terminating-the-terminator-what-to-do-about-autonomous- weapons/.

2 As advocated by Yale ethicist Wendell Wallach, *A Dangerous Master: How to Keep Technology From Slipping Out of Our Control* (New York: Basic Books, 2015).

3 The U.S. Department of Defense (DoD), for example, unilaterally initiated a five-year moratorium on research and development of fully autonomous systems in effect from 2012 to 2017 and issued DoD Directive 3000.09 governing the employment of autonomy in weapons systems in November 2012. See Paul Scharre, *An Army of None: Autonomous Weapons and the Future of War* (New York: W.W. Norton & Co., 2018): 89ff.

4 See William J. Buckley, ed., *Kosovo: Contending Voices on Balkan Interventions* (Grand Rapids, MI: William B. Eerdmans, 2000).

5 See George R. Lucas, Jr., "'This Is Not Your Father's War': Confronting the Moral Challenges of 'Unconventional' War," *Journal of National Security Law and Policy* 3 (2) (2009): 331–342; "Postmodern War," in *New Warriors and New Weapons: Ethics & Emerging Military Technologies*," *Journal of Military Ethics* 9 (4) (December 2010): 289–298.

6 Robert Sparrow, "Killer Robots," *Journal of Applied Philosophy* 24 (1) (2007): 62–77; "Predators or Plowshares? Arms Control of Robotic Weapons," *IEEE Technology and Society Magazine* 28 (1) (2009): 25–29; "Robotic Weapons and the Future of War," in *New Wars and New Soldiers: Military Ethics in the Contemporary World*, eds. Paolo Tripodi and Jessica Wolfendale (London: Ashgate Publishing Ltd, 2011): 117–133. See also Noel Sharkey, "Robot Wars are a Reality," *The Guardian* (18 August 2007): 29; "Automated Killers and the Computing Profession," *Computer* 40 (2007): 122–124; "Cassandra or False Prophet of Doom: AI Robots and War," *IEEE Intelligent Systems* (July/August 2008): 14–17; "Grounds for Discrimination: Autonomous Robot Weapons," *RUSI Defence Systems* 11 (2) (2008): 86–89; "Saying 'No!' to Lethal Autonomous

Targeting," in "New Warriors and New Weapons: Ethics & Emerging Military Technologies," ed. G.R. Lucas, Jr. *Journal of Military Ethics* 9 (4) (December 2010): 299–313.

7 See Major General Robert H. Latiff, "Ethical Issues in Defense Systems Acquisition," in *The Routledge Handbook of Military Ethics,* ed. George R. Lucas (London: Routledge, 2015): 209–219. See also his *Future War: Preparing for the New Global Battlefield* (New York: Alfred Knopf, 2017), and *Future Peace: Technology, Aggression and the Rush to War* (South Bend, IN: Notre Dame University Press, 2022).

8 Peter W. Singer, *Wired for War* (New York: Penguin Press, 2009); "The Ethics of 'Killer Apps'," in "New Warriors and New Weapons: Ethics & Emerging Military Technologies," ed. G.R. Lucas, Jr., *Journal of Military Ethics* 9 (4) (December 2010): 314–327.

9 Bradley J. Strawser, "Moral Predators: The Duty to Employ Uninhabited Vehicles," in "New Warriors and New Weapons: Ethics & Emerging Military Technologies," ed. G.R. Lucas, Jr., *Journal of Military Ethics* 9 (4) (December 2010): 357–383. This principle essentially holds that when they are engaged in otherwise morally justifiable military or security missions, military and security personnel are owed as much safety and minimized risk of harm as military technology can afford them.

10 This section is indebted in particular to Guglielmo Tamburrini and Daniele Arnoroso, "Autonomous Weapons Systems and Meaningful Human Control: Ethical and Legal Issues," *Current Robotics Reports* 1 (24 August 2020): 187–194. https://doi.org/10.1007/s43154-020-00024-3 [accessed 4 May 2022].

11 Mary L. Cummings et al., "The Role of Human-Automation Consensus in Multiple Unmanned Vehicle Scheduling," *Human Factors: The Journal of the Human Factors and Ergonomics* 52 (1) (2010); "Assessing Operator Workload and Performance in Expeditionary Multiple Unmanned Vehicle Control," in *Proceedings of the 48th AIAA Aerospace Sciences Meeting* (Orlando, FL, January 2010).

12 Readers may observe drone and personnel in an operating station at: www.youtube.com/watch?v=8rzkgFAFMTI

13 See the works previously cited for the first three authors. Note that this is also a theme woven throughout Paul Scharre's more recent exposé: *An Army of None* (New York: W.W. Norton, 2018). See also George Bekey, *Autonomous Robots: From Biological Inspiration to Implementation and Control* (Cambridge, MA: MIT Press, 2005); George Bekey, Patrick Lin, and Keith Abney, *Autonomous Military Robotics: Risk, Ethics, and Design* (U.S. Department of the Navy, Office of Naval Research, 20 December 2008), www.semanticscholar.org/paper/Autonomous-Military-Robotics%3A-Risk%2C-Ethics%2C-and-Lin-Bekey/e1387638132f50fc9e2dbe6bccf4f705e53b166b.

14 See, for example, Ronald Craig Arkin, Patrick Lim, and Alana R. Wagner, "Moral Decision Making in Autonomous Systems: Enforcement, Moral Emotions, Dignity, Trust, and Deception," *Proceedings of the IEEE* 100 (3) (March 2012): 571–589.

15 Philosophy and technology scholar John P. Sullins describes the nature of this fundamental misunderstanding in terms of the engineering prerequisites for achieving any sort of machine moral reasoning: these be development of machine (artificial) consciousness, followed by *artificial phronesis*, which Aristotle first described as an ability to reason practically about problems for which there is no algorithmic solution. While agnostic on the prospects for all of this, Sullins observes that what he terms "the problem of attaining artificial phronesis in machine behavior" has not even been properly conceptualized by researchers. See J.P. Sullins, "The Role of Consciousness and Artificial Phronēsis in AI Ethical Reasoning," *AAAI Spring Symposium: Towards Conscious AI Systems* (2019), http://ceur-ws.org/Vol-2287/paper11.pdf.

16 IHL itself comprises statutes devised and imposed by human beings interested in limiting the extent of death, destruction, and suffering that otherwise attend armed conflict. The five basic principles, or "pillars," of IHL pertaining to armed conflict are variously described as (i) military necessity; (ii) proportionality or the economy of force; (iii) distinction (or discrimination) of noncombatants and their property from enemy belligerents; (iv) prohibition against inflicting superfluous injury or unnecessary suffering; and (v) the catchall provision of *humanity* that extends general protections to all

persons in wartime against injury or abuse not specifically covered in black letter statutes, "consistent with the laws of nations and the dictates of public conscience." International Committee of the Red Cross (ICRC), https://casebook.icrc.org/glossary/fundamental-principles-ihl.

17 See Neil Davidson, "A Legal Perspective: Autonomous Weapons Systems under International Humanitarian Law," UNDOA Occasional Papers, #30. N.d. (2018?) 18 pp, www.icrc.org/en/download/file/65762/autonomous_weapon_systems_under_international_humanitarian_law.pdf.

18 See, for example, Armin Krishnan, *Killer Robots: Legality and Ethicality of Autonomous Weapons* (London: Ashgate Press, 2009); Peter Asaro, "How Just Could a Robot War Be?" in *Current Issues in Computing and Philosophy,* eds. P. Brey, A. Briggle, and K. Waelbers (Amsterdam: IOS Press, 2008): 50–64.

19 Asaro (2008) and Sparrow (2011). See Matthew S. Larkin, *Brave New Warfare: Autonomy in Lethal UAVs.* Master's Thesis (Monterey, CA: Naval Postgraduate School), https://wiki.nps.edu/download/attachments/15073701/Brave+New+Warfare+(Larkin,+Matthew+Thesis).pdf?version=1&modificationDate=1301324368000.

20 This presumed lack of accountability for the commission of "war crimes" by robots was first raised by Robert Sparrow (2007) and Peter Asaro (2008), and is a principal motivation behind their founding, with Noel Sharkey, the International Committee for Robot Arms Control (ICRAC).

21 Aron Dombrovszki, "The Unfounded Bias Against Autonomous Weapons Systems," *Információs Társadalom* XXI (2) (2021): 13–28, https://dx.doi.org/10.22503/inftars.XXI.2021.2.2 [accessed May 13 2022].

22 A very sensible and levelheaded assessment of the potential threat to human dignity posed by LAWS engaging in unsupervised targeting is found in Michael C. Horowitz, "The Ethics and Morality of Robotic Warfare: Assessing the Debate Over Autonomous Weapons," *Daedalus: Journal of the American Academy of Arts & Sciences* 145 (4) (Fall 2016): 25–36.

23 These kinds of "autonomy" scenarios are described and debated among defense experts in Chapters 6 and 7 of Scharre (2018). See also D. Purves, R. Jenkins, and B.J. Strawser, "Autonomous Machines, Moral Judgment, and Acting for the Right Reasons," *Ethical Theory and Moral Practice* 18 (2015): 851–872, https://doi.org/10.1007/s10677-015-9563-y [accessed 12 May 2022].

24 Kalashnikov's KUB-BLA "loitering suicide drone," currently deployed by the Russian Army in their invasion of Ukraine, claims to be equipped with AI that can enable it to identify and attack targets autonomously. But in fact the "autonomous AI-enhanced operation" appears to allow only flight corrections and maneuvering that permit the unpiloted drone to strike targets that are preselected by a human operator (much as a semiautonomous cruise missile can do). That is far from the full autonomy described here. See Will Knight, "Russia's Killer Drone in Ukraine Raises Fears About AI in Warfare," *Wired Magazine* (17 March 2022), http://wired.com/story/ai-drones-russia-ukraine [accessed 3 April 2022].

25 Audrey Kurth Cronin, *Power to the People: How Open Technological Innovation Is Arming Tomorrow's Terrorists* (New York: Oxford University Press, 2020).

26 As Robert Sparrow observes, many IHL experts already interpret the "Martens Clause" along these lines. See "Ethics as a Source of Law: The Martens Clause and Autonomous Weapons," in *Humanitarian Law and Policy* (Geneva: International Committee of the Red Cross, 14 November 2017), https://blogs.icrc.org/law-and-policy/2017/11/14/ethics-source-law-martens-clause-autonomous-weapons/. The clause reads

> Until a more complete code of the laws of war is issued, the High Contracting Parties think it right to declare that in cases not included in the Regulations adopted by them, populations and belligerents remain under the protection and empire of the principles of international law, as they result from the usages established between

civilized nations, from the laws of humanity and the requirements of the public conscience.

www.icrc.org/en/doc/resources/documents/article/other/57jnhy.htm [accessed 30 April 2022]

27 The investigation and prosecutions attending the public release of the Boeing 737–800 "Max" demonstrates how the consequences of machine malfunction redound back to human agents, even when the latter attempt to escape their liability for reckless or negligent design. The attitude that Singer, Sharkey, and others discern among engineers and defense industries all too ready to pursue autonomy without adequate investigation of these problems would constitute one glaring example of "criminal negligence," which is why I argue that attention must be paid to the "safety, reliability, risk" design specification for any armed unmanned systems endowed with any degree of autonomy.
28 In the same article (Lucas 2009), I argue that the dilemma of military robotics in this regard differs little from that of human combatants, who must be similarly "trained" (rather than "educated") to follow the applicable rules of engagement for a given conflict, that in turn represent the translations by military lawyers of IHL and law of armed conflict into actionable mission parameters in given conflicts. Failure to comply due to misjudgments, accidents, and mistakes (that are not attributed to criminal negligence or recklessness, in the human case) are then acknowledged by the respective militaries and their governments: apologies are issued, and compensation for damages (ineffectual though that may be) is offered, in analogy with similar kinds of product liability situations in domestic law.
29 See Michael Walzer, *Just and Unjust Wars* (New York: Basic Books, 1977; 4th ed., 2010).
30 This criterion – that robots comply as or more effectively with applicable constraints of LOAC on their use of force and doing of harm than human combatants under similar circumstances – constitutes what I originally defined in (Lucas 2010) as the Arkin test for robot "morality" (although that is likewise somewhat misleading, as the criterion pertains straightforwardly to compliance with international law, not with actually exhibiting the capacities for moral reasoning or judgment). In this sense, the test for "morality" (i.e., for the limited ability to comply with legal restrictions on the use of force) is similar to the Turing test for machine intelligence: we have satisfied or exceeded the standard when machine behavior is indistinguishable from (or better than) human behavior in any given context.
31 Naval engineer John Canning argued several years ago that this targeting of an adversary's weapons systems (rather than the adversaries themselves) is the proper objective of lethally armed, fully autonomous uncrewed systems. Otherwise, such systems should at most be armed with nonlethal weapons or programmed to undertake evasive action rather than use force in self-defense. See John Canning, G.W. Riggs, O. Thomas Holland, and Carolyn Blakelock: "A Concept for the Operation of Armed Autonomous Systems on the Battlefield," in *Proceedings of Association for Unmanned Vehicle Systems International's (AUVSI) Unmanned Systems North America* (Anaheim, CA, August 3–5, 2004); John Canning, "Weaponized Unmanned Systems: A Transformational Warfighting Opportunity, Government Roles in Making it Happen," in *Proceedings of Engineering the Total Ship (ETS)* (Falls Church, VA, 23–25 September 2008).
32 For the current status of international law respecting the development and use of uncrewed systems, as well as constructive proposals for strengthening this legal regime, see the exhaustive review by Gary Marchant et al., "International Governance of Autonomous Military Robotics," *Columbia Science and Technology Law Review* 12 (272) (2011), www.stlr.org/cite.cgi?volume=12&article=7.
33 Peter W. Singer (2009, 2010).
34 In an earlier article, "Industrial Challenges of Military Robotics" (2011), I proposed that the time had come to move beyond speculation about the relative efficacy of LOAC compliance of autonomous uncrewed systems, to the development and testing of such

systems, designed to operate effectively within the constraints of specific "Rules of Engagement" (ROE). ROE are specific findings and interpretations specifying lawful conduct in a specific theater of combat operations. I obtained a grant from the Office of the Secretary of Defense via our robotics consortium at the Naval Postgraduate School on the topic "operationalizing the laws of war for unmanned systems," in which I sought to enlist engineering, computer science, and robotics graduate students and faculty to develop testable guidance software for specific systems we are developing, for example, for autonomous underwater warfare, to determine whether such systems could be made "safe and reliable" with respect to compliance with international law. I was not, however, able to encourage any of my colleagues in engineering to sponsor or supervise master's- or doctoral-level research in this topic, as they found it "insufficiently empirical and not really focused on engineering." I believe this attitude reflects not just a bias against the unfamiliar but also an abject failure to remain current in scholarship and research in the field. Leading roboticists, engineers, and scientists engaged in robotics (like Ron Arkin) have persuaded the field that this is among the most important scientific challenges faced and published their work to this effect in leading peer-reviewed technical journals. It strikes me as inexcusable academically, as well as professionally dangerous, to continue to fail to acknowledge the significance of designing and testing alternative models for achieving an acceptable level of legal and moral guidance and compliance in future uncrewed systems.

References

Arkin, Ronald Craig; Ulam, Patrick; Wagner, Alana R. "Moral Decision Making in Autonomous Systems: Enforcement, Moral Emotions, Dignity, Trust, and Deception," *Proceedings of the IEEE* 100 (3) (March 2012): 571–589.

Asaro, Peter. "How Just Could a Robot War Be?" in *Current Issues in Computing and Philosophy*, eds. P. Brey, A. Briggle, and K. Waelbers (Amsterdam: IOS Press, 2008): 50–64.

Bekey, George. *Autonomous Robots: From Biological Inspiration to Implementation and Control* (Cambridge, MA: MIT Press, 2005).

Bekey, George; Lin, Patrick; Abney, Keith. *Autonomous Military Robotics: Risk, Ethics, and Design* (Washington, DC: U.S. Department of the Navy, Office of Naval Research, 20 December 2008).

Buckley, William J., ed. *Kosovo: Contending Voices on Balkan Interventions* (Grand Rapids, MI: William B. Eerdmans, 2000).

Canning, John. "Weaponized Unmanned Systems: A Transformational Warfighting Opportunity, Government Roles in Making It Happen," in *Proceedings of Engineering the Total Ship (ETS)* (Falls Church, VA, 23–25 September 2008).

Canning, John; Riggs, G.W.; Holland, O. Thomas; Blakelock, Carolyn. "A Concept for the Operation of Armed Autonomous Systems on the Battlefield," in *Proceedings of the Association for Unmanned Vehicle Systems International's (AUVSI) Unmanned Systems North America* (Anaheim, CA, August 3–5, 2004).

Clare, Andrew; Hart, Christin; Cummings, Mary. "Assessing Operator Workload and Performance in Expeditionary Multiple Unmanned Vehicle Control," in *Proceedings of the 48th AIAA Aerospace Sciences Meeting* (Orlando, FL, January 2010). Published Online: 25 June 2012, https://doi.org/10.2514/6.2010-763.

Cronin, Audrey Kurth. *Power to the People: How Open Technological Innovation Is Arming Tomorrow's Terrorists* (New York: Oxford University Press, 2020).

Cummings, M.L.; Clare, A.; Hart, C. "The Role of Human – Automation Consensus in Multiple Unmanned Vehicle Scheduling," *Human Factors: The Journal of the Human Factors and Ergonomics Society* 52 (1) (29 June 2010): 17–27.

Cummings, M.L. "Assessing Operator Workload and Performance in Expeditionary Multiple Unmanned Vehicle Control," in *Proceedings of the 48th AIAA Aerospace Sciences Meeting* (Orlando, FL, January 2010).

Davidson, Neil. "A Legal Perspective: Autonomous Weapons Systems under International Humanitarian Law," UNDOA Occasional Papers, #30. N.d. (2018?), www.icrc.org/en/download/file/65762/autonomous_weapon_systems_under_international_humanitarian_law.pdf.

Dombrovszki, Aron. "The Unfounded Bias Against Autonomous Weapons Systems," *Információs Társadalom* XXI (2) (2021): 13–28, https://dx.doi.org/10.22503/inftars.XXI.2021.2.2 [accessed May 13 2022].

Horowitz, Michael C. "The Ethics and Morality of Robotic Warfare: Assessing the Debate over Autonomous Weapons," *Daedalus: Journal of the American Academy of Arts & Sciences* 145 (4) (Fall 2016): 25–36.

International Committee of the Red Cross (ICRC). "Fundamental Principles of IHL," https://casebook.icrc.org/glossary/fundamental-principles-ihl.

Knight, Will. "Russia's Killer Drone in Ukraine Raises Fears About AI in Warfare," *Wired Magazine* (17 March 2022), http://wired.com/story/ai-drones-russia-ukraine [accessed 3 April 2022].

Krishnan, Armin. *Killer Robots: Legality and Ethicality of Autonomous Weapons* (London: Ashgate Press, 2009).

Larkin, Matthew S. *Brave New Warfare: Autonomy in Lethal UAVs*. Master's Thesis (Monterey, CA: Naval Postgraduate School), https://wiki.nps.edu/download/attachments/15073701/Brave+New+Warfare+(Larkin,+Matthew+Thesis).pdf?version=1&modificationDate=1301324368000.

Latiff, Robert H. "Ethical Issues in Defense Systems Acquisition," in *The Routledge Handbook of Military Ethics*, ed. George Lucas (London: Routledge, 2015): 209–219.

Latiff, Robert H. *Future War: Preparing for the New Global Battlefield* (New York: Alfred Knopf, 2017).

Latiff, Robert H. *Future Peace: Technology, Aggression and the Rush to War* (South Bend, IN: Notre Dame University Press, 2022).

Lucas, George R. Jr. " 'This Is Not Your Father's War': Confronting the Moral Challenges of 'Unconventional' War," *Journal of National Security Law and Policy* 3 (2) (2009): 331–342.

Lucas, George R., Jr. "Postmodern War," in *New Warriors and New Weapons: Ethics & Emerging Military Technologies*, ed. George R. Lucas, Jr., *Journal of Military Ethics* 9 (4) (December 2010): 289–298.

Lucas, George R., Jr. "Industrial Challenges of Military Robotics," *Journal of Military Ethics* 10 (4) (December 2011): 274–295.

Marchant, G.E.; Allenby, B.; Arkin R.; et al. "International Governance of Autonomous Military Robotics," *Columbia Science and Technology Law Review* 12 (272) (2011).

Purves, D.; Jenkins, R.; Strawser, B.J. "Autonomous Machines, Moral Judgment, and Acting for the Right Reasons," *Ethical Theory and Moral Practice* 18 (2015): 851–872.

Scharre, Paul. *An Army of None: Autonomous Weapons and the Future of War* (New York: W.W. Norton & Co., 2018).

Sharkey, Noel. "Automated Killers and the Computing Profession," *Computer* 40 (2007): 122–124.

Sharkey, Noel. "Robot Wars Are a Reality," *The Guardian* (18 August 2007): 29.

Sharkey, Noel. "Cassandra or False Prophet of Doom: AI Robots and War," *IEEE Intelligent Systems* (July/August 2008): 14–17.

Sharkey, Noel. "Grounds for Discrimination: Autonomous Robot Weapons," *RUSI Defence Systems* 11 (2) (2008): 86–89.

Sharkey, Noel. "Saying 'No!' to Lethal Autonomous Targeting," in *New Warriors and New Weapons: Ethics & Emerging Military Technologies*, ed. George R. Lucas, Jr., *Journal of Military Ethics* 9 (4) (December 2010): 299–313.

Singer, Peter W. *Wired for War* (New York: Penguin Press, 2009).

Singer, Peter W. "The Ethics of 'Killer Apps'," in *New Warriors and New Weapons: Ethics & Emerging Military Technologies*, ed. George R. Lucas, Jr., *Journal of Military Ethics* 9 (4) (December 2010): 314–327.

Sparrow, Robert. "Killer Robots," *Journal of Applied Philosophy* 24 (1) (2007): 62–77.

Sparrow, Robert. "Predators or Plowshares? Arms Control of Robotic Weapons," *IEEE Technology and Society Magazine* 28 (1) (2009): 25–29.

Sparrow, Robert. "Robotic Weapons and the Future of War," in *New Wars and New Soldiers: Military Ethics in the Contemporary World*, eds. Paolo Tripodi and Jessica Wolfendale (London: Ashgate Publishing Ltd, 2011): 117–133.

Sparrow, Robert. "Ethics as a Source of Law: The Martins Clause and Autonomous Weapons," in *Humanitarian Law and Policy* (Geneva: International Committee of the Red Cross, 14 November 2017), https://blogs.icrc.org/law-and-policy/2017/11/14/ethics-source-law-martens-clause-autonomous-weapons/.

Strawser, Bradley J. "Moral Predators: The Duty to Employ Uninhabited Vehicles," in *New Warriors and New Weapons: Ethics & Emerging Military Technologies*, ed. George R. Lucas, Jr., *Journal of Military Ethics* 9 (4) (December 2010): 357–383.

Sullins, J.P. "The Role of Consciousness and Artificial Phronēsis in AI Ethical Reasoning," in *AAAI Spring Symposium: Towards Conscious AI Systems* (2019), http://ceur-ws.org/Vol-2287/paper11.pdf.

Tamburrini, Guglielmo; Arnoroso, Daniele. "Autonomous Weapons Systems and Meaningful Human Control: Ethical and Legal Issues," *Current Robotics Reports* 1 (24 August 2020): 187–194, https://doi.org/10.1007/s43154-020-00024-3 [accessed 4 May 2022].

Ticehurst, Rupert. "The Martens Clause and the Laws of Armed Conflict," *International Review of the Red Cross* (317), www.icrc.org/en/doc/resources/documents/article/other/57jnhy.htm [accessed 30 April 2022].

Wallach, Wendell. "Terminating the Terminator: What to Do About Autonomous Weapons," *Science Progress* (29 January 2013), http://scienceprogress.org/2013/01/terminating-the-terminator-what-to-do-about-autonomous- weapons/.

Wallach, Wendell. *A Dangerous Master: How to Keep Technology From Slipping Out of Our Control* (New York: Basic Books, 2015).

Walzer, Michael. *Just and Unjust Wars* (New York: Basic Books, 1977; 4th ed., 2010).

3

ETHICS AND AUTOMATED WARFARE

> The "electric dog" which now is but an uncanny scientific curiosity may within the very near future become in truth a real "dog of war," without fear, without heart, without the human element so often susceptible to trickery, with but one purpose; to overtake and slay whatever comes within range of its senses at the will of its master.
>
> – *B.F. Miessner (1916)*[1]

The electric dog was an early twentieth-century uncrewed ground vehicle built to follow a moving light signal to its source, as part of a larger project to develop a self-guided surface torpedo for the U.S. Navy during World War I, in the era just prior to the invention of radar. It has taken nearly a century for this prediction concerning the use of killer robots in war, made on the concluding page of a book by the young Yale University electrical engineering student who invented the electric dog, to come to pass.[2] The first two decades of the twenty-first century have seen an enormous outpouring of work devoted to the ethical and (far less frequently) the legal implications of military robotics, in response to a virtual explosion in military robotics technology and battlefield applications during this period.[3]

Conceptual Foundations of Ethics and Law for Remotely Operated Systems

It is worth pausing to reflect on what we have learned about the legal, moral, and policy implications of these trends as a result of these numerous and substantial efforts. First, while the technologies themselves are designed to operate in the domains of air, land, and sea, as well as in space, the majority of the discussions has centered on remotely piloted, lethally armed aerial platforms, such as Predators

DOI: 10.4324/9781003273912-4

and Reapers. That in turn stems from the highly effective use of these aerial platforms in surveillance operations, sometimes resulting in targeted killing of selected high-value adversaries by the United States and its allies. Indeed, it is often difficult to disentangle the discussions of aerial robotic technologies either from their controversial tactical deployment in such operations or from the long-term strategic consequences of the United States' willingness to engage in such tactics. The tactical uses and strategic consequences of these policies involving remotely operated systems, however, are quite distinct from the moral dilemmas posed by the vastly wider development and use of these systems themselves.

It is particularly unfortunate that the otherwise important policy discussions and moral debates surrounding the long-standing practice of targeted killing tend to obscure the fact that some of the most effective and justifiable uses of military robotics have been in unarmed ground operations, ranging from exploration of booby-trapped caves in Tora Bora, to battlefield rescue and casualty extraction, to dismantling improvised explosive devices (IEDs) or assisting in humanitarian relief operations.[4] Meanwhile, some of the most promising future developments in military robotics will likely be realized in the maritime and underwater environment (in surface combat or antisubmarine warfare, for example), as well as when some of these systems return home from the warfront and are employed in a variety of domestic or regional security operations such as border security, immigration control, drug and human trafficking, kidnapping, or disaster response and relief following hurricanes, floods, earthquakes, and massive wildfires – to which scant attention has thus far been paid (apart from implied threats to individual privacy).

During the Cold War, for example, it was often the case that submarines from rival superpowers engaged in intelligence, surveillance, and reconnaissance (ISR) missions in contested waters, keeping an eye on the adversary's movements and interests in a particular sector, and perhaps playing games of cat and mouse and even chicken to assess everything from noise detection to the maneuverability and other technical capabilities of different models of submarines as well as to test the effectiveness of coastal defenses. With the demise of the superpower rivalry and the Cold War, however, it has been some time since any naval force could routinely expend the resources necessary to continue such Tom Clancy-like macho underwater scenarios. They are simply too risky and resource-intensive.

Prior to the Russian Federation's 2022 invasion of Ukraine, strategic focus in the rest of the world shifted from the Atlantic to the Pacific, and from Russia to China, as treaty partners like Japan, South Korea, and the Philippines contend with one another and with the Chinese mainland for control of resource-rich areas of the South China Sea. Here, a more typical scenario would involve an underwater ISR mission near the Diayou/Senkaku islands, carried out by the United States in support of the interests of one of our principal allies, like Japan or South Korea. Today, that operation can be more efficiently and cost-effectively undertaken by deploying a single crewed vessel as an ISR command center, equipped with a variety of unmanned underwater vehicles (UUVs), each programmed to operate semiautonomously in carrying out a series of task-oriented maneuvers in much the same way and even following much the same command or decision tree script that human commanders would have followed in an earlier era.

In an underwater runtime environment, for example,[5] robots behave, or are programmed to behave, with about the same degree of autonomy as a human commander of an individual crewed ISR platform: that is, the operational or mission orders are for either type of vehicle to search, find, report, and either continue the mission or return to the command center or specified rendezvous point. This kind of mission can prove to be dull, dirty, routinely dangerous (for the crewed platform), and certainly boring, until, that is, an adversary's submarine is observed carrying out exploratory mining surveys on the ocean floor. In a plausible war game scenario, we might posit that the adversary then attempts to evade detection by fleeing into a prohibited marine sanctuary under the administrative control of yet another party to the dispute (e.g., the Philippines). The hypothetical semiautonomous UUV would then face exactly the same legal and moral dilemma as would confront the human commander of a conventional crewed submarine under otherwise identical circumstances: namely, to continue the military mission of tracking the enemy or refuse to violate international law and norms by hesitating to enter these prohibited, no-go waters. Standard operating procedures and standing orders defining the mission would require the human commander to contact operational headquarters for clearance or else discontinue the mission. The UUV can relatively easily be programmed to do likewise, thereby incorporating the constraints of law and morality within the parameters of the rules of engagement defining this well-defined (and what I have elsewhere termed highly scripted) mission.[6]

This seems a clear and relatively straightforward situation for which we have unfortunate precedent in the human case.[7] The underlying question of this hypothetical case is whether (perhaps as a result of this precedent) to build a corresponding rule of engagement constraint for this mission that would override the tactical priorities of military necessity in deference to the requirements of law and good international relations. What seems equally clear at present is that we lack the technical capability to design a UUV with sufficient independent decision-making capacity to simulate the swagger of one of Tom Clancy's human commanders during the Cold War era and decide on its own to override this legal constraint and venture into the no-go zone in search of the bogie.

Happily, meeting the normal demands of law and morality does not require such a complicated, and likely infeasible, feat of engineering. Moreover, were we to design and program our remotely operated undersea system to perform in the more or less straightforward manner otherwise described, we would have both duplicated the conventional behavior of a fully crewed system while simultaneously fulfilling what I have frequently defined as the Arkin test or Arkin constraint for robot morality: that is, we would have succeeded in designing, programming, and deploying a well-governed, reliable remotely operated system that could almost certainly perform as well as or even better (from a moral and legal perspective) than human beings under similar or identical circumstances.[8]

Even if I am correct in this claim, it may seem that I have cheated or fudged the boundary conditions to arrive at this result. Apart from whales, dolphins, and perhaps the intrepid underwater explorer James Cameron, there are not a large number of civilian noncombatants wandering the undersea environment. Just as with Russian and American submarines during the Cold War, it is primarily adversaries (and some military allies) that one is likely to encounter there, lessening considerably the prospect of accidentally or unintentionally doing harm to innocents (collateral damage). On balance, that is to say, the undersea environment affords a relatively uncomplicated moral context within which to operate in comparison, say, to that of soldiers in a brigade combat team (or lethally armed robots) entering a local village in search of insurgents, let alone of a UAV making its own, wholly unsupervised targeting decisions and executing a full-blown kill-chain command unilaterally in midflight. It is the latter prospects that have raised the specter of uncontrolled and morally unaccountable killer robots run amok and led ethicists like Wendell Wallach (Yale University) to propose having such systems declared *mala in se*[9] while roboticists like Noel Sharkey and his colleagues in ICRAC demand that the very development, let alone deployment, of lethally armed autonomous systems be outlawed altogether.[10]

The UUV in the present example, however, is not lethally armed (at least, not yet), and it is only semiautonomous (although, as described, it possesses essentially as much autonomy as a human operator or commander is authorized to exercise). This may seem to make consideration of moral dilemmas and legal challenges appear overly simplified. But that is not a bad thing. If the issue of military or security robots behaving ethically, let alone of their coming to exercise a computational analogue of human moral judgment, seems a complex and controversial matter as well as a formidable engineering challenge, then why not start with something simpler? What this example of the underwater runtime environment demonstrates is that we might feasibly design, build, program, test, and ultimately deploy reliable systems with only minimal intelligence and autonomy that nonetheless meet the demands of law and morality when operating in their defined battlespace.

Developing Appropriate Hypothetical Case Studies

By continuing to focus our work even more precisely on this somewhat simplified moral environment, we might learn lessons about how subsequently to approach the much more complicated problems on the water's surface, as well as on land and in the air, in addition to learning what to anticipate when we do.

For example, we can add a bit more complexity to our working underwater scenario. What if our UUV continues to tail the enemy and is fired upon? Do we arm it defensively against this possibility, and if so, does it return fire? Or does it take evasive action only? Or does it abort the mission and return to the host ship? Once again, in another era, human commanders, both on the surface and underwater, routinely confronted such decisions and were guided in making them both by situational awareness and by knowledge of both the conflict-specific and general (or standing) rules of engagement that constrain and inform such activities. The key similarity is that full autonomy to act without external restraint was seldom granted to the human commanders. That is to say, despite the human commanders possessing a wide range of complex and varying capacities – intuitive judgment, leadership, moral scruples, conscience – that would be extremely difficult to replicate in machine behavior, the humans in fact usually simply acted in accordance with these standing orders – that is, within a regulatory and governance framework ranging over a set of considerations from the international law of the sea to humanitarian law and a range of treaty obligations, all the way to specific rules of engagement designed to remove as much ambiguity and personal responsibility or accountability as possible from their actions (even if that is not exactly how they saw it, thought about it, or would have described it at the time). The human commanders had some situational autonomy but not full (let alone unlimited) autonomy. Hence, their behaviors might be far easier to simulate with remotely operated systems in this environment. Here, in this more clearly defined arena (as opposed to a range of other, more complex environments), we might hope at least to develop remotely operated semiautonomous systems that could function at a level of reliability and safety equivalent to humans, even absent the advances in programming and governance technology that would otherwise be required to literally duplicate or replace the human presence or involvement in these scenarios.

If this vastly less presumptuous and far more attainable objective seems feasible in the case of underwater systems, might we then return to the even more complex, land-based scenario of the brigade combat team engaged in a recon mission, searching for insurgents in a nearby village? Like the underwater ISR mission, this scenario is for the most part dull, dirty, and dangerous, as well as tedious and unrewarding, and on those grounds alone it is in principle amenable to the use of remotely operated systems. The dull, dirty, and boring aspects cease, however, whenever something dramatic and unexpected occurs, like a small child bursting out of a house and running in fear across the path of an enemy insurgent who is about to fire his rifle or escape. Could a remotely operated ground system conceivably cope with that foreseeable but unexpected circumstance, and others like it, with the degree of flexibility and sound judgment we demand of human combatants? Specifically, could it reliably and safely recognize the child as a noncombatant and appropriately withhold fire, even if the legitimate target is thereby allowed to fire freely or escape capture?

In the underwater case, we compared the degree of autonomy and sophistication required for the remotely operated system to duplicate not the full capacities of the human commander but what we might term the capacities specifically authorized for use by that commander (which are considerably less than the full range available in the human case). Likewise, in the village scenario, we would compare the capacities required of a functioning and semiautonomous ground system to those required and expected of, say, a young Army private, recently recruited, trained, oriented to the applicable rules of engagement and deployed in this conflict zone. Do we have a reasonable prospect of designing a remotely operated ground system to function as well as, say, a relatively new Army private? More generally, is there a reasonable prospect for designing and integrating remotely operated ground systems into the force mix of brigade combat teams to work reliably alongside, or even replace, some of the Army privates (if not the sergeant or lieutenant)?

There are many more instances as well as variations of these types of unexpected encounters or unforeseen developments in the land-based case than in the underwater environment. The robot has some surprising advantages over the Army private when it comes to its potential reaction time and especially with respect to the risk of harm it can tolerate in comparison to the human combatant. Where the remotely operated system currently lags far behind the Army private – and why the deployment of safe and reliable land-based systems may require a much longer period of development – is in what I described in the underwater instance as its degree of situational awareness. Automatic target recognition or pattern recognition software employed in the uncrewed system needs to be able to interact quickly and reliably with hardware sensors to enable the system to distinguish between a child and an adult, between an insurgent and a shepherd, and between an AK-47 and a child's toy or a shepherd's crook. While this can in fact be done at present, such distinctions cannot yet be made at a rapid operational pace with anything like the reliability of the Army private, even when allowing for the occasional errors in the latter's situational awareness amidst the fog of war.

But what if one day soon such systems could reliably and consistently demonstrate the requisite degree of situational awareness? Or what if, in the meantime, we chose to develop and deploy land-based systems only in combat environments that resembled the very clearly structured underwater environment – that is, characterized by very precise boundary conditions with little likelihood of the anomalous events and concomitant mistakes of judgment or perception that lead in turn to tragedy? The development of fully effective and reliable target and pattern recognition software and friend or foe systems may well lie in the reasonably near future. And meanwhile, as noted, robots have in fact been deployed in highly scripted contexts, such as serving as sentries and border guards in prohibited demilitarized or no-go zones. Robot sentries are currently used effectively in Israel as border guards in remote, strictly entry-forbidden areas, as well as by South Korea in the demilitarized zone with the North.[11] While Fire Scouts are primarily used for ISR at sea, the U.S. Navy has experimented with arming and deploying smaller versions of Fire Scouts – unmanned and semiautonomous helicopters – to provide force protection to ship convoys or aircraft carriers to shield them from insurgent attacks when approaching ports of call.[12] The development and increased use of remotely operated systems in such environments could well lead to effective and relatively low-cost force multiplication with lower risk for combatants and noncombatants alike. If we can do these things, and if doing so works at least as well as our current practice, then perhaps we should pursue more fully our capabilities to do so. Moreover, if we determine that we can and should make these modifications, and if it is feasible to do so, ought we not to be trying as hard as we can to bring about these marked improvements in the conduct of armed conflict?

Underlying Philosophical Considerations

This last line of reasoning describes another dimension of the Arkin test: a remotely operated platform fulfills the demands of law and morality (and may therefore be permissibly deployed) when it can be shown to comply with the requirements or constraints imposed by both and/or better than a human under similar circumstances. Arkin, to whom we owe the benchmark, observes that this principle may also serve to generate a *technological obligation* to move forward with the development and use of robotic technology that would render war itself and the conduct of armed hostilities less destructive, risky, and indiscriminate.[13] The prospects for increasingly automated warfare turn critically on this moral claim.

Satisfying the Arkin test, however, requires that we identify, analyze, and replicate the range of requisite behaviors in question, even in the relatively simplified underwater runtime command scenario, for example, sufficiently well enough to generate a reliable program script for an unmanned system that will emulate or duplicate the kind of human judgment and action called for in these situations. In the underwater case, we can foresee, for example, that a human commander might be tempted to override the rules of engagement prohibition against venturing into the international marine preserve because he or she notices something that our limited and literal-minded UUV would miss. But, of course, the human commander might also override rules of engagement out of pride, ego, ambition, or just plain poor judgment. Likewise, in the village, the Army private might exercise what partisans of folk psychology would label intuitive judgment to spare innocent lives but might equally well instead react in just the opposite fashion – motivated perhaps by confusion and fear, racism, hatred, resentment, or mental disturbance – leading to an excessive and indiscriminate use of force resulting in the tragic injury or death of noncombatants.

While, on the one hand, we probably cannot analyze the intuition and situational awareness of the human into simplified Boolean logic, we have the compensating reassurance, on the other hand, that remotely operated systems could not conceivably emulate any of the other, undesirable human reactions described earlier, simply because UUVs or UGVs do not care; they have no interests, intentions, or self-regard; they harbor no ambitions or hatred; and they are utterly incapable of the interiority (to use another metaphor of folk psychology) characteristic of self-consciousness. The German philosopher Martin Heidegger famously maintained that "Care [*Sorge*] is the Being of Dasein," a complex manner of depicting that such interior features – concern and compassion, as well as hatred and ambition, self-deception and self-regard – constitute the essence of being human.[14]

Heidegger's insight pertains especially well to the elusive folk-term conscience, which seems to integrate several of the components I have mentioned specifically alongside others: for example, I care about others than just myself; I have attachments of friendship, love, and loyalty; I sense that there are bonds and expectations connected to these that generate a range of duties and obligations to act in certain ways and avoid others. And, when tempted to override those constraints for the sake of immediate mission accomplishment (alternatively described more straightforwardly and less euphemistically as self-interest, expediency, or personal gain), my acknowledgment of these other concerns causes cognitive dissonance, resulting in uncertainty about how to proceed. Because I *care* about these other matters and persons, I feel guilt, which may intervene to impede my attempts to override those concerns for the sake of expediency – or, failing to do so, the resulting guilt may function as a kind of biofeedback to improve my behavior in the future. This is quintessentially human. Our own human caring is one (highly effective?) manner of behavioral governance, in both an individual and a social sense. We might just as well say that this trait of caring, along with the constellation of intentional and emotional states surrounding it, constitutes the unique software package with which we have come from the factory preloaded and that this particular software package works with our particular hardware effectively in most cases to generate responsible, intentional, accountable individual behavior within a wider social or cultural context. And whether we might additionally speculate that God, or evolution, or both – or something else entirely – has produced this arrangement, still it remains the case from a purely functional standpoint that emotions like guilt and concomitant phenomenal experiences like conscience function as behavior modifiers, part of an elaborate and complex human feedback system that serves to modulate, constrain, and modify our individual behavior in a social context.

One strategy in robotics that takes account of the foregoing observations is, accordingly, to pursue the path of strong artificial intelligence (AI), in which human engineers and computer scientists seek to develop computational models of human moral behavior by attempting to replicate emotions like guilt as part of a larger effort to develop a fully functioning machine analogue of human moral conscience. This highly ambitious strategy might entail trying to replicate other features of the complex palette of human mental states or human tactics associated with the phenomenon of morality (and immorality), such as ambition, self-regard, or the ability to engage in deceptive and misleading behavior.[15] The ambitious agenda of strong AI has been advocated by a number of scientists and engineers, from Marvin Minsky[16] to Arkin himself, as the most promising avenue to designing machine morality.[17] As an ambitious long-range research project, such initiatives have much to commend them.[18] It would be fascinating to analyze guilt as an effective form of system feedback and behavioral modification and self-correction or machine learning. Likewise, it seems clear that some machine analogue of deceptive behavior might sometimes prove necessary in a robotic system designed for sophisticated battlefield extraction or perhaps elder care (guiding the machine's actions toward reducing fear, bewilderment, and shock in the treatment of battlefield casualties or in the care of dementia patients). Do we now need to reproduce exactly, or even approximately, these identical capacities in unmanned systems to make them reliable and safe and effective?

From the previous (albeit simplified) scenarios, it would appear not.

Robots in this sense are not, nor could they be, nor would we need or wish them to be human in this sense. In contrast to Arkin's stated research agenda in particular, such ambitions do not seem to constitute a logically necessary preliminary step toward guaranteeing safety, reliability, and the most basic compliance on the part of present-day remotely operated systems with prevailing legal and moral norms of behavior in combat or security operations.[19] Once again, as the foregoing scenarios demonstrate, satisfactory results can be obtained by employing existing software, hardware, and programming languages. Those modest successes in relatively uncomplicated situations might well lead researchers and end users toward further, fully feasible, and largely conventional engineering solutions to the more complex behavioral challenges in remotely operated systems governance.

We might usefully compare this alternative research agenda with the history of aviation, in which initially ambitious and largely unsuccessful attempts to model animal behavior directly gave way to more modest and ultimately successful attempts to attain flight through the use of conventional materials and system designs that bore little resemblance to the actual behavior of birds or insects. Indeed, it is only within the past few years that engineering and materials sciences (including miniaturization of powerful computing) have enabled engineers to actually model and duplicate the flight behaviors of birds and insects directly. Had we, however, demanded adherence to this strict narrow-minded correspondence of principle at the dawn of the aviation age (rather than rightly abandoning it at the time as unattainable), we would likely still be awaiting our first successful flight, and, through this lack of creative imagination, have missed out on an entire intervening century of exciting aviation developments, uses, and benefits that bear only the most rudimentary resemblance to animal behavior.

Moral and Legal Implications of a Less Complex Research Agenda

The foregoing observations and insights are essential to addressing the host of controversies that have otherwise arisen in the field of military robotics in particular. Indeed, from the emergence and increasing use of remotely piloted vehicles to the advent of cyber war and conflict, the development of new and exotic military technologies has provoked fierce and divisive public debate regarding the ethical challenges posed by such technologies. Peter Singer and Noel Sharkey, in particular, have focused their criticisms especially upon Ronald Arkin, whom they accuse in effect of offering false and technologically unattainable promises as justification for his advocacy of greater use of military robots in combat.

Their argument is, in effect, in line with the foregoing observation regarding uniquely human capacities, traits, and behaviors that seem constitutive of moral reasoning and effective moral judgment and decision-making. The computational machine analogues of these human behaviors and mental states have not yet been attained and will not likely be so in the near future, if ever. Indeed, both Singer and Sharkey think the promises of strong AI researchers in these areas, in particular, are hyperbole and pure science fiction.[20] As a result, they claim there is no warrant for continuing to develop autonomous, lethally armed military hardware and that it is deceptive and cynical to offer such vague promises as grounds for continuing to support and fund such research. Absent these requisite guidance systems, lethally armed and otherwise autonomous (i.e., self-guided, independent of ongoing human executive oversight, and capable of making and executing kill-chain targeting decisions unilaterally) systems would invariably prove dangerously unreliable, and the very pursuit of such research is reckless, if not criminally negligent.[21] Sharkey and Singer go so far as to claim, as a result, that attempts to design such systems, let alone deploy them, should be outlawed altogether. Wendell Wallach has proposed a somewhat different strategy that would designate the use of such systems wholly apart from any form of human supervision, executive oversight, or accountability as off limits. In this way of thinking, if the use of wholly unsupervised autonomous systems is thought to be inappropriate, Wallach argues, one could place a legal limit on the use of lethally armed versions of remotely operated systems by having them designated *mala in se* under international law. This legal designation would have the effect of grouping the use of lethally armed autonomous systems alongside the use of chemical and biological weapons of mass destruction, as serving no legitimate military purpose whatever. Armed uncrewed systems could circumvent this legal restriction only if they remained fully under human control, with accountability for targeting decisions (including errors and any resulting collateral damage) ascribed solely to human agents. Apart from the sensitive legal terminology entailed in this proposal, it would otherwise have consequences largely indistinguishable from the current ban on the development and use of unsupervised lethally armed autonomous systems established in the Department of Defense Directive 3000.09 of November 2012.[22] The designation would have the additional effect of making the current ban permanent rather than temporary.[23]

Such ongoing and intractable controversies may point toward an altogether different problem. These intractable moral dilemmas, ironically, may be taken as evidence that the language of morality and ethics is serving us poorly in this context, further confusing us, rather than helpfully clarifying or enlightening us on how best to cope with the continuing development and deployment of seemingly exotic new military technologies. To the complaint of opponents of military uses of robotics that such uses are immoral and are, or ought to be, declared illegal, proponents respond by attempting to promise, at least, that their creations will be able to behave as ethically as or more ethically than humans. In fact, however, opposing parties involved in these discussions harbor distinctive and incompatible – and sometimes conceptually confused and unclear – notions of what ethics entails. From individual and culturally determined intuitions regarding right conduct, through the achievement of beneficial outcomes, all the way to equating ethics merely to legal compliance, this conceptual confusion results in frequent and virtually hopeless equivocation. Moreover, many scientists and engineers (not to mention military personnel) tend to view the wider public's concern with ethics as misplaced and regard the invocation of ethics in these contexts as little more than a pretext for technologically and scientifically illiterate, fearmongering, nay-saying Luddites who simply wish to impede the progress of science and technology.

But why should we insist on invoking fear and mistrust, and posing allegedly moral objections to the development and use of remotely operated systems, instead of defining clear engineering design specifications and operational outcomes that incorporate the main ethical concerns? Why not simply require that engineers and the military either design, build, and operate their remotely operated systems to these exacting standards, if they are able, or else desist from manufacturing or deploying such systems until they succeed in satisfying these engineering specifications? Why engage in a science-fiction debate over the future prospects for artificial machine intelligence that would incorporate analogues of human moral cognition, when (as I have demonstrated earlier in the case of UUVs) what is required is far more feasible and less exotic: namely, machines that function reliably, safely, and fully in compliance with applicable international laws, such as the law of armed conflict, when operating in wartime. And why insist that the development and use of such systems would constitute a game changer that ushers in a new mode of unrestricted warfare, in which all the known laws and moral principles of armed conflict are rendered obsolete, when what is required is merely appropriate analogical reasoning to determine how the known constraints on conventional armed conflict might be usefully extrapolated to provide effective governance for these novel conditions?

The prospects for machine models of moral cognition, as we have discovered to this point, constitute a fascinating but as yet futuristic and highly speculative enterprise. The goal of developing working computational models of reasoning, including moral reasoning, might not prove altogether impossible, but the effort required will surely be formidable. Morality and moral deliberation for the present (as critics of military robotics contend) remain firmly in the domain of human experience and likely will so for the foreseeable future. In any event, discussions of ethics and morality pertaining to remotely operated systems at present are largely irrelevant. We neither want nor need our uncrewed systems to be ethical, let alone "more ethical" or "more humane" than human agents. We merely need them to be safe and reliable, to fulfill their programmable purposes without error or accident, and to have that programming designed to conform to relevant international law (LOAC) and specific rules of engagement. With regard to legal compliance, that is to say, machines should be able to pass the Arkin test: autonomous uncrewed systems must be demonstrably capable of meeting or exceeding behavioral benchmarks set by human agents performing similar tasks under similar circumstances, as we have thus far shown them quite capable in the case of UUVs.

On the other hand, proposals at this juncture simply to outlaw research, development, design, and manufacture of autonomous weapons systems seem at once premature, ill-timed, and ill-informed – classic examples of poor governance. Such proposals do not reflect the concerns of the majority of stakeholders who would be affected; they misstate and would attempt to overregulate relevant behaviors.[24] Ultimately, such regulatory statutes would prove unacceptable to and unenforceable against many of the relevant parties (especially among nations or organizations with little current regard for international law) and would thus serve merely to undermine respect for the rule of law in international relations. Machines (lacking the requisite features of folk psychology, such as beliefs, intentions, and desires) by definition cannot themselves commit war crimes, nor could a machine itself be held meaningfully accountable for its actions under the law. Instead, a regulatory and criminal regime, respecting relative legal jurisdictions, already exists that holds human individuals and organizations who might engage in reckless and/or criminally negligent behavior in the design, manufacture, and end use of uncrewed systems of any sort fully accountable for their behavior and its consequences. We will revisit this vital topic in the concluding chapter of this book.

Notes

1 Benjamin Franklin Miessner, *Radiodynamics: The Wireless Control of Torpedoes and Other Mechanisms* (New York: Van Nostrand, 1916).

2 E.V. Everett, *Unmanned Systems of WW I & II* (Cambridge, MA: MIT Press, 2014), ch. 5.

3 These studies encompass Australian philosopher Robert Sparrow's inaugural essay, "Killer Robots" (IEEE Proceedings, 2007), and a subsequent, similarly titled book by Arman Krishnan (Ashgate, 2009). A detailed and pathbreaking survey of the ethical dilemmas posed by the increased use of such technologies prepared for the U.S. Office of Naval Research (ONR) by renowned computer scientist and roboticist George Bekey and his philosophy colleagues Patrick Lin and Keith Abney at California State Polytechnic University (ONR 2008) heralded, in turn, the widely read and enormously influential treatment of the emerging ethical challenges and foreign policy implications of military robotics, *Wired for War,* by Brookings Institution senior fellow, Peter W. Singer (Penguin, 2009).

The vast majority of these works focus on the ethical ramifications attendant upon the increased military uses of robotic technologies, reflecting the relevant lack of attention by legal scholars to the status of robotics in international law. The current status of domestic and international law governing robotics, however, together with a range of proposals for effective future governance of these technologies, was recently coauthored by Arizona State University Law Professor Gary Marchant and several colleagues in the "Consortium on Emerging Technologies, Military Operations, and National Security" (CETMONS), published in the Columbia Science and Technology Law Review (2011). The legal and moral implications of military robotics constituted the main focus of a special issue of the *Journal of Military Ethics* (9, no. 4, 2010), and of subsequent anthologies edited by Lin, Abney, and Bekey and Bradley J. Strawser (Killing by Remote Control, 2013), along with a book-length treatment of aerial robotics ("drones") from an operational perspective by Col. M. Shane Riza, USAF (2013). See: Keith Abney, Patrick Lin, and George Bekey, *Autonomous Military Robotics: Risk, Ethics, and Design* (U.S. Department of the Navy, Office of Naval Research, 20 December 2008): 112 pp, http://ethics.calpoly.edu/ONR_report.pdf.

Peter W. Singer, *Wired for War* (New York: Penguin Press, 2009).

Gary E. Marchant, Braden Allenby, Ronald Arkin, Edward T. Barrett, Jason Borenstein, Lyn M. Gaudet, Orde Kittrie, Patrick Lin, George R. Lucas, Richard O'Meara, and Jared Silberman, "International Governance of Autonomous Military Robots," *Columbia Science and Technology Law Review* 12 (2011), www.stlr.org/cite.cgi?volume=12&article=7. More recently, see Jeffrey S. Thurnher, "The Law That Applies to Autonomous Weapon Systems," *ASIL Insights* 17 (4) (18 January 2013); Michael N. Schmitt, "Autonomous Weapon Systems and International Humanitarian Law: A Reply to the Critics," *Harvard National Security Journal* 4 (1) (2013): 1–37.

"New Warriors and New Weapons: Ethics & Emerging Military Technologies," a special issue of *Journal of Military Ethics* 9 (4) (December 2010).

Patrick Lin, Keith Abney, and George Bekey, eds., *Robot Ethics: The Ethical and Social Implications of Robotics* (Cambridge, MA: MIT Press, 2011); Bradley J. Strawser, *Killing by Remote Control* (New York: Oxford University Press, 2013); M. Shane Riza, *Killing without Heart* (Potomac, MD: Potomac Books, 2013).

4 A sense of the range of applications available can be found in many places, from the Unmanned Systems Roadmap of the U.S. Department of Defense to the online newsletter of the Unmanned Aerial Systems (www.uasvision.com/), containing articles documenting the present and near-future use of unmanned systems for mapping coral reefs, monitoring the arctic environment, and apprehending drug trafficking. An upcoming small systems business expo (http://susbexpo.com/) includes feature articles on the uses of unmanned systems in humanitarian relief operations in Haiti, fighting forest fires, and agricultural crop spraying. A recent GAO report (September, 2012), www.gao.gov/assets/650/648348.pdf) detailing FAA preparations for these uses also cites risks and abuses, ranging from unsafe operations of model aircraft operating too close to pedestrians at the University of Virginia, to apprehension of a domestic terrorist who was rigging a similar model system to carry plastic explosives in a planned attack on the White House. Descriptions of uses of remotely operated systems for multiple purposes in the marine environment can be found in the 2012 annual report of the multi-institutional Consortium on Unmanned Systems Education and Research (CRUSER), http://lgdata.s3-website-us-east-1.amazonaws.com/docs/1314/612480/CRUSER_Annual-Report_FY2012.pdf. An enormous archive of three-dimensional visual prototypes in all relevant environments can be found at: https://savage.nps.edu/Savage/#Section16. (Viewing these will require installation of an extension 3-D (X#D) plug-in, available on this site.)

5 Donald P. Brutzman, Duane T. Davis, George R. Lucas Jr., and Robert B. McGhee, "Run-Time Ethics Checking for Autonomous Unmanned Vehicles: Developing a Practical Approach," in *Proceedings of the 18th International Symposium on Unmanned Untethered Submersible Technology* (Portsmouth, NH, 13 August 2013), http://auvac.org/uploads/publication_pdf/Table%20of%20Contents.pdf; full text at: https://savage.nps.edu/AuvWorkbench/documentation/papers/UUST2013PracticalRuntimeAUVEthics.pdf.

6 I define highly scripted security missions utilizing lethally armed autonomous systems in G.R. Lucas, Jr., "Industrial Challenges of Military Robotics," *Journal of Military Ethics* 10 (4) (2011): 274–295. A similar account of where and how to attain design success in ethical machine behavior can be found in Robert Sparrow, "Building a Better Warbot: Ethical Issues in the Design of Unmanned Systems for Military Applications," *Journal of Science and Engineering Ethics* 15 (2009): 169–187. The appeal for human executive oversight provides for the possibility of overriding the legal prohibition but renders the unmanned system in this instance merely "semi-autonomous" rather than fully autonomous, in which case the accountability for the decision rests with the human commander approving the action, not the unmanned platform.

7 An actual U.S. Navy minesweeper took such a detour with unfortunate and widely publicized results: www.cbsnews.com/8301-202_162-57564485/u.s-navy-ship-runs-aground-in-the-philippines/.

8 This criterion – that robots comply as or more effectively with applicable constraints of LOAC on their use of force and doing of harm than human combatants under similar circumstances – constitutes what I have termed the Arkin test for robot morality (although that is likewise somewhat misleading, as the criterion pertains straightforwardly to compliance with international law, not with the exhibiting of moral judgment). In this sense, the test for "morality" (i.e., for the limited ability to comply with legal restrictions on the use of force) is similar to the Turing test for machine intelligence: we have satisfied the demand when machine behavior is indistinguishable from (let alone better than) human behavior in any given context. I have outlined this test in several places: see "Postmodern War," in "New Warriors and New Weapons: Ethics & Emerging Military Technologies," a special issue of *Journal of Military Ethics* 9 (4) (December 2010): 289–298, and in much greater detail in G.R. Lucas, "Engineering,

Ethics and Industry: The Moral Challenges of Lethal Autonomy," in *Killing by Remote Control*, ed. B.J. Strawser (New York: Oxford University Press): 211–228.

9 Wendell Wallach, "Terminating the Terminator: What to Do About Autonomous Weapons," *Science Progress* (29 January 2013), http://scienceprogress.org/2013/01/terminating-the-terminator-what-to-do-about-autonomous-weapons/.

10 Noel Sharkey, "Saying 'No!' to Lethal Autonomous Targeting," *Journal of Military Ethics* 9 (4) (December 2010): 299–313. For an account of the work of ICRAC, see Nic Fleming, "Campaign Asks for International Treaty to Limit War Robots," *New Scientist* (30 September 2009), www.newscientist.com/article/dn17887-campaign-asks-for-international-treaty-to-limit-war-robots.html. See also the 2010 "Berlin Statement" of ICRAC at: http://icrac.net/statements, as well as the ICRAC mission statement at: http://icrac.net/who/.

11 "South Korea Deploys Robot Capable of Killing Intruders along Border with North," *The Telegraph* (13 July 2010), www.telegraph.co.uk/news/worldnews/asia/southkorea/7887217/South-Korea-deploys-robot-capable-of-killing-intruders-along-border-with-North.html.

12 Christopher P. Cavas, "U.S. Navy's New, Bigger Fire Scout to Fly This Fall," *Defense News* (Washington, DC, 13 June 2013), www.defensenews.com/article/20130611/DEFREG02/306110009/.

13 Ronald C. Arkin, "The Case for Ethical Autonomy in Unmanned Systems," *Journal of Military Ethics* 9 (4) (December 2010): 347–356. See also his definitive work on this topic, *Governing Lethal Behavior in Autonomous Robots* (Boca Raton, FL: Chapman & Hall/Taylor & Francis Group, 2009).

14 This famous line occurs in Chapter 6 of Heidegger's first major work, *Being and Time* (1929). This is likely not the proper venue for entering into an extensive analysis of what this may portend for human existence, save to say that all the subtle forms of experience Heidegger describes in his own, Husserlian-like account of time-consciousness in the human case just clearly are *not* part of the "experience" of machines, including robots. Indeed, one account of the essence of such artifacts is that they don't "*have*" experiences. And insofar as these experiences are (as both Heidegger, and his teacher, Edmund Husserl, aver) constitutive of human being, robots are not at all like, nor likely to be like, human beings.

15 Deception is a fascinating case in point, in that behavioral scientists have known for decades that deception is not unique to humans, that it occurs in a variety of species, and is utilized as a tactic in pursuit of a variety of ends, from simple survival to the fulfilling of desires and ambitions (whether for food, sex, or power or to elicit the affection of others). Daniel Dennet, an eminent cognitive scientist and philosopher of mind, is perhaps best known for his accounts over the years of the role of deception as an important dimension of intentionality in animal and human behavior: for example, in his classic work, *The Intentional Stance* (Cambridge, MA: MIT Press, 1989). In the human case, deception is a powerful tactic to operationalize strategies with a variety of objectives that might be defined as "successful mission outcome": for example, in calming a terrified wounded combatant with reassuring words so that he may be brought back from the front to a military hospital for treatment, or, in quite a different sense building some sort of "Potemkin Village" (such as General George Patton's "First United States Army Group" (FUSAG) during World War II) so that the enemy might be deceived regarding troop strength, placement, or tactical intentions.

16 Marvin Minsky, *The Emotion Machine: Commonsense Thinking About Artificial Intelligence and the Future of the Human Mind* (New York: Simon and Schuster, 2006).

17 Ronald C. Arkin and Patrick Ulam, "An Ethical Adaptor: Behavioral Modification Derived from Moral Emotions," *IEEE International Symposium on Computational Intelligence in Robotics and Automation* (CIRA-09), Dajeon (Korea), December 2009; R. Arkin, P. Ulam, and A. Wagner, "Moral Decision Making in Autonomous Systems:

Enforcement, Moral Emotions, Dignity, Trust, and Deception," *Proceedings of the IEEE* 100 (3) (March 2012): 571–589.

18 See John Sullins, "The Role of Consciousness and Artificial Phronesis in AI Ethical Reasoning," in *AAAI Spring Symposium: Towards Conscious AI Systems*, AAAIS-SSS (Stanford, CA, 25–27 March 2019), http://ceur-ws.org/Vol-2287/ [accessed 12 May 2022].

19 This observation is *not meant* to gainsay either the significance or utility of such research. Rather, I merely mean to indicate that Arkin's research agenda does not represent the only way forward on the question of robot morality. His is an example of what one might term a visionary approach, as opposed, frankly, to a more pedestrian (or workmanlike) approach making use of available technological capacity in the present to address the pressing questions of law and ethics with respect to unmanned systems.

20 Noel Sharkey, "March of the Killer Robots," *London Telegraph* (15 June 2009); Noel Sharkey, "The Automation and Proliferation of Military Drones and the Protection of Civilians," *Law, Innovation and Technology* 3 (December 2011): 236–237.

21 In addition to his comments in *Wired for War* (2009) on the bad faith and deceptive nature of moral reassurances from engineers like Arkin engaged in promoting the values and virtues of autonomous systems, see Peter W. Singer, "The Ethics of Killer Apps: Why Is It So Hard to Talk About Morality When It Comes to New Military Technology?" *Journal of Military Ethics* 9 (4) (December 2010): 314–327.

22 Department of Defense Directive 3000.09, "Autonomy in Weapons Systems," 13 (21 November 2012), www.dtic.mil/whs/directives/corres/pdf/300009p.pdf.

23 The legal sensitivity stems from the association of lethally armed autonomous systems with other means and methods of warfare that are "evil in themselves" (*mala in se*), such as rape. It is less clear or convincing, however, that the reasons adduced for this classification would prove compelling, both because the analogy between autonomous systems and other familiar examples of means *male in se* (rape, in particular) do not appear obvious, while the author's argument still seems to rest in part on the objection I have tried in this chapter to discredit: namely, that machines cannot be held accountable for their actions. Biological and chemical weapons of mass destruction, in addition, are not so designated on account of the design or type of the weapon itself but because the use of such weapons is thought to cause unnecessary injury and superfluous suffering. It is hard to see how this could possibly be the case with lethally armed, autonomous drones, where the death or injury from a missile is presumably identical to that experienced from the same missile fired from a crewed aircraft or an RPV (drone). See Wendell Wallach, "Terminating the Terminator: What to Do about Autonomous Weapons," *Science Progress* (29 January 2013), http://scienceprogress.org/2013/01/terminating-the-terminator-what-to-do-about-autonomous-weapons/.

24 In addition to proposals to outlaw armed or autonomous military robotic systems by ICRAC itself, see the report from Human Rights Watch, "Losing Humanity: The Case Against Killer Robots" (2012), ww.hrw.org/sites/default/files/reports/arms1112ForUpload_0.pdf. While unquestionably well-intentioned, the report is often poorly or incompletely informed regarding technical details and highly misleading in many of its observations. Furthermore, its proposal for states to collaborate in banning the further development and use of such technologies would not only prove unenforceable but likely would impede other kinds of developments in robotics (such as the use of autonomous systems during natural disasters and humanitarian crises) that the authors themselves would not mean to prohibit. It is in such senses that these sorts of proposals represent "poor governance." For a well-informed and clearly argued rejoinder to this report, critiquing the legal efforts to ban autonomous systems, see Kenneth Anderson and Matthew Waxman, "Law and Ethics for Autonomous Weapon Systems: Why a Ban Won't Work, and Why the Laws of War Can," Task Force on National Security and Law, Hoover Institution (Stanford, CA: Hoover Institution Press, 2013), www.scribd.com/doc/134765163/Law-and-Ethics-for-Autonomous-Weapon-Systems.

References

Anderson, Kenneth; Waxman, Matthew. "Law and Ethics for Autonomous Weapon Systems: Why a Ban Won't Work, and Why the Laws of War Can," in *Task Force on National Security and Law, Hoover Institution* (Stanford, CA: Hoover Institution Press, 2013), www.scribd.com/doc/134765163/Law-and-Ethics-for-Autonomous-Weapon-Systems.

Arkin, Ronald C. *Governing Lethal Behavior in Autonomous Robots* (Boca Raton, FL: Chapman & Hall/Taylor & Francis Group, 2009).

Arkin, Ronald C. "The Case for Ethical Autonomy in Unmanned Systems," *Journal of Military Ethics* 9 (4) (December 2010): 347–356.

Arkin, Ronald C.; Ulam, Patrick. "An Ethical Adaptor: Behavioral Modification Derived From Moral Emotions," *IEEE International Symposium on Computational Intelligence in Robotics and Automation* (CIRA-09), Dajeon (Korea), December 2009.

Arkin, Ronald C.; Ulam, Patrick; Wagner, A. "Moral Decision Making in Autonomous Systems: Enforcement, Moral Emotions, Dignity, Trust, and Deception," *Proceedings of the IEEE*, 100 (3) (March 2012): 571–589.

Bekey, George; Lin, Patrick; Abney, Keith. *Autonomous Military Robotics: Risk, Ethics, and Design* (Washington, DC: U.S. Department of the Navy, Office of Naval Research, 20 December 2008).

Brutzman, Donald P.; Davis, Duane T.; Lucas, George R. Jr.; McGhee, Robert B. "Run-Time Ethics Checking for Autonomous Unmanned Vehicles: Developing a Practical Approach," in *Proceedings of the 18th International Symposium on Unmanned Untethered Submersible Technology* (Portsmouth, NH, 13 August 2013), http://auvac.org/uploads/publication_pdf/Table%20of%20Contents.pdf; full text at: https://savage.nps.edu/AuvWorkbench/documentation/papers/UUST2013PracticalRuntimeAUVEthics.pdf.

Cavas, Christopher P. "U.S. Navy's New, Bigger Fire Scout to Fly this Fall," *Defense News* (Washington, DC, 13 June 2013), www.defensenews.com/article/20130611/DEFREG02/306110009/.

Department of Defense Directive 3000.09. "Autonomy in Weapons Systems," 13 (21 November 2012), www.dtic.mil/whs/directives/corres/pdf/300009p.pdf.

Everett, E.V. *Unmanned Systems of WW I & II* (Cambridge, MA: MIT Press, 2014): ch. 5.

Fleming, Nic. "Campaign Asks for International Treaty to Limit War Robots," *New Scientist* (30 September 2009), www.newscientist.com/article/dn17887-campaign-asks-for-international-treaty-to-limit-war-robots.html.

Heidegger, Martin. *Being and Time*. Trans. John Macquarrie and Edward Robinson (Oxford: Blackwell, 1962 [1929]).

Human Rights Watch. "Losing Humanity: The Case Against Killer Robots" (2012), www.hrw.org/sites/default/files/reports/arms1112ForUpload_0.pdf.

Krishnan, Armin. *Killer Robots: Legality and Ethicality of Autonomous Weapons* (London: Ashgate Press, 2009).

Lin, Patrick; Abney, Keith; Bekey, George, eds. *Robot Ethics: The Ethical and Social Implications of Robotics* (Cambridge, MA: MIT Press, 2011).

Lucas, George R., Jr. "Postmodern War," in *New Warriors and New Weapons: Ethics & Emerging Military Technologies*, ed. George R. Lucas, Jr., *Journal of Military Ethics* 9 (4) (December 2010): 289–298.

Lucas, George R., Jr. "Industrial Challenges of Military Robotics," *Journal of Military Ethics* 10 (4) (2011): 274–295.

Lucas, George R., Jr. "Engineering, Ethics and Industry: The Moral Challenges of Lethal Autonomy," in *Killing by Remote Control*, ed. B.J. Strawser (New York: Oxford University Press, 2013): 211–228.

Marchant, G.E.; Allenby, B.; Arkin R.; et al. "International Governance of Autonomous Military Robotics," *Columbia Science and Technology Law Review* 12 (272) (2011).

Miessner, Benjamin Franklin. *Radiodynamics: The Wireless Control of Torpedoes and Other Mechanisms* (New York: Van Nostrand, 1916).

Minsky, Marvin. *The Emotion Machine: Commonsense Thinking about Artificial Intelligence and the Future of the Human Mind* (New York: Simon and Schuster, 2006).

Riza, M. Shane. *Killing Without Heart* (Potomac, MD: Potomac Books, 2013.

Schmitt, Michael N. "Autonomous Weapon Systems and International Humanitarian Law: A Reply to the Critics," *Harvard National Security Journal Features* 4 (1) (2013): 1–37.

Sharkey, Noel. "March of the Killer Robots," *London Telegraph* (15 June 2009).

Sharkey, Noel. "Saying 'No!' to Lethal Autonomous Targeting," *Journal of Military Ethics* 9 (4) (December 2010): 299–313.

Sharkey, Noel. "The Automation and Proliferation of Military Drones and the Protection of Civilians," *Law, Innovation and Technology* 3 (December 2011): 236–237.

Singer, Peter W. *Wired for War* (New York: Penguin Press, 2009)

Singer, Peter W. "The Ethics of Killer Apps: Why Is It So Hard to Talk About Morality When It Comes to New Military Technology?" *Journal of Military Ethics* 9 (4) (December 2010): 314–327.

"South Korea Deploys Robot Capable of Killing Intruders Along Border With North," *The Telegraph* (13 July 2010), www.telegraph.co.uk/news/worldnews/asia/southkorea/7887217/South-Korea-deploys-robot-capable-of-killing-intruders-along-border-with-North.html.

Sparrow, Robert. "Killer Robots," *Journal of Applied Philosophy* 24 (1) (2007): 62–77.

Sparrow, Robert. "Building a Better Warbot: Ethical Issues in the Design of Unmanned Systems for Military Applications," *Journal of Science and Engineering Ethics* 15 (2009): 169–187.

Strawser, Bradley J. *Killing by Remote Control* (New York: Oxford University Press, 2013).

Sullins, John. "The Role of Consciousness and Artificial Phronesis in AI Ethical Reasoning," in *AAAI Spring Symposium: Towards Conscious AI Systems*, AAAIS-SSS (Stanford, CA, 25–27 March 2019), http://ceur-ws.org/Vol-2287/ [accessed 12 May 2022].

Thurnher, Jeffrey S. "The Law That Applies to Autonomous Weapon Systems," *ASIL Insights* 17 (4) (18 January 2013).

Wallach, Wendell. "Terminating the Terminator: What to Do About Autonomous Weapons," *Science Progress* (29 January 2013), http://scienceprogress.org/2013/01/terminating-the-terminator-what-to-do-about-autonomous-weapons/.

4

WHEN ROBOTS RULE THE WAVES

In contrast to the use of uncrewed systems in the domains of air and land, significantly less attention has been paid to the prospect of autonomous submersibles and/or autonomous surface vessels.[1] Once again, as he did with "killer" aerial and ground robots, Robert Sparrow first identified and sought to address this lacuna. This chapter is based on our subsequent collaboration to catalog some of the most distinctive uncrewed maritime systems and their current and proposed uses in a preliminary report for the United Nations Institute for Disarmament Research (UNIDIR) in 2015, subsequently published in the *U.S. Naval War College Review*.[2] In this condensed digest, I have retained and highlighted some of our contrasting views on the rapid development and military potential of autonomous uncrewed underwater vehicles (UUVs) and uncrewed surface vehicles (USVs).

Unsurprisingly, there are several ethical dilemmas specific to these technologies, owing to the unique and distinctive character of war at sea. Likewise, there are several unique and complex legal questions that are likely to arise regarding the applications of autonomous UUVs and USVs, including

- whether (as the comparatively modest body of legal literature to date has posed the problem) armed autonomous UUVs and USVs should be understood as "vessels" or as "weapons";
- the sorts of operations autonomous UUVs and USVs might legitimately be tasked with in international, as opposed to territorial, waters;
- whether the operation of armed autonomous systems is compatible with freedom of navigation in international waters; and
- the capacity of future maritime and underwater autonomous systems, when weaponized, to abide by the requirements of distinction and proportionality in naval warfare.

DOI: 10.4324/9781003273912-5

Accordingly, this chapter begins with a brief account of the reasons for believing that uncrewed systems will come to play an increasingly vital role in future naval combat and describes a number of UUVs and USVs already deployed by the U.S. Navy or currently under development by way of illustration.[3] Then we consider the argument that war at sea has a distinctive ethical character. Consequently, the use of uncrewed – and especially autonomous – systems in this context can generate ethical issues that the preceding chapter's summary discussion of the ethics of uncrewed systems may have missed. We then highlight the importance of a question about the appropriate way to conceptualize armed USVs and UUVs, suggesting that whether we think of individual systems as "vessels" or "weapons" will have implications for our understanding of the ethics of their applications, beyond merely the distinct legal regimes that apply to each.

The fourth section of this chapter examines a range of issues that will arise about the operations of UUVs and USVs in different sorts of waters (territorial, international, etc.). We examine at length the implications of the operations of armed autonomous weapon systems for freedom of navigation on the high seas. The chapter then turns to consideration of the ethical issues raised by the requirements of the principle of distinction for the operations of maritime lethally armed autonomous weapons systems (LAWS). There are several reasons to believe that the international humanitarian law (IHL) problem of distinction (discrimination of combatants from noncombatants) poses fewer problems for LAWS on and under the seas than in other domains of warfare, owing in large part to the comparative absence of noncombatants in the maritime operational space. Nevertheless, this chapter highlights five different specific cases where the ability to make such distinctions reliably remains a profound challenge. We subsequently consider the question of proportionality. As will have proven to be the case with distinction, there are some reasons to expect proportionality calculations regarding civilian casualties to be easier in the context of war at sea than in other forms of warfare. However, once we acknowledge that both damage to the environment and enemy combatant casualties are relevant to the ethical (if not the legal) requirement of proportionality, that requirement will also look very difficult for machines, even at sea.

In conclusion, we add some further complexity to the preceding discussion by considering

- the standard of compliance with the principle of distinction and proportionality that we should require of maritime LAWS;
- the possibility that maintaining a human being in the loop or (perhaps) on the loop could help to largely prevent attacks on illegitimate targets; and
- the implications of the remotely operated systems for the requirement of precautions in attack.

Robotic Weapons for Conflict on and Under the Sea

While aerial drones have largely been hogging the limelight when it comes to the military uses of robotics, there is currently an enormous amount of interest in the development and application of remotely piloted, semiautonomous, and autonomous weapons to carry out combat on and under the sea (Berkowitz 2014; Matthews 2013; United States Navy 2007; Department of Defense 2014, 8, 80–91).[4]

The existence of waves, currents, tides, and submerged obstacles, and the difficulties of maintaining reliable communications through water, in some ways makes the oceans a more difficult environment for robots than the air. However, remaining afloat or submerged at a given depth is less technically demanding than remaining airborne, whereas surface vessels need to move in only two dimensions rather than the three required of aerial and submersible vehicles. The relatively small number of terrain types in war at sea, the virtual nonexistence of legitimate commercial traffic beneath the sea, as well as the fact that blue-water operations often proceed without regard to concerns about running aground, also collectively mean that the oceans are a more tractable environment for robots than aerial or land conflict. Moreover, the results that might be achieved through the further development and deployment of UUVs and USVs are substantial. Operations at sea – and especially underwater – are always dangerous and often dull, and they are arguably also often "dirty" (in the sense of being wearing and uncomfortable for those involved in them). Thus, many missions at sea are well suited to being assigned to robots. Consequently, the military advantages to be secured by the development of autonomous systems for armed conflict on and under the seas are enormous (Matthews 2013). Our focus in this chapter will be on UUV and USV programs undertaken largely by the U.S. Navy, but it is important to emphasize that such systems are currently being developed by several other nations.[5]

Uncrewed *surface* vehicles (USVs) have enormous potential in naval operations, although this potential is just beginning to be explored. The fact that these USVs operate on the surface means that maintaining a human being in (or on) the loop is more feasible than it is for submersibles. Nevertheless, as in the case of remotely operated maritime vehicles more generally, there are still powerful military and economic dynamics pushing toward the development of USV systems that are capable of fully autonomous operations.

The USV inventory for the United States already includes several systems of different sizes – and intended for different roles – with more under development. Navy scientists are using self-propelled, self-guided, and self-sufficient wave gliders (essentially modified solar- and-wave-powered surf boards) manufactured by Liquid Robotics to gather meteorological and oceanographic data. In the future, these systems might be used for intelligence, surveillance, and reconnaissance (ISR) missions.[6] The U.S. Navy has conducted trials for several models of USVs for maritime security and fleet protection. The Spartan Scout, for example, is an aluminum rigid-hull inflatable boat that is capable of remote-controlled and semiautonomous operations. Software called CARACaS (Control Architecture for Robotic Agent Command and Sensing), which allows one human supervisor to oversee the operations of several USVs, has been used to provide USVs with the capacity for swarming to intercept enemy vessels.[7] Of course, the same systems might serve as weapons platforms that could be deployed in aggressive forward postures without placing crews at risk. The U.S. Navy tested a version of Spartan Scout armed with .50 caliber machine guns as early as 2002 and successfully demonstrated the firing of missiles from it in 2012.[8] The technology that makes possible defensive swarming also enables uncrewed craft to swarm offensively, with the aim of thereby overwhelming enemy ship-based defenses.

The U.S. Navy is also actively interested in developing an antisubmarine warfare capability using USVs. The Defense Advanced Research Projects Agency (DARPA) has responded to the threat posed to U.S. vessels by the new generation of quiet diesel submarines by initiating a program to build and test an autonomous trimaran capable of tracking submerged enemy submarines for extended periods.[9] The Anti-Submarine Warfare Continuous Trail Uncrewed Vessel (ACTUV), or Sea Hunter, underwent initial trials beginning in 2016, while the key navigational and anticollision avoidance systems for this vessel underwent successful trials using a test boat in January 2015.[10] Should this project come to fruition, one might expect to see extended range autonomous navigation and collision avoidance capabilities rolled out to any number of other surface vessels.

Submarine operations are notoriously dangerous, so removing human crews from submersibles wherever possible is arguably a moral imperative under the principle of unnecessary risk (PUR). There are several other benefits as well. Because uncrewed systems don't carry a crew, they can be significantly smaller than the crewed systems required to carry out similar operations. In turn, this permits UUVs to operate more quietly, for longer periods, and with a longer range. Autonomous UUVs in particular show enormous potential for operating for very long periods without needing to surface to replenish oxygen or fuel supplies or to return to base to rotate crews. This renders them ideal for roles in which the capacity to loiter undetected is an advantage. Also, emissions from the vessel's fuel source risk giving away two of the most vital secrets of a submersible: its presence and its location. Hence, according to the PUR, the capacity to operate autonomously is a requirement for an effective uncrewed submersible.

It was therefore no surprise to learn that the U.S. Navy has for some time had an ambitious program of research and development of UUVs and especially autonomous UUVs, as well as a number of existing systems already deployed.[11] UUVs' capacity for stealth and also their ability to be used in circumstances where it might be too expensive or dangerous to deploy a crewed vessel makes them ideal for ISR. Almost every UUV discussed in the literature is advertised as having a valuable role to play in ISR. For instance, the Sea Maverick and Sea Stalker UUVs are small(ish) semiautonomous submarines intended to carry out reconnaissance missions in depths of up to 1,000 feet.[12] The Littoral Battlespace Sensing-Glider uses an innovative propulsion system involving changes of buoyancy to travel the oceans for up to a month at a time and return oceanographic data useful for submarine warfare.[13] The U.S. Navy is also experimenting with more speculative systems such as Cyro, a robotic jellyfish, with the thought that a network of small submersible low-cost but hard-to-detect systems could provide valuable intelligence on enemy activities in contested waters.[14]

Similarly, UUVs have an obvious utility in countermine warfare, a role that can prove especially dangerous for crewed vehicles. The U.S. Navy possesses a number of systems intended for this role, including the Mark 18 (mod 1) Swordfish, the Mark 18 (mod 2) Kingfish, and the Littoral Battlespace Sensing UUV, all derived from variants of the REMUS Autonomous Undersea Vehicle manufactured by Hydroid, as well as the AN/BLQ-11 autonomous UUV (formerly called the Long-term Mine Reconnaissance System), which may be launched from the torpedo tubes of Los Angeles – and Virginia-class submarines.[15] The mine countermeasure package for the Littoral Combat Ship is based around an autonomous Remote Multi-Mission Vehicle (RMMV), which detects mines with a variable-depth towed sonar array.[16]

Armed UUVs themselves share much in common with naval mines (one might think of an autonomous torpedo as a "swimming" mine, for example) and may be used in a similar role. Indeed, mine warfare is on the verge of a profound revolution made possible by the capacity to separate the sensor packages that detect enemy vessels from the submerged ordnance that is tasked with destroying them. While CAPTOR had already provided proof of principle of this possibility, recent innovations in sensors, marine propulsion, and autonomous navigation have radically expanded the prospects for the development of such systems. In the future, nations may defend themselves – or deny the sea to others – using large arrays of networked sensors that communicate targeting information directly to a smaller number of autonomous armed UUVs lurking in the depths nearby.[17]

Finally, perhaps the most ambitious roles anticipated for any UUV are those that the large displacement uncrewed undersea vehicle (LDUUV) is supposed to fulfil. The LDUUV is an experimental autonomous submarine intended to be able to navigate and operate underwater for extended periods after being launched from a shore-based facility or an appropriately equipped nuclear submarine or a surface vessel. The tasks envisioned for it include underwater reconnaissance and mine countermeasures but also extend to carrying and deploying smaller UUVs or even launching aerial drones for surface reconnaissance.[18] The U.S. Department of Defense has announced a tender process to provide LDUUVs with an antisubmarine warfare capability (Kelly 2014). It seems clear that the ultimate conclusion of the technology trajectory being explored in this system is a fully autonomous submersible capable of the same range of operations as a crewed submarine.[19] In the discussion that follows, it is often variations of the LDUUV that are envisioned when examining the issues raised by the prospect of armed autonomous UUVs.

The Distinctive Ethical Character of War at Sea

There is a small but fruitful discussion in the literature of the legal status of UUVs and USVs (see, e.g., Gogarty and Hagger 2008; Henderson 2006; McLaughlin 2011; Norris 2013). However, to date there has been little discussion of the ethical issues raised by these systems. Insofar as legal instruments reflect, at least in part, the existing consensus on the duties and obligations of those whose activities they govern, we will sometimes refer to legal texts and precedents during the course of our argument. Nevertheless, as explained in previous chapters, the law does not exhaust ethics. Provisions of the law not only fail to address ethical concerns; indeed, those very legal constraints may pose their own unique moral dilemmas that will need to be addressed in operational policy and naval warfare strategy. In addition, there may be obvious ethical demands on warfighters that are yet to be adequately codified in the existing law. Finally, there may be activities that are legally permitted but that are not morally permissible. Ethical principles may therefore provide useful guidance to warfighters where the current law is silent or lacking. They may also motivate and inform attempts to revise, extend, or supplement the existing law.

One reason to believe that the development of robotic weapons for naval warfare might raise new ethical issues is that war at sea differs in important respects from war in (most) other environments.[20] As a result, the moral norms and customs that have evolved to regulate naval warfare are arguably more demanding than those regulating warfare elsewhere, are more deeply entrenched in the consciousness of warfighters, and have distinctive elements. Four features of war at sea play a key role in shaping the ethical (and legal) codes that regulate the activity of naval combatants.[21] First, in wartime as in peacetime, the sea itself is a deadly adversary of those who travel on or under it. Even in peacetime, hazards in the form of strong winds, rough seas, and hidden reefs abound while shipwreck and drowning are an ever-present danger. In wartime, seafarers who are forced to abandon ship after an enemy attack may find themselves facing nearly certain doom alone in freezing waters or floating in a small life raft thousands of miles from land. Second, because of the hostile nature of the marine environment, life at sea is primarily a collective life in which men and women are thrown together in a mutual endeavor framed by the possibility of misadventure.[22] Few people go to sea by themselves. Rather, people go to sea together in vessels, which then form miniature – or even, on modern capital ships, quite large – societies amid a hostile environment.

These first two facts already have two important consequences for ethical understandings regarding war at sea. First, the collective nature of life at sea and the shared vulnerability of all seafarers to misadventure and drowning means that a strong expectation of mutual aid has grown among those who go to sea. In particular, all those who go to sea are understood to have a duty to come to the aid of those who are lost at sea wherever possible and when they can do so without incurring serious danger to themselves. This is a particular duty that transcends ordinary national loyalties and has no direct analogue in land warfare.[23] The development of this expectation may be accounted for as a function of the need for a form of social insurance for this risky endeavor. Every individual at sea is safer if there is an expectation that everyone will come to the rescue of anyone as required. Consequently, it is in each and every individual's interests if this expectation is widely promulgated and if failures to live up with it are subject to sanctions, both formal and informal.

Obviously, war – and the dehumanization of the enemy that often accompanies it – places this expectation under stress. Nevertheless, because enemy sailors in the water are no longer combatants by virtue of being *hors de combat* – and because the risk of being in need of rescue is higher for all seafarers during wartime – the expectation remains that vessels will render aid to, and will attempt to rescue, individuals lost at sea regardless of their nationality when they have the capacity to do so and as long as doing so would not jeopardize the safety of the vessel and those on board. Moreover, the extent to which all those who go to sea share a distinct way of life compared to those who remain on land – and the solidarity that this encourages – along with the constant danger posed by the sea to all combatants ensures that this duty of rescue remains central to maritime culture even in wartime.[24]

In addition, the ethical and legal codes that govern war at sea are primarily concerned with the activities and fate of "vessels." As the operations of a ship are the result of a cooperative activity, it is often not possible to distinguish between the intentions of the commanding officer and that of his or her crew. Nor is it usually possible to attack some persons on board a vessel without targeting the vessel as a whole and thus risking the lives of everyone aboard. For these reasons, maritime combatants literally sink or swim together. Thus, it is both natural and appropriate that the vessel be the primary focus of attention in ethical (as well as legal) deliberation about naval warfare.

There are two additional features of war at sea that are important to bear in mind when thinking about its ethics, which concern the unique relation between combatants and noncombatants in naval combat: population density and geographical features. The sea is more sparsely populated than land, and in wartime, the vessels that sail on or under it divide more or less naturally into those who are actively participating in the conflict and those who are not (Walzer 2006, 147). Especially with the benefits of modern sensor packages, military vessels are more easily distinguished from civilian vessels than are groups of soldiers from civilians in land warfare, and it is more difficult for combatants to hide among the noncombatant population. Thus, except for merchant vessels that might have been pressed into service to carry cargo or personnel for military purposes, it is generally much easier to distinguish legitimate from illegitimate targets at sea than it is in other forms of warfare.[25] On the other hand, the comparatively featureless nature of the oceans and the lack of local geographical reference for national and other relevant political boundaries means that it is harder to separate combatants and noncombatants geographically. This problem is exacerbated by the fact that oceangoing commerce is essential to the flourishing – and even to the survival – of modern nations, with the consequence that, even during wartime, merchants will continue to ply the seas with their goods and passenger ships and ferries will continue to transport civilians (von Heinegg 2003, 402). At least partially in recognition of this fact, the high seas remain a commons, owned by no one and available for use by everyone.

These latter two features of war at sea have led to the development of a sophisticated set of practices and agreements around the activities of belligerent and neutral parties intended to allow peaceful navigation of the seas by neutral parties to continue even when wars are being fought. Customary international law relating to naval warfare attempts to balance the competing demands of national sovereignty and freedom of navigation, it distinguishes between belligerent and neutral nations' internal waters, territorial waters, and exclusive economic zones and the high seas, and it places limits on the sorts of activities that may be legitimately pursued in each (von Heinegg 2003). Understanding the competing considerations informing these treaties will also, as we shall see, prove useful to resolving ethical issues relating to the areas and roles in which UUVs and USVs may legitimately be deployed.

It does not serve us to exaggerate the extent to which the ethics of war at sea differs from the ethics of fighting wars in other environments. Indeed, the fundamental moral framework for naval warfare, as for land or air warfare, is outlined in just war theory. The special features highlighted here may be accounted for as consequences of the application of just war theory to the peculiar character of war at sea. Moreover, each of the various features of war at sea highlighted earlier may have some counterparts in other domains of warfare.[26] Nevertheless, drawing attention to the way the ethics of war is structured by its special contextual circumstances may productively inform deliberation about the ethics of the development and deployment of robotic weapons in this context.

Vessels Versus Weapons

The legal and ethical codes that govern war at sea are mostly concerned with the activities of ships and submarines and place demands on individuals primarily, although not exclusively, through their role on these vessels.

Several legal authorities have already begun to consider whether or when UUVs and USVs should be considered "vessels" under the law of the sea. The emerging consensus seems to be that autonomous UUVs and USVs, at least above a certain size, should be classed as vessels.[27] While RPVs might plausibly be held to be extensions of the vessel from which they are operated (McLaughlin 2011, 108–109), systems capable of extended autonomous operations should be understood as vessels in their own right (Gogarty and Hagger 2008, 114–116; von Heinegg 2008, 146; Henderson 2006, 66; McLaughlin 2011, 112; Norris 2013).[28]

The question of how we understand USVs and UUVs is also central to the ethics of their design and application. The more we think of these systems as autonomous and controlled by an onboard computer, and the more roles they become capable of fulfilling, the more natural it is to think of them as vessels. However, as the discussion later highlights, understanding them as vessels appears to impose demanding ethical requirements on their capacities and operations, especially relating to distinction, proportionality, and the duty of rescue.

An alternative way of addressing these requirements, in the light of such conundrums, is to think of armed autonomous USVs and UUVs themselves instead as weapons, which may be deployed by warfighters, who then become responsible for ensuring that the use of the weapon meets the requirements of distinction, proportionality, and other applicable *jus in bello* requirements (Rawley 2014). Yet, this way of proceeding generates its own challenges. A great deal of work remains to be done to clarify the best way of understanding the status of armed UUVs and

USVs in the context of larger ethical framework governing war at sea (as opposed merely to their current legal status).

Deployment

The Law of the Sea Convention attempts to balance the competing claims of national sovereignty and freedom of navigation in peacetime by distinguishing between the status of different sorts of waters and the permissibility of different sorts of activities therein. Customary international law relating to naval warfare extends this to regulate the relations between belligerent and neutral parties insofar as possible. The research and analysis required to assess the operations of USVs and UUVs within these frameworks is now beginning to be undertaken and some initial results are starting to emerge (Gogarty and Hagger 2008). Henderson (2006) suggests, for example, that "UUVs may operate freely in both the high seas and 'exclusive economic zones'" (EEZs) while "exercising due regard for the interests of other vessels and posing no threat to the territorial integrity of the coastal state" (68–69), and remain submerged while exercising transit passage in international straits and in archipelagic sea lanes (69). In territorial seas, he suggests, UUVs must operate on the surface to exercise the right of innocent passage and display appropriate lights and make sound signals to facilitate safety of navigation. Gogarty and Hagger (2008, 117–118) also suggest that USVs and UUVs would be restricted in the activities that they can undertake while exercising the right of innocent passage. McLaughlin (2011) emphasizes that USVs and UUVs are clearly subject to the Convention on the International Regulations for Preventing Collisions at Sea (COLREGs) and must be capable of avoiding collisions to such a degree that they could be said to maintain a "proper and sufficient lookout." He also allows that the presence of a foreign submerged UUV within a nation's territorial waters might constitute a sovereign affront justifying the use of armed force (113–114).

Some important ethical questions underpinning and surrounding the relevant legal frameworks might prove useful in informing this nascent ongoing legal debate. It does seem reasonable, for instance, that the moral right nations have over their territorial waters and (to a lesser extent) continental shelves and exclusive economic zones should exclude USVs and UUVs conducting – or perhaps even just capable of conducting – certain sorts of operations. If nations have a right against other nations that others may not conduct mining or survey operations in their EEZs or carry out operations injurious to their security in their territorial waters, then (according to the principle we adduced in Chapter 1 regarding the negligible legal impact of removing a crew at a distance from an aircraft) this right would surely carry over consistently to exclude uncrewed vessels just as much as crewed vessels. Arguably, the fact that UUVs and USVs are not crewed makes their use in these sorts of waters more suspicious and threatening to the interests of sovereign governments (on the assumption that other nations will be more likely to deploy vessels in hazardous environments that might generate a military response, given that doing so will not place a human crew at risk of death or capture). Requiring such systems to confine themselves to innocent passage through territorial waters is at least a partial solution to this problem.

The ethics of the use of autonomous UUVs and USVs on the high seas remains an open and controversial matter. At first sight at least, the right to freedom of navigation in international waters appears to extend to include these systems, presuming that they do not pose too much of a navigational hazard to other vessels. This presumption rests, however, on a clear understanding of them as vessels. That presumption may be unsettled when considering the prospect of armed autonomous UUVs and USVs and whether such systems should be thought of, instead, as weapons. Simply arming a vessel (e.g., a naval vessel) does not transform its status into that of a weapon, of course. But the fact that the armed "vessel" is also uncrewed or autonomous may affect our final judgment of its status.

Roughly speaking, the operations of vessels in international waters are permissible as long as they are compatible with the right of free navigation of other vessels through the same waters. Thus, if they are to operate on the high seas, UUVs and USVs must have the capacity to reliably avoid posing a hazard to other vessels. At a bare minimum, this requires taking the appropriate measures to minimize the risk of collision. While the COLREGs spell this out as requiring all vessels to "at all times maintain a proper lookout by sight and hearing" (which phrasing encourages the reader to presume a human being either physically on board or maintaining continuous supervision remotely), there is no reason why a fully autonomous system that proved equally capable of avoiding collision with other vessels without onboard human supervision shouldn't be judged to meet the appropriate standard.

Of course, armed UUVs and USVs operating on the high seas would appear to pose risks to commercial shipping and to the warships of neutral nations beyond simply the risk of collision: they might (accidentally) fire upon those other vessels, for example. Their significance for the right of freedom of navigation is therefore likely to depend on their capacity (and the faith of other navigators in their capacity) to distinguish between legitimate and illegitimate targets of attack (as discussed further later).

A key question in the larger debate about the ethics of autonomous weapons concerns whether they, too, might prove capable of satisfying what, in Chapter 3, was defined as the Arkin test. That is, would their use as weapons of war be deemed permissible if maritime LAWS proved themselves equally capable of complying with the IHL standards currently required of human mariners regarding *distinction* and *proportionality*? And contrariwise, if land-based and aerial LAWS were finally deemed *male in se* or otherwise prohibited, would not this ban extend to maritime LAWS as well? If so, then naval forces would be prohibited from arming autonomous maritime systems and likely would also require restricting their use as vessels (and never as weapons) when engaged, for example, in ISR.

Some (like this book's author), attempting to adhere strictly to the original moral intentions of the Law of Armed Conflict (*jus in bello*) to provide protections for war's most vulnerable victims, are prone to believe that satisfaction of the Arkin test would be sufficient to render the use of LAWS permissible. Indeed, owing to the (thus far unrealized) promise of LAWS to comply more perfectly with legal demands of proportionality and distinction than human combatants under identical circumstances, one might even conclude that their use would become mandatory (e.g., Lucas 2014). On the other hand, a number of authors (e.g., Sparrow, Sharkey, Wallach) have suggested that a strict focus on the requirement of human autonomy and accountability central to the moral (as opposed to the legal) structure of *jus in bello* itself may lead us to conclude that the absence of a human *will* (moral agency) at the moment the attack is carried out means that the Arkin test is irrelevant, since autonomous weapons cannot ever be said to comply with that stipulation (Asaro 2012; Sparrow 2016). Insofar as the principal concern in this chapter is with the compatibility of the operations of maritime LAWS with the right to freedom of navigation (rather than with the wider conceptual debate concerning the ethics of autonomous targeting), it appears that the relevant standard of discrimination is precisely and only that required of human beings in similar circumstances, as the Arkin test seems to stipulate.

There is another reason to worry, however, that achieving a high standard when it comes to the capacity to distinguish between legitimate and illegitimate targets may not by itself prove sufficient to render the use of maritime LAWS ethical on the high seas. The presence of LAWS operating in certain waters might exercise a chilling effect on commercial shipping over a wide area and thus impinge on the right of freedom of navigation. This might prove to be the case, even if the chance of an accidental attack by LAWS was extremely remote (given the level of demonstrable reliability required for the legal deployment of these systems, for example). This possibility seems especially likely if we think of autonomous UUVs and USVs as weapons rather than vessels. Indeed, one might well argue that armed autonomous UUVs, at least, should be understood as sophisticated versions of free-floating mines and consequently should be prohibited (Berkowitz 2014).[29] The use of drifting mines that do not disarm themselves within an hour is currently prohibited under international law precisely because of the threat they pose to freedom of navigation.[30] The fact that the chance of any particular ship being struck by any particular drifting mine is small does not seem to affect the force of this concern.

An important point of reference for our intuitions here is the United States' Mk 60 CAPTOR deepwater mine, which is a moored torpedo launch system capable of detecting the acoustic signature of approaching enemy submarines and firing a torpedo to destroy them.[31] This system is arguably already autonomous insofar as the "decision" to launch a torpedo is made without direct human input at the moment of launch. Versions of the system have been in use since 1979 without causing significant international outcry, which suggests that concerns about freedom of navigation in the open waters need not rule out the deployment of autonomous weapons systems. There are at least three reasons to be cautious about this conclusion, however. First, because as the CAPTOR is itself fixed – even if its range of operations is extended – the system would appear to pose less of a danger to navigation than hypothetical free-ranging maritime LAWS.[32] Second, insofar as this weapon is advertised as an antisubmarine system, those plying the surface of the waters may feel that they have little to fear from it. International opinion might be very different should similar systems come to be tasked with destroying surface vessels. Finally, the absence of any outcry against CAPTOR and similar systems should likely be understood in the context of a history where, to date, they have not been responsible for any noncombatant casualties. The first time an autonomous weapon system deployed at sea attacks a commercial or – even worse – a passenger vessel, we might expect public and international opinion about their legitimacy to change dramatically.

Even very reliable autonomous weapons systems may therefore jeopardize freedom of navigation if vessels are unwilling to put to sea in waters in which maritime LAWS are known to be operating. While fear of (accidental) attack by an LAWS might appear to be irrational when compared to the risks posed by crewed systems, beliefs about risk are notoriously complex and difficult to assess because they often contain hidden value judgments. In this case, a reluctance to risk attack by maritime LAWS may express the value judgment (as Sparrow and Asaro noted, earlier) that *human beings alone should be responsible for decisions to take human lives.* Insofar as what matters for the sustaining of the international commerce that the right of freedom of navigation exists to protect is the willingness of ships to ply the oceans, subjective judgments of risk may be just as significant – indeed more – for the existence of freedom of navigation as the objective risks that ships actually take when they leave port.

It may, therefore, turn out that the international community will be required to adjudicate on the balance of the interests of states in deploying maritime LAWS with the desire of operators of civilian vessels not to be put at risk of attack by an autonomous weapon. Any attempts to embed this judgment in legislation will also need to consider what is realistically achievable in this regard, especially given the military advantages associated with uncrewed systems and the force of the military requirements driving their adoption and use. In many ways, such a debate would hark back to that which took place with the advent of submarine warfare, which was effectively resolved in favor of permitting the operations of military submersibles. This might well prove to be the outcome with regard to armed autonomous UUVs and USVs as well. However, it is important to acknowledge the competing considerations in this debate, as attempted here.

A number of further questions may arise concerning the operations of armed autonomous UUVs and USVs in various waters that at least deserve mention in passing. The difficulty in imagining autonomous weapons having the capacity to capture enemy or neutral vessels, for example, suggests that they could at most play a limited role in naval blockades or taking neutral merchant vessels as prizes (von Heinegg 2008, 149). The requirement to record the locations of mines so that they may be removed or rendered harmless after the cessation of conflict, by contrast, would appear to be moot, since the "mines" under consideration in this instance are themselves mobile and autonomous. The considerations motivating this requirement itself (i.e., to reduce the subsequent hazards to shipping following conflict) imply that autonomous weapons must reliably be able to render themselves harmless upon direct instruction by human supervisors or else after some defined period has elapsed. There are undoubtedly also other issues that, along with these, require further investigation.

Distinction

Perhaps, the most fundamental ethical requirement in wartime is to confine one's attacks to enemy combatants and as much as possible to try to avoid civilian casualties. Thus, the *jus in bello* principle of distinction requires warfighters to refrain from targeting noncombatants and take appropriate care to try to minimize the noncombatant casualties caused by attacks targeted at combatants.

As noted in Chapter 1, much of the past criticism of autonomous weapons systems involved the charge that robotic weapons were unlikely to be capable of meeting the requirements of distinction, at least for the foreseeable future. In counterinsurgency warfare, identifying whether someone is a combatant or not required a complex set of contextual judgments that seemed beyond the capacity of machines at the time (Guarini and Bello 2012; Sharkey 2012b). Whether this problem is insurmountable or exists in all the roles in which we might imagine LAWS being used remains deeply controversial. It led the U.S. Navy in 2021 to postpone plans to deploy large uncrewed surface vehicles (LUSV) armed with strike missiles, for example, until further analysis of the safety, security, and reliability of such systems can be completed.[33]

In the present context of maritime systems, however, suffice it to say that the problem of distinction is arguably less demanding in naval warfare because there are fewer potential targets and because sonar and radar are more capable of distinguishing between military and civilian vessels than image recognition, radar, and lidar are at distinguishing between targets for robots engaged in land warfare (Brutzman et al. 2013, 3). Indeed, one reason advanced for favoring the use of autonomous systems on or under the sea, especially in blue-water missions, is that (when compared with land or air), the civilian footprint on the high seas is comparatively small, even allowing for commercial shipping and recreational boating. Moreover, the problem of distinction looks especially tractable in the context of antisubmarine warfare, given the relative paucity of civilian submarines with tonnage and/or acoustic signatures comparable to those of military submarines, together with the fact that those few civilian systems that do exist tend to operate in a limited range of roles and locations (primarily around oil rigs and submarine cables or in isolated and well-defined deep-sea explorations). We might therefore expect that if robots are to become capable of distinction in any context, they will become capable of it in war on and under the sea.

Nevertheless, there are at least five sorts of cases where the requirements of distinction pose a formidable challenge for the legal and ethical operation of autonomous weapons in naval warfare. First, to avoid attacks on military ships of neutral nations, maritime LAWS will need to be able to identify the nature and the nationality of potential targets, not just the fact that they are warships. In some cases, where the ships in the enemy's fleet are easily distinguishable from those of other nations due to distinctive radar or acoustic profiles, this problem may not arise. However, in some circumstances, identifying that a ship carries guns or torpedoes and/or is of a certain tonnage or class will not be sufficient to establish that it is an enemy warship. Instead, making this identification will require the ability to form reasonable conclusions about its identity based on its historical pattern of activity and threat posture within the battlespace.

One obvious way to solve this problem would be to program autonomous UUVs and USVs to confine their attacks to targets that are themselves actively firing weapons (Canning 2006). However, this would significantly reduce the military utility of LAWS, especially in strike and area-denial roles. Whether computers will ever be able to make the necessary judgments to avoid the need for this restriction remains an open question.

Second, maritime LAWS must be able to recognize when warships are repurposed as hospital ships and declared as such, in which case they cease to be legitimate targets. This sometimes happens in the course of a particular engagement, when, for instance, the enemy is forced to draft a ship into service as a hospital ship to treat a large number of their warfighters who have been wounded during the course of battle. The new role of the ship will be communicated by prominently displaying the Red Cross (or its various equivalents) and directly, by radio, to the other forces involved in the battle. Maritime LAWS will need to have the capacity to recognize these signals and the change of status in the vessel concerned.

Third, enemy vessels that have clearly indicated their surrender are not legitimate targets (cf. Additional Protocol I to the Geneva Conventions 1977, Article 43). All maritime LAWS must therefore be able to recognize surrender (Sparrow 2015). It is possible that in the future warships may be expected to carry a surrender beacon that is capable of communicating to any LAWS operating in the area that they have in fact surrendered. Until that day, however, maritime LAWS will need to have the capacity to recognize and respond to the existing conventions about communication of surrender through changes in threat posture and via the display of signal lights or flags. Again, at this stage it is unclear whether robots will ever be able to do this reliably.

Fourth, maritime LAWS must be able to identify when an enemy ship is *hors de combat* by virtue of being so badly damaged as to be incapable of posing any military threat. In rare circumstances, it may not be possible for a badly damaged and listing ship to signal surrender. Thus, morally – if not legally – speaking, even an enemy warship that has not indicated surrender is not necessarily a legitimate target if it is no longer capable of engaging in hostilities.[34] Human beings are (sometimes) able to discern when this circumstance applies using their rich knowledge of the world and of the motivations and likely actions of people in various situations. Once again, applying the Arkin test at minimum, maritime LAWS would need to be at least as capable as human beings at making such discriminations before their use would be ethical.

Importantly, these last three issues appear in a different light depending on whether we think of maritime LAWS as vessels or as weapons. If an enemy warship surrenders after a torpedo is launched from a crewed submarine, for instance, the ship's destruction would be a tragedy but not a crime. However, if a ship fires upon an enemy vessel that has clearly indicated surrender, this action constitutes a war crime. If we think of LAWS as a weapon, then as long as the officer who deploys it does not do so knowing the intended targets have surrendered or otherwise become *hors de combat* or been repurposed as hospital ships, its use will be legitimate even if there is some chance that the status of its target(s) may change after it is deployed.

On the other hand, if we think of the USV or UUV as a vessel, then it seems it must have the capacity to detect whether potential targets have surrendered or otherwise become *hors de combat* (or been repurposed as a hospital ship) to avoid further attack. If the delay between deploying a maritime LAWS understood as a weapon and its carrying out an attack is too long – a matter of days rather than hours, for instance – then this might shake our conviction that it is sufficiently discriminating to be ethical.[35]

Fifth, when it comes to operations to interdict or attack merchant shipping, the problem of distinction is especially challenging precisely because it is so context sensitive. LAWS would seem particularly unsuited to make these contextual judgments about whether, for example, merchant vessels were carrying enemy troops or "otherwise making an effective contribution to military action." The fact that LAWS are unlikely to be capable of searching or capturing merchant ships also limits their utility in making this discrimination.

Proportionality

The ethical stipulation of proportionality in *jus in bello* requires that the military advantage to be gained by an attack on an otherwise legitimate military target proves sufficient to justify the death and destruction that might reasonably be expected to be caused by the attack. Importantly, the legal requirement of proportionality is usually understood to demand only that the likely foreseeable (but wholly unintended) noncombatant casualties ("collateral damage") resulting from the attack be minimized. The ethical requirement is more stringent, requiring consideration of the lives of combatants, including even enemy in this calculation as well (Walzer 2006, 156). Thus, for instance, a deliberate attack on a military installation housing a large number of enemy warfighters who posed no immediate threat, when it was already known that the enemy had signed an agreement to surrender effective the next day, would be unethical by virtue of being disproportionate.

Sparrow (2007) has argued that the requirements of proportionality stand as a profound barrier to the ethical use of LAWS.[36] The calculations of military advantage required to assess whether a given number of civilian (or military) casualties is proportionate are extremely complex and context sensitive and require a detailed understanding of the way the world works that is likely to remain beyond the capacities of autonomous systems for the foreseeable future (Sparrow 2016). This author's position (e.g., Lucas 2014), somewhat in contrast, is less pessimistic, believing that their potential to exceed the limited abilities of human beings when it comes to making judgments of proportionality is an important part of the promise of LAWS.

Again, however, there are reasons to believe that these sorts of calculations of proportionality are likely to be easier in the context of war at sea than in the remaining domains. To begin with, as noted earlier, the relative lack of civilian clutter on the oceans means that the risk of civilian casualties in attacks on legitimate military targets in naval engagements is much lower than in land warfare, thereby reducing the number of circumstances in which a judgment of the proportionality of anticipated civilian casualties is required. There are also typically fewer units involved in naval engagements than land warfare and the scope of operations available to individual units is less, which makes it more plausible to think that a computer could calculate the military advantage associated with a particular attack and, accordingly, whether a given number of military deaths would be justified.[37]

On the other hand, there is a distinctive proportionality calculation that is especially difficult in the context of war at sea. Military operations may have significant and long-term implications for civilian life via their impact on the environment.[38] Consequently, combatants are now also held to be under an obligation to consider and, where possible, minimize the damage to the environment caused by their activities. These obligations must be balanced against considerations of military necessity. In practice, then, combatants are required to make a calculation of proportionality when contemplating an attack to determine whether or not the environmental damage it is likely to cause is justified by the military advantage it will achieve.[39] However, the role played by wind, waves, and tides in distributing the debris resulting from war at sea and the complex nature of marine ecosystems make calculations of the environmental impacts of naval operations especially difficult. Moreover, both the intrinsic value of significant features of the environment (such as, for instance, clean rivers, healthy coral reefs, spawning grounds of fish, and so on) and the instrumental value they have in terms of their contribution to human well-being are controversial. Judgments about such matters inevitably involve balancing a range of complex considerations as well as arguments about matters of (moral) value. For both these reasons, calculations of proportionality in attack in relation to damage to the environment seem likely to remain beyond the capacity of computers for many years to come.

Thus, once we admit in this context that both the marine environment and enemy combatant casualties (Walzer 2006, 156) are relevant to the proportionality calculation (in ethics, if not in law) and we take the broader strategic context into account, as well as the possible interactions of naval, ground, and air forces, it once more appears that judgments of proportionality are fiendishly difficult and require knowledge of the world and reasoning capacities that computer systems currently lack. Thus, at the very least, proportionality appears to remain a more difficult issue for autonomous weapons systems in naval warfare than distinction.

Supervised Autonomy and Precautions in Attack at Sea

Human beings have significant limitations when it comes to their capacity to achieve distinction and make judgments of proportionality, so still it might be argued that machines will eventually be able to perform at least as well as humans at these tasks (Arkin 2010, 2013; Arkin et al. 2012). This is an empirical matter. However, there is also a deeper philosophical question here regarding the nature and force of the ethical imperatives underpinning the requirements of *jus in bello*. While human beings often fail to behave ethically, when it comes to the duty to avoid taking human life unnecessarily, morality demands that agents aim at perfection, or complete compliance, and not at some lesser standard. Consequently, we must not seem to countenance justifying the use of an autonomous weapon solely on the basis that it makes as few mistakes as, or fewer than, the alternative (Sparrow 2015, 2016; Lucas 2011, 2013).

A partial solution to the problems of distinction and proportionality might be achieved by requiring maritime LAWS to seek input from a human supervisor whenever the risks of attacking an illegitimate target exceeded some predetermined threshold. A few authorities already advocate supervised autonomy as a way of attempting to combine the benefits of autonomous operations and human decision-making in complex environments (Arkin 2009; Brutzman et al. 2013; Leveringhaus and de Greef 2015). Yet, there are obvious limitations of this proposal as well. To begin with, it presumes that the task of accurately assessing the risk of inadvertently attacking an illegitimate target is easier than identifying a potential target as legitimate or not in the first place. That is certainly not always the case. Perhaps, more importantly, relying on human supervision to carry out combat operations ethically would sacrifice two of the key benefits of autonomous operations. It would require maintaining a robust communications infrastructure sufficient to allow the LAWS to transmit the relevant data to a base station and receive instructions from a human operator. That is especially challenging in the context of operations under water. It would also jeopardize the capacity of autonomous systems to conduct stealth operations. Submersibles would need to transmit and receive signals in real time – and thus risk giving away their location – to allow a human supervisor to provide input into their decisions. While supervised autonomy may be a solution in the context of operations against technologically unsophisticated adversaries without the capacity to contest the electronic battlespace or launch kinetic attacks against communications infrastructure, it seems unlikely to be an attractive solution in the longer term or more general case.

There is still a further complexity here. The *jus in bello* principles of distinction and proportionality not only distinguish between legitimate and illegitimate targets but also demand that warfighters make all feasible efforts to avoid attacking illegitimate targets in circumstances where, for various reasons, it proves difficult to distinguish between the two. Thus, as the *San Remo Manual* notes, warfighters "must take all feasible measures to gather information which will assist in determining whether or not objects which are not military objectives are present in an area of attack" and "take all feasible precautions in the choice of methods and means in order to avoid or minimize collateral casualties or damage" (Doswald-Beck 1995, 16). The question of what sorts of measures or precautions are "feasible" in a given context is obviously complex and often controversial, and the level of risk to warfighters involved in the various options available to them is clearly relevant. There must be some limit to the amount of risk that we can reasonably expect warfighters to take on to achieve any given degree of confidence about the nature of the targets they intend to attack. The fact that no further human lives would be placed directly at risk by requiring autonomous UUVs and USVs to undertake inherently more risky measures to minimize the chance of inadvertently attacking civilian targets or causing disproportionate casualties suggest that these legal requirements to take all feasible measures and all feasible precautions might prove to be significantly more demanding for these systems.

For instance, uncrewed submersibles might be required to launch sensor buoys, to use active sonar, or even to surface to facilitate identification of targets. Indeed, maritime LAWS might even be required to await authorization from human supervisor before carrying out an attack. In that case, according to the strongest version of this line of argument, fully autonomous (or "unsupervised") operations of a UUV for USV would prove *de facto* unethical. There are two obvious ways this conclusion might be resisted.

First, given the military utility of uncrewed systems – and an argument from military necessity – it might be argued that the risk to the "vessel," regardless of the absence of any crew on board, is properly relevant to judgments about feasibility. It would be unreasonable to include within the range of feasible precautions those that would almost certainly result in the destruction of the system if carried out during an engagement. Second, in addition, while exposing an uncrewed system to risk may not directly threaten any lives, the destruction of the vessel would jeopardize the safety of friendly forces who might have been relying upon it carrying out its mission. Thus, human lives may well be at stake when we risk the safety of a UMS. These two considerations speak in favor of allowing autonomous systems to prioritize their own safety over the safety of those whose lives they potentially threaten through their targeting decisions.

The capacity of UMS to take more precautions prior to launching an attack is often cited as an argument in favor of developing and deploying them (Arkin 2009, 29–30, 108–109; 2010). The fact that they are uncrewed means that they might plausibly be used in more risky operations to try to achieve any worthwhile goal. Perversely, when the goal is the preservation of the lives of noncombatants, this might even mean placing (what would otherwise be) autonomous systems at risk by requiring them to seek authorization for each attack from a human operator. Yet, this would vitiate many of the military advantages of autonomous operations, including the extent to which the use of UMS reduces the risk to the lives of friendly forces. The advent of armed autonomous systems will therefore require a potentially difficult conversation among the international community about the balance to be struck between military necessity and humanitarian considerations and the role of human supervision of autonomous systems in securing this balance.[40] As we can now discern, that is likely to prove extraordinarily challenging.

Notes

1 Those few discussions we are aware of include Matthews 2013 and Brutzman et al. 2013.
2 Robert Sparrow and George R. Lucas, "When Robots Rule the Waves?" *Naval War College Review* 69 (4) (Autumn 2016): 49–78.
3 A subsequent and even more detailed account of the types of maritime systems currently in use or under development can be found in Arthur Holland Michel, "(Uncrewed) Maritime Systems: State of the Operational Art," in *One Nation Under Drones: Legality, Morality, and Utility of Uncrewed Combat Systems*, ed. John E. Jackson (Captain, U.S. Navy, retired) (Annapolis: Naval Institute Press, 2018): 54–74.
4 A particularly interesting – and arguably problematic – category of autonomous weapon systems would be vessels that were autonomous in some of their operations but that were also staffed by human beings. Thus, we might imagine an autonomous submersible that navigated and chose targets autonomously but that relied upon onboard human engineers to maintain its mechanical and hydraulic systems. Similarly, we might imagine autonomous light attack craft that require human beings to carry out these roles. Finally, one might imagine vessels that were controlled by humans but that carried guns or missile systems that chose targets and fired autonomously (indeed, on some accounts any vessel that carries the Phalanx CWIS or Aegis system is already in this category). To our knowledge, there has been little discussion anywhere in the literature to date of the issues raised by these classes of systems.
5 Somewhat ominously, for example, our original coauthored report of 2015 was quickly translated into Chinese. It also bears mention that drones launched from land, ships, or submersibles clearly have tremendous potential in the context of war at sea. Given that the ethics of the military uses of drones has been extensively discussed in general in Chapter 3, there is no need to discuss sea-based drones of similar type here, save to say that unique features of their activities in this alternative domain may be subsumed under the discussions in this chapter of the ethics of attacks on vessels on or under the water.
6 www.navaldrones.com/Waveglider.html; http://fortune.com/2013/04/11/drones-come-to-the-high-seas/; http://liquidr.com/technology/waveglider/sv3.html.
7 http://spectrum.ieee.org/automaton/robotics/military-robots/us-navy-robot-boat-swarm.
8 Martinic 2014; www.navaldrones.com/Spartan-Scout.html; Israel has deployed an armed USV, "The Protector," which is a nine-meter 4,000-kg displacement remotely operated vessel manufactured by Raphael, since 2009. See www.naval-technology.com/projects/protector-uncrewed-surface-vehicle/; www.atimes.com/atimes/Southeast_Asia/NH29Ae02.html.
9 See www.darpa.mil/program/anti-submarine-warfare-continuous-trail-uncrewed-vessel.
10 "Leidos Anti-submarine Warfare Drone Surrogate Completes Voyage" (26 January 2015), www.navaldrones.com/ACTUV.html [accessed 29 July 2015].
11 UUVs may be divided up by tonnage/displacement or by intended role; we have chosen the latter schema to better bring out the ethical issues that might be raised by operations in each role.
12 www.navaldrones.com/Sea-Maverick.html, www.navaldrones.com/Sea-Stalker-UUV.html
13 http://auvac.org/newsitems/view/1399.
14 "Robot Jellyfish Patrolling the Ocean," *Defense News* (6 April 2013), www.dailymail.co.uk/sciencetech/article-2300966/Man-sized-robot-jellyfish-silicone-patrol-US-waters-aquatic-spy-study-life-ocean-floor.html.
15 www.navaldrones.com/Remus.html; http://auvac.org/configurations/view/14
16 Strictly speaking, the RMMV is semisubmersible rather than fully submersible, www.navy.mil/navydata/fact_display.asp?cid=2100&tid=453&ct=2;

17 An early proposal along these lines is documented here: www.navy.mil/navydata/cno/n87/usw/issue_29/predator.html. Sea Predator was later cancelled. For discussion of ongoing research into distributed networks and their potential for area denial, see www.usni.org/magazines/proceedings/2014-08/mine-and-undersea-warfare-future; Clark 2015; Truver 2012.
18 www.navytimes.com/story/military/tech/2015/04/16/lduuv-test-san-fransisco-san-diego-2016/25839499/. 16 April 2015 [accessed 29 September 2015]; Clark 2015, 13.
19 See, for instance, *Defense Science Board* 2012, 85.
20 For another account of these differences, along similar lines, see Corn et al. (2012), 418–419.
21 Note that we are here primarily concerned with war among ships and submarines and not munitions fired from oceangoing systems directed at targets on the land or in the air.
22 War itself, more generally, has always been a collective endeavor to be sure. However, the boundaries of the social collectivity in naval warfare are inevitably if not exclusively the physical confines of particular vessels.
23 This obligation is reflected in SOLAS, Ch. V, Reg. 10(a); UNCLOS Article 98 (1). For a useful discussion, see Davies (2003). Walzer seems to suggest, in his discussion of the Laconia affair (2006, 147), that the duty of rescue applies only to noncombatants and thus in the context of attacks on merchant shipping. On the other hand, Article 18 of Geneva Convention (II) 1949 refers specifically to shipwrecked members of the armed forces, a matter that for decades complicated the formation of international law governing submarine warfare.
24 The legal formulation of this duty, in Article 18 of Geneva Convention (II) 1949, specifies that it applies "after each engagement," but it is hard to see why this duty should lapse before or between engagements, and this restriction is most naturally understood as acknowledging that parties to the conflict are unlikely to have the capacity to safely conduct rescue in the midst of combat rather than as denying the existence of a generalized duty to rescue. For some discussion, see von Heinegg (2008, 160–161).
25 The legal right of warships to fly false flags during wartime complicates this claim somewhat when it comes to the challenges faced by human combatants. However, it is unlikely that autonomous systems will be relying upon visual sightings of national flags to identify the nationality of vessels; they are much more likely to rely upon acoustic signatures or radar silhouettes, which are harder to disguise.
26 Thus, for instance, identification of legitimate targets in air-to-air combat is also arguably easier than in land warfare, while an obligation to aid those who are *hors de combat* may also exist in other extreme environments such as deserts and snowfields.
27 There is also a debate about when/if such systems can be considered warships, especially in relation to the status of merchant shipping (see, for example, McLaughlin 2011).
28 McLaughlin thinks they should be granted sovereign immunity on the basis that they are "government ships operating for non-commercial purposes" even though he thinks it is a stretch to argue that they are themselves "warships." He agrees, however, that they are "vessels" under COLREGs. The question he raises of whether uncrewed systems are "warships" is an issue with implications mostly for the ethics of attacks *on* these systems rather than attacks *by* them and as such is of less interest to us here.
29 *San Remo Manual*, Part 4, Section 1, 79, "it is prohibited to use torpedoes which do not sink or otherwise become harmless when they have completed their run" (Doswald-Beck 1995, 25). See also Part 4, Section 1, 82, on free-floating mines, which are prohibited unless they are directed against military objectives and become harmless an hour after being deployed.
30 The 1907 Hague Convention VIII prohibited the use of "automatic contact mines." However, as Heintschel von Heinegg (2003, 415) notes, these principles "are generally recognized as customary international law and thus also govern the use of modern naval mines."
31 www.fas.org/man/dod-101/sys/dumb/mk60.htm.
32 The *San Remo Manual* notes that the CAPTOR should arguably be considered a system capable of delivering a weapon rather than a weapon itself (Doswald-Beck 1995, 169).

W. Heintschel von Heinegg 2008, 154, also argues that this system should be governed by the rules applicable to torpedoes.

33 Megan Eckstein, "U.S. Navy Considers Alternatives to Uncrewed Boats with Missiles," *Defense News* (22 March 2022), www.defensenews.com/naval/2022/03/22/us-navy-considers-alternatives-to-uncrewed-boats-with-missiles/ [accessed 24 March 2022].

34 The destruction of a crewed ship in these circumstances would generate disproportionate casualties.

35 McLaughlin (2011) offers a useful discussion of relevant considerations in this and similar contexts in pp. 105–106. See also Sparrow 2015.

36 See also Roff 2013; Human Rights Watch 2012; Wagner 2011.

37 On the other hand, to the extent that is difficult to predict whether a given munition will sink or merely damage a vessel, the number of combatant deaths likely to result from any given attack is *harder* to calculate in naval warfare than in land or air warfare.

38 For an extended discussion of the legal obligations on combatants in this regard, see Dinstein 2010, 197–217. See also: Doswald-Beck 1995, 15; Antoine 1992; Desgagné 2000; Tarasofsky 1993.

39 This requirement appears to have escaped the notice of RF President Putin in the case of land warfare.

40 See, for discussion, Anderson and Waxman 2012; Johnson and Axin 2013; Kanwar 2011; Wagner 2011.

References

Adams, Thomas K. "Future Warfare and the Decline of Human Decisionmaking," *Parameters* 31 (4) (2001): 57–71.

Additional Protocol I to the Geneva Conventions. 1977. "Protocol Additional to the Geneva Conventions of 12 August 1949, and Relating to the Protection of Victims of International Armed Conflicts (Protocol I)" (8 June 1977), www.icrc.org/ihl.nsf/INTRO/470?OpenDocument.

Altmann, J. "Arms Control for Armed Uninhabited Vehicles: An Ethical Issue," *Ethics and Information Technology* 15 (2) (2013): 137–152.

Anderson, K.; Waxman, M. "Law and Ethics for Robot Soldiers," *Policy Review* 176 (2012): 35–49.

Anderson, K.; Waxman, M. "Law and Ethics for Autonomous Weapon Systems: Why a Ban Won't Work and How the Laws of War Can" (10 April 2013). Jean Perkins Task Force on National Security and Law Essay Series, The Hoover Institution, Stanford University; American University, WCL Research Paper 2013–11; Columbia Public Law Research Paper 13–351, http://dx.doi.org/10.2139/ssrn.2250126.

Antoine, P. "International Humanitarian Law and the Protection of the Environment in Time of Armed Conflict," *International Review of the Red Cross* 32 (291) (1992): 517–537.

Arkin, R.C. *Governing Lethal Behavior in Autonomous Robots* (Boca Raton: CRC Press, 2009).

Arkin, R.C. "The Case for Ethical Autonomy in Uncrewed Systems," *Journal of Military Ethics* 9 (4) (2010): 332–341.

Arkin, R.C. "Lethal Autonomous Systems and the Plight of the Noncombatant," *AISB Quarterly* 137 (July 2013): 1–9.

Arkin, R.C.; Ulam, Patrick; Wagner, Alan R. "Moral Decision Making in Autonomous Systems: Enforcement, Moral Emotion, Dignity, Trust and Deception," *Proceedings of the IEEE* 100 (3) (2012): 571–589.

Asaro, P. "On Banning Autonomous Weapon Systems: Human Rights, Automation, and the Dehumanization of Lethal Decision-Making," *International Review of the Red Cross* 94 (886) (2012): 687–709.

Berkowitz, Bruce. "Sea Power in the Robotic Age," *Issues in Science and Technology* 30 (2) (2014): 33–40.

Borenstein, J. "The Ethics of Autonomous Military Robots," *Studies in Ethics, Law, and Technology* 2 (1) (2008).

Brutzman, D.P.; Davis, D.T.; Lucas, G.R. Jr.; McGhee, R.P. 2013. "Run-time Ethics Checking for Autonomous Uncrewed Vehicles: Developing a Practical Approach," in *Proceedings of the 18th International Symposium on Uncrewed Untethered Submersible Technology (UUST)* (Portsmouth, New Hampshire), https://savage.nps.edu/AuvWorkbench/website/documentation/papers/UUST2013PracticalRuntimeAUVEthics.pdf.

Canning, J.S. "A Concept of Operations for Armed Autonomous Systems," Paper presented at the 3rd Annual Disruptive Technology Conference, Washington, DC, 2006, www.dtic.mil/ndia/2006disruptive_tech/canning.pdf.

Clark, Bryan. *The Emerging Era in Undersea Warfare* (Washington, DC: CSBA, 2015).

Corn, G.S.; Hansen, V.; Jackson, R.B.; Jenks, C.; Jensen, E.T.; Schoettler, J.A. *The Law of Armed Conflict: An Operational Approach* (New York: Wolters Kluwer Law & Business, 2012).

Davies, M. "Obligations and Implications for Ships Encountering Persons in Need of Assistance at Sea," *Pacific Rim Law and Policy Journal* 12 (1) (2003): 109–141.

Defense Science Board: US Department of Defense. *The Role of Autonomy in DoD Systems* (Washington, DC: Office of the Under Secretary of Defense for Acquisition, Technology and Logistics, 2012).

Department of Defense. *Uncrewed Ground Systems Roadmap* (Washington, DC: Robotic Systems Joint Project Office, 2011).

Department of Defense. *Uncrewed Systems Integrated Roadmap: FY2013–2038* (Washington, DC: Department of Defense, 2014).

Desgagné, R. "The Prevention of Environmental Damage in Time of Armed Conflict: Proportionality and Precautionary Measures," *Yearbook of International Humanitarian Law* 3 (2000): 109–129.

Dinstein, Yoram. *The Conduct of Hostilities under the Law of International Armed Conflict*. 2nd ed. (Cambridge: Cambridge University Press, 2010).

Doswald-Beck, L., ed. *San Remo Manual on International Law Applicable to Armed Conflicts At Sea* (Cambridge: Cambridge University Press, 1995).

Geneva Convention (II) for the Amelioration of the Condition of Wounded, Sick and Shipwrecked Members of Armed Forces at Sea. Geneva, 12 August 1949, www.icrc.org/ihl/INTRO/370?OpenDocument.

Gogarty, B.; Hagger, M. "The Laws of Man Over Vehicles Uncrewed: The Legal Response to Robotic Revolution on Sea, Land and Air," *Journal of Law, Information and Science* 19 (1) (2008): 73–145.

Guarini, M.; Bello, P. "Robotic Warfare: Some Challenges in Moving From Noncivilian to Civilian Theaters," in *Robot Ethics: The Ethical and Social Implications of Robotics*, eds. P. Lin, K. Abney, and G.A. Bekey (Cambridge, MA: MIT Press, 2012): 129–144.

Henderson, A.H. "Murky Waters: The Legal Status of Uncrewed Undersea Vehicles," *Naval Law Review* 53 (2006): 55–72.

Human Rights Watch. "Losing Humanity: The Case against Killer Robots" (2012), www.hrw.org/sites/default/files/reports/arms1112ForUpload_0_0.pdf [accessed 1 September 2013].

International Convention for the Safety of Life at Sea, Nov. 1, 1974, 32 U.S.T. 47, 1184 U.N.T.S. 278.

Johnson, Aaron M; Axinn, Sidney. "The Morality of Autonomous Robots," *Journal of Military Ethics* 12 (2) (2013): 129–141.

Kanwar, V. "Post-Human Humanitarian Law: The Law of War in the Age of Robotic Weapons," *Harvard National Security Journal* 2 (2) (2011): 616–628.

Kelly, John. "Navy Researchers Consider Arming Future Large Unmanned Submersible With Anti-submarine Weaponry," *Military and Aerospace Electronics* (18 November 2014), https://www.militaryaerospace.com/computers/article/16718810/navy-researchers-consider-arming-future-large-unmanned-submersible-with-antisubmarine-weaponry [accessed 22 August 2022].

Krishnan, A. *Killer Robots: Legality and Ethicality of Autonomous Weapons* (Farnham, England: Ashgate Publishing, 2009).

Larter, David. "ONR: Large Underwater Drone Set for 2016 West Coast Cruise," *Navy Times* (16 April 2015), www.navytimes.com/story/military/tech/2015/04/16/lduuv-test-san-fransisco-san-diego-2016/25839499/ [accessed 29 September 2015].

Leveringhaus, Alex; de Greef, Tjerk. "Keeping the Human 'in-the-Loop': A Qualified Defence of Autonomous Weapons," in *Precision Strike Technology and International Intervention: Strategic, Ethico-Legal and Decisional Implications*, eds. Mike Aaronson, Wali Aslam, Tom Dyson, and Regina Rauxloh (Abingdon; New York: Routledge, 2015).

Lucas, George R., Jr. "Industrial Challenges of Military Robotics," *Journal of Military Ethics* 10 (4) (2011): 274–295.

Lucas, George R., Jr. "Engineering, Ethics, and Industry: The Moral Challenges of Lethal Autonomy," in *Killing by Remote Control: The Ethics of an Uncrewed Military,* ed. B.J. Strawser (New York: Oxford University Press, 2013): 211–228.

Lucas, George R. Jr. "Automated Warfare," *Stanford Law and Policy Review* 25 (2) (2014): 317–339.

Marchant, G.E.; Allenby, B.; Arkin, R.; Barrett, E.T.; Borenstein, J.; Gaudet, L.M.; Kittrie, O.; Lin, P.; Lucas Jr., G.R.; O'Meara, R. "International Governance of Autonomous Military Robots," *Columbia University Review of Science & Technology Law* 12 (2011): 272–315.

Martinic, Gary. "Uncrewed Maritime Surveillance and Weapons Systems," *Headmark* 151 (2014): 86–91, http://navalinstitute.com.au/uncrewed-maritime-surveillance-and-weapons-systems/.

Matthews, W. "Murky Waters: Seagoing Drones Swim Into New Legal and Ethical Territory," *Defense News* (9 April 2013), www.defensenews.com/article/20130409/C4ISR02/304090014/Murky-Waters-Seagoing-Drones-Swim-Into-New-Legal-Ethical-Territory.

McLaughlin, R. "Uncrewed Naval Vehicles at Sea: USVs, UUVs, and the Adequacy of the Law," *Journal of Law Information and Science* 21 (2) (2011): 100–115.

Norris, A. *Legal Issues Relating to Uncrewed Maritime Systems* (Newport, RI: U.S. Naval War College, 2013), www.hsdl.org/?view&did=731705.

O'Connell, M.E. "Banning Autonomous Killing: The Legal and Ethical Requirement That Humans Make Near-time Lethal Decisions," in *The American Way of Bombing: Changing Ethical and Legal Norms, From Flying Fortresses to Drones,* ed. M. Evangelista and H. Shue (Ithaca, NY: Cornell University Press, 2014).

Rawley, Chris. "Return to Trust at Sea Through Uncrewed Autonomy," U.S. Naval Institute (2014), www.usni.org/return-trust-sea-through-uncrewed-autonomy [accessed 7 May 2014].

Roff, H.M. "Killing in War: Responsibility, Liability, and Lethal Autonomous Robots," in *Routledge Handbook of Ethics and War: Just War Theory in the 21st Century*, ed. F. Allhoff, N.G. Evans, and A. Henschke (New York: Routledge, 2013): 352–364.

Schmitt, M. "Autonomous Weapon Systems and International Humanitarian Law: A Reply to the Critics," *Harvard National Security Journal* (2013), http://harvardnsj.org/2013/02/autonomous-weapon-systems-and-international-humanitarian-law-a-reply-to-the-critics/.

Schmitt, M.N.; Thurnher, J.S. "'Out of the Loop': Autonomous Weapon Systems and the Law of Armed Conflict," *Harvard National Security Journal* 4 (2) (2013): 231–281.
Sharkey, N. "The Evitability of Autonomous Robot Warfare," *International Review of the Red Cross* 94 (886) (2012a): 787–799.
Sharkey, N. "Autonomous Robots and the Automation of Warfare," *International Humanitarian Law Magazine* 2 (2012b): 18–19.
Singer, P.W. *Wired for War: The Robotics Revolution and Conflict in the 21st Century* (New York: Penguin Books, 2009).
Singer, P.W.; Cole, August. *Ghost Fleet* (New York: Houghton, Mifflin & Harcourt, 2015).
Sparrow, R. "Killer Robots," *Journal of Applied Philosophy* 24 (1) (2007): 62–77.
Sparrow, R. "Twenty Seconds to Comply: Autonomous Weapon Systems and the Recognition of Surrender," *International Law Studies* 91 (2015): 699–728.
Sparrow, R. "Robots and Respect: Assessing the Case Against Autonomous Weapon Systems," *Ethics and International Affairs* 30 (1) (2016): 93–116, https://doi.org/10.1017/S0892679415000647.
Strawser, B.J., ed. *Killing by Remote Control: The Ethics of an Uncrewed Military* (New York: Oxford University Press, 2013).
Tarasofsky, R.G. "Legal Protection of the Environment during International Armed Conflict," *Netherlands Yearbook of International Law* 24 (1993): 17–79.
Truver, Scott C. "Taking Mines Seriously: Mine Warfare in China's near Seas," *Naval War College Review* 65 (2) (2012): 30–66.
United Nations Convention on the Law of the Sea. 1982. UN Doc. A/CONF.62/122 and Corr.
United States Air Force. *RPA Vector: Vision and Enabling Concepts 2013–2038* (Washington, DC: United States Air Force, 2014).
United States Army. *U.S. Army Uncrewed Aircraft Systems Roadmap 2010–2035: Eyes of the Army* (Fort Rucker, AL: US Army UAS Center of Excellence, 2010).
United States Navy. *The Navy Uncrewed Surface Vehicle (USV) Master Plan* (Washington, DC: Department of the Navy, 2007).
von Heinegg, W. Heintschel. "The Protection of Navigation in Case of Armed Conflict," *The International Journal of Marine and Coastal Law* 18 (3) (2003): 401–422.
von Heinegg, W. Heintschel. "Submarine Operations and International Law," in *Law at War: The Law as It Was and the Law as It Should Be*, eds. O. Engdahl and P. Wrange (Leiden: E.J. Brill NV, 2008): 141–162.
Wagner, M. "Taking Humans Out of the Loop: Implications for International Humanitarian Law," *Journal of Law Information and Science* 21 (2) (2011): 155–165.
Walzer, Michael. *Just and Unjust Wars: A Moral Argument With Historical Illustrations*. 4th ed. (New York: Basic Books, 2006).

5

ARTIFICIAL INTELLIGENCE AND CONVENTIONAL MILITARY OPERATIONS

In what manner does the introduction of ever more sophisticated forms of artificial intelligence (AI) exacerbate, help to resolve, or otherwise change the complexion of the moral and legal challenges encountered in the development and use of lethally armed autonomous weapons systems (LAWS)? AI certainly has come to play an ever-expanding role in the context of war (e.g., Scharre 2018). Its impact is felt not only in the enhanced capabilities of LAWS that operate on land, on and under the sea, and in the air but also in the domain of space as well as in the cyber sphere. AI analysis of big data sets enables vast improvements in our abilities to conduct instructive war games and engage in strategic military planning and even training for future contingencies.

The effort to design algorithms so that the machines operate in conformity with recognized laws of war constitutes a new multidisciplinary research domain involving mathematicians, engineers, philosophers, lawyers, and military strategists collaborating in specially dedicated labs. Current uses of modular AI (i.e., AI tailored for specific tasks and involving closely supervised machine learning) already pervade both defensive and offensive military operations and (increasingly) weapons systems with varying degrees of efficiency and success. As we shall later observe, AI has proved especially promising in both defensive and offensive cyber operations. This chapter focuses on several proposed uses of general AI, including deep learning enabling expanded autonomous operations, along with the attendant risks and prospective moral dilemmas arising from each.

Raising these questions helps us segue from the previous focus on military robotics specifically to other areas of concern, such as cyber conflict, which we will begin to take up in this chapter. We will then turn to conflict and the military use of AI in the remaining realms of concern in subsequent chapters. We begin with the problem of understanding the specific capabilities that AI introduces, and

DOI: 10.4324/9781003273912-6

the legal and moral questions raised in military robotics, before turning at greater length to AI-enhanced cyber conflict.

Comprehending AI

There is no settled and universally agreed-upon definition of AI.[1] For purposes of this analysis, AI will be understood broadly to designate a varying degree of capacity for intelligent behavior embedded within (and/or guiding or enhancing the operations of) mechanical artifacts. Intelligence, in turn, designates an ability to recognize and unilaterally attempt to resolve complex problems, while artificial is simply meant to exclude from consideration such capacities that are already found in naturally occurring biological or organic systems (natural as opposed to artificial intelligence).

Importantly, in light of considerations arising in previous chapters, this definition of AI is meant to encompass its use in both autonomous and non-autonomous systems. An artificially intelligent system is autonomous if the selection of the means for reaching a preset goal is left to the system itself or can otherwise be modified or changed (as in machine learning). A system is nonautonomous (semiautonomous or *less-than-fully* autonomous) if, despite its capacity for unsupervised or remotely supervised operation, the means to reaching an established goal have been unalterably fixed or predetermined by an external agent.

Yet, even these attempted distinctions are imprecise. IBM's Deep Blue and Watson supercomputers, for example, were both able to learn and improve their abilities to play chess or Jeopardy and challenge or defeat some of the world's leading experts. In that sense, they might seem to be both intelligent and autonomous, in that they engage in these behaviors by themselves. But neither machine suddenly decided to storm out of the television studio to express contempt for their human opponents nor did they change their own programming to, say, initiate a world war. While engaging in their competition with human opponents, however, both machines often inadvertently illustrated the way artificial reasoning and problem-solving may develop entirely novel and utterly different strategies for solving complex problems, in a manner that would likely never occur to a human chess or Jeopardy player. And of course, their ability to examine and analyze enormous amounts of information, far beyond the capacity of a human mind, proved useful in succeeding at Jeopardy or envisioning the implications of a vast array of moves that resulted in winning a strategic game like Go. Such novel reasoning patterns and big data analysis clearly would aid policymakers and strategic planners to develop enhanced methods for forecasting the behavior of adversaries or determining new ways of prevailing in armed conflicts. Thus, it does seem the case that, while intelligence and self-direction are distinct capabilities, *adding intelligence* augments capacities for autonomy (just as it does in humans and many animals endowed with the capacity to reason).

There are several definitions of AI, none of which is definitive. High-level doctrine in the EU defines AI systems as

> [S]oftware (and possibly also hardware) systems designed by humans that, given a complex goal, act in the physical or digital dimension by perceiving their environment through data acquisition, interpreting the collected structured or unstructured data, reasoning on the knowledge, or processing the information, derived from this data and deciding the best action(s) to take to achieve the given goal.[2]

The U.S. Department of Defense joint doctrine employs a definition first developed by the U.S. Air Force Research Lab:

> the ability of machines to perform tasks that normally require human intelligence – for example, recognizing patterns, learning from previous experience, drawing conclusions, making predictions, or taking action – whether digitally or as the smart software behind autonomous physical systems.[3]

NATO has not issued any joint doctrine pertaining specifically to use of AI in cyberspace or conventional combat operations. However, NATO's "Allied Joint Doctrine for Cyberspace Operations,"[4] to be cited more extensively later, appears in all relevant respects fully compatible with the EU doctrine, in which the high-level description of the operations and capacities of AI systems "either rely on the use of symbolic rules or (learning) a numeric model, and . . . can also adapt their behavior by analyzing how the environment is affected by their previous actions" (p. 1).

As a scientific discipline, AI includes several approaches and techniques,[5] including various degrees of machine learning (of which deep learning and reinforcement learning are specific examples), machine reasoning (which includes planning, scheduling, knowledge representation and reasoning, search, and optimization), and robotics (which includes control, perception, sensors, and actuators, as well as the integration of all other techniques into cyber and/or physical systems).

Currently, as we are increasingly becoming aware, AI applications are all around us. We use them on a daily basis whether we actively notice them or not. Easy examples include digital home assistants, online searches, product recommendations, and the vast array of algorithms that increasingly enable self-driving cars and similar machines. In cybersecurity, as we shall observe in more detail shortly, common examples are malware detection and classification, network intrusion detection, file type identification, network traffic identification, spam identification, insider threat detection, and user authentication.[6]

These AI-supported applications are examples of modular AI (also sometimes termed narrow or weak AI). This mode of AI can be phenomenally good at single tasks in strictly defined environments, such as at playing complex games like Chess or Go, but narrow AI is useless where more general intelligence is needed in broader contexts and unfamiliar environments.[7] General AI (often termed strong AI) is closer to human intelligence in operating across a variety of cognitive tasks. A key element of general AI is the ability to improve the overall knowledge and performance of the system in which it is embedded, *entirely on its own*. Unsupervised machine learning systems, for instance, do not merely follow a predetermined algorithm. Instead, they generate their own algorithms from information they gather.[8] As of yet, however, it is important to emphasize that nothing approaching general AI has yet been attained or achieved in any of its ultimately envisioned forms. There are a variety of quite remarkable AI applications, however, that might accurately be characterized as falling somewhere between modular and general AI in their distinct and innovative paradigms of machine learning.[9]

Another significant observation and clarification is that AI systems, wherever they are employed, have been rightly described by AI experts themselves as brittle (Missy Cummings), and even stupid (Dave Barnes) in entirely random and seemingly perverse fashion. That is to say, AI systems are *subject to error, failures, and (sometimes spectacular) accidents*, and wherever implanted or used, they introduce vulnerability to deliberate and malicious attacks upon their host systems. One straightforward recent example is that of a Predator drone equipped with intelligent object and target recognition software that should have enabled it to distinguish between cars and tanks and human beings and other objects in a war zone. It was trained using an enormous, labeled data set of discrete items, and it seemed to function effectively in extensive testing – until it was tested in an Arctic environment, where it failed miserably. The drone had initially been trained and tested in a desert environment and simply could not translate its acquired knowledge into a different context. AlphaGo reported a similar problem with its game-focused system: oddly, when the dimensions of the game board were changed, even in the slightest degree, and even while preserving the overall board symmetry, the computer proved utterly unable to duplicate its earlier mastery of Go.

Data *set labeling* for AI design is another huge problem. Much has been made of the implicit bias contained in big data sets, in which facial recognition software proves much less reliable, for example, in correctly identifying women rather than men or distinguishing among persons of color. This may reflect the problem that amassing and correctly labeling discrete items in such data sets is itself a massive, time-consuming, and (for humans, at least) incredibly tedious and boring task. As a result, in a kind of vicious circle, other intelligent machines must be employed to carry out the labeling of new data sets, thereby increasing the risk of error and mistakes. Anyone familiar with voice recognition software, such as dictating text on a smartphone, will be familiar with the amusing and sometimes bizarre weaknesses still found embedded in such capacities, even after decades of development (even admitting how remarkably they can perform in other respects).

AI experts generally describe three waves of AI development. Initially, systems were largely rule-based (expert systems utilizing algorithms oriented toward specific task performance). These have been followed by statistically based systems (drawing inferences from big data sets, as described earlier). The third wave, introducing the greatest chance for errors and unpredictable emergent behaviors, would incorporate some sort of machine analogue of conceptual reasoning. This third wave aims at developing some of the capacities considered for moral machines in earlier chapters. However, knowledgeable AI experts point out once again that we are nowhere near attaining this third wave of AI. Military and defense AI experts have added repeatedly, perhaps to quell public anxiety or misunderstanding, that "no one in the Defense Department wants or needs to go there."[10]

Moral War Machines

The military efficacy of AI systems has been studied extensively (e.g., Lopez 2020). Ethical issues have also surfaced, many of these focused on problems associated with the use of uncrewed autonomous machines as platforms for delivering lethal attack or active defense (as in the various forms of LAWS described in previous chapters). Some critics, as we have already observed, are asking whether these platforms should be used at all (e.g., the Campaign to Stop Killer Robots and ICRAC [the International Committee for Robot Arms Control]; Sharkey 2017).

Most frequently, as we observed earlier, ethicists have focused on the moral status of these machines as autonomous agents. Ethicists have explored variously

- whether autonomously functioning machines can be designed to act morally (Arkin 2010);
- what constitutes an accurate description of machine morality or computational morality (Wallach and Allen 2008); and
- whether these machines might one day come to exercise moral agency, and if so, whether they should be recognized themselves as morally considerable (i.e., deserving of moral consideration) or as possessing limited moral rights (Wallach 2015).

Despite their autonomous mode of operation, AI-based weapons systems function only within a wider context involving collaboration with human agents. This human–machine integration and interaction within the conduct of hostilities is referred to in military jargon as the *force mix* (Lucas 2016). Ethics research into the human and machine force mix, especially into the moral implications for the human agents who use AI-based weapons systems, has often failed to keep pace with accelerating technological developments (e.g., Vallor 2017).

The specific research project of which this book is a part, "Artificial Intelligence in the Battlefield," or "Warring with Machines," aims to remedy this. That larger project, undertaken by the Peace Research Institute in Oslo (PRIO) and funded by the Norwegian Research Council, takes as its primary referent the people – military personnel at varying levels of the command structure – who serve in combat settings alongside these AI-enhanced military weapons and operational systems. We collectively aim to examine the extent to which the new technologically enhanced force mix affects the moral character of the human personnel involved in carrying out military strategic planning, combat operations, logistics, and even professional military education (Riza 2013). In this connection, the PRIO project (including this book) examines questions related to the impact of increased reliance on AI on the moral agency of human combatants (the end users of these AI-enhanced weapons and systems). In particular, we want to inquire whether human moral responsibility is *diffused* or *seriously attenuated* when combat initiatives (such as target recognition and attack) are increasingly delegated to machines – a phenomenon increasingly made possible through the use of AI enhancements. Likewise, we want more optimistically to inquire whether the aid and operations assistance that these machines can provide can promote improved legal compliance and discerning moral conduct on the battlefield (enabling, for instance, better discrimination between combatants and noncombatants). And of course, we wish to determine insofar as possible the ways the new military-and-technology (human–machine) force mix transforms human moral agency in combat settings (for example, by enhancing human awareness, capacity for data analysis, and consequent reasoning abilities).

To begin with, consider the impact of our increasing reliance on AI on some of the ethical and legal concerns within the sphere of military robotics (i.e., when integrating AI into the spheres of military operations examined in the previous chapters). The prospect of fully autonomous, AI-enhanced weapons within the next few decades requires a serious consideration of their unique impact on those earlier moral and legal debates. Some of the most serious moral and legal objections to fully autonomous weapons, as we noted, already pose two *jus in bello* issues.

- Autonomous weapons, even with AI-augmented operation, will not be able to abide by the laws of armed conflict, because they will not be able to meet basic requirements of LOAC, such as the principles of distinction, proportionality, and precaution.
- The existence of autonomous weapons, especially if equipped with AI, will likely further distort or short-circuit any system of accountability for violations of LOAC, creating a "responsibility gap."

Likewise, we noted that any new technology of warfare, whether autonomous or otherwise, must be compatible with LOAC in its use. Thus, as with all other weapons, AI-augmented LAWS must be capable of performing in ways consistent with the principles of LOAC like distinction and proportionality, and due care (what Michael Walzer (1977) originally defined as *double intention* or deliberate precaution) must be exercised in ensuring this compliance in good faith. The central issue of exercising due care or precaution, in turn, was whether fully autonomous weapons, acting on their own, could reasonably be expected to operate in accordance with these *jus in bello* principles.

Just as with claims that self-driving automobiles will have fewer accidents than human drivers, it is frequently suggested that AI-enhanced lethal autonomous robots may increasingly demonstrate themselves to be *better* able to follow the laws of armed conflict than human soldiers. As we saw, one of the most prominent advocates of this position is the roboticist and computer scientist Ronald Arkin at the Georgia Institute of Technology. He now suggests that AI-enhanced autonomous weapons may be able to meet the legal standards of LOAC (IHL) and follow rules of engagement and all applicable ethical requirements. Framing this claim as a research hypothesis, Arkin states:

> It is not my belief that an autonomous unmanned system will be able to be perfectly ethical in the battlefield, but I am convinced that they [sic] can perform more ethically than human soldiers are capable of performing.[11]

Arkin began his earlier advocacy of military robotics by noting that soldiers do not always adhere to the laws of war. He now points to a study by the U.S. Surgeon General's office of military personnel engaged in the Iraq War (2006) showing that large percentages of Army soldiers and Marines held beliefs and attitudes that are directly contrary to LOAC. Arkin does not blame the men and women in combat. To the contrary, he sympathizes:

> [T]hey are placed into situations where no human has ever been designed to function. This is exacerbated by the tempo at which modern warfare is conducted. Expecting widespread compliance with IHL given this pace and resultant stress seems unreasonable and perhaps unattainable by flesh and blood warfighters.[12]

Arkin believes that autonomous robots with capabilities afforded by ever more sophisticated AI may be able to do better. He lists a number of advantages robots would have over human soldiers, including some of the pro-considerations we covered earlier. These include the following.

- An ability to act conservatively when faced with only a low level of confidence in the identification of a target. A robot can afford to hold its fire because it will have no need to protect itself. Instead of a shoot first, ask questions later approach, it can operate on a do-no-harm strategy.
- Possession of a broad range of robotic sensors that can produce better battlefield observation than humans can. These include super-high-resolution camera lenses and electro-optics, wall-penetrating radars, acoustics, and seismic sensing, the reliable operation of which is significantly enhanced with the introduction of (and further improvements in) AI governance software.
- The lack of emotions that cloud human judgment or can lead to illegal actions out of anger and frustration. AI-enhanced LAWS would be able to operate with a cool, impartial, calculated rationality.
- Freedom from psychological biases like the problem of scenario fulfillment in which a person interprets present perceptions to fit with his or her preconceived picture of what is going on. This form of machine bias (deferring to

the results of AI-driven data analysis) is a factor that likely contributed to the downing of the commercial Iranian airliner by the USS *Vincennes* in 1988.

- Ability to penetrate the fog of war better than human soldiers because of the ability to integrate vastly more information from more sources far faster than a human possibly could before responding with lethal force. Additionally, Arkin believes weapons on the horizon will be too fast, too small, and too numerous and will create an environment that is too complex for humans to handle.

Along with the foregoing points, Arkin suggests that LAWS with AI-augmented operational capabilities will prove better at policing the behavior of their human comrades in arms because they can (in principle) monitor and dispassionately report the illegal behavior of their human counterparts.[13] In view of humanity's track record, Arkin cautions that we are forced to assume that humans will persist both in entering into warfare and in behaving poorly in the midst of it. The 2022 outbreak of conventional kinetic interstate hostilities between Ukraine and the Russian Federation (and the deliberate atrocities against civilians inflicted by the latter), on a scale not seen since the 1950s, seems to prove him correct on that point, at least. Given this dire prediction, he argues, we must continually try to "protect innocent noncombatants in the battlespace far better than we currently do."[14] Research in AI in particular should be ever-more-fully incorporated into military robotics and can and should be applied toward achieving ultimate goal of moral war machines.

Arkin considers that earliest conventional LAWS can be even further augmented with abilities to operate within legal constraints by incorporating certain features of AI architecture in the design of autonomous weapons. He envisions a set of ethical and legal control components on top of more conventional robotic control systems. These hierarchically supervening components would impose a specific *set of rules* on the robot's otherwise autonomous functioning that would discern legally (and possibly even morally) appropriate courses of action.[15] An autonomous weapons system equipped with these controls would evaluate the information it receives through its sensing devices and determine whether an attack is prohibited under LOAC or rules of engagement. If an attack violates any of these rules, then it could not proceed. Assuming an attack would not violate any of the rules, then it would be able to be carried out but only if attacking the target were required by operational orders (military necessity).[16]

A key component of the robotic weapon's overall architecture is what Arkin refers to as an Ethical Governor. Just as a governor on a steam engine shuts it down when it runs at a dangerously elevated temperature, the Ethical Governor is designed to prevent unethical or illegal actions the autonomous robot might produce in reaction to stimuli it receives through its sensors. To achieve this, the laws of war and rules of engagement are encoded, respectively, in the robot's long-term and short-term memory. Then, in actual operations, the Ethical Governor evaluates the ethical and legal appropriateness of any lethal response that is within the robot combatant's decision matrix prior to its being enacted, intervening and overriding that choice to prevent an illegal or morally illegitimate response.

Should a target initially be assessed as an otherwise legitimate, legally-permissible target, a proportionality assessment is quickly conducted with the help of a collateral damage estimator within the Ethical Governor.[17] For this test, the Ethical Governor quantifies a variety of criteria, especially the likelihood of a militarily effective strike and the possibility of harm or damage to civilians and/or civilian objects, based on the presumably vast amount of available technical data. The LAWS then defaults to an algorithm that combines statistical data with incoming perceptual information (in military jargon, battlespace awareness) to evaluate the proposed strike *in a utilitarian manner.*[18] It remains to be seen, however, whether what is known in moral philosophy as utilitarian calculus is the only, let alone the preferred or best, option available to an AI-enhanced weapons system. But note how quickly the discussion defaults to a purely quantitative, calculative form of moral reasoning, which might prove to be the most straightforward to encode within a software program.

A second component within the overall architecture as Arkin envisions it is the Ethical Adaptor. Although it is preferable that unethical or illegal behavior should not occur in the first place, the autonomous robot might on occasion, just like a human combatant, make a lethal mistake. If an act by the robot is determined to have been illegal or unethical, then the robot's subsequent operation must, at minimum, be modified or adjusted in response to reduce or prevent the recurrence of the undesired behavior. The Ethical Adaptor is specifically designed to modify the autonomous robot's future action in light of past errors. It can update and optimize the LAWS's set of constraints by further restricting the use of its weaponry. The adjustment can be made autonomously within the LAWS operating system if it is equipped with sufficiently robust AI-enhancements. Of course, such modifications can also be made by a human operator during an ongoing mission by interfacing directly with the operational architecture during the mission's execution.

In a hypothetical test scenario, an aerial drone is equipped with three weapons systems: precision-guided ordnance, hellfire missiles, and a chain gun. As the scenario begins, the robot engages an enemy unit in the first kill zone with the precision-guided bombs, estimating that neither civilian casualties nor excessive structural damage will result. In after-action review, however, it is determined that a small number of noncombatants were killed, and the robot also detects that a nearby civilian building was badly damaged by the blast. Upon self-assessment following the engagement, the Ethical Adaptor determines an adjustment is required and restricts the robot's weapons choices by deactivating the precision-guided bombs. The robot continues the mission. When engaging another target in the second kill zone, the robot is now forced to use its hellfire missiles because the previous choice of ordnance was determined to be insufficiently discriminate and has therefore been deactivated by the Ethical Adaptor. After the second engagement, the Adaptor again determines actual collateral damage. In the scenario, additional noncombatant casualties occur. This time, the resulting adjustment reaches the maximum, and all weapon systems are deactivated – unless or until the human operator deliberately overrides the Ethical Adaptor.[19]

As Arkin sees it, AI-enhanced autonomous killer robots should operate alongside soldiers rather than as complete replacements. A human presence in the battlespace should be maintained. The autonomous weapons should be designed with human overrides to ensure the legal requirement of meaningful human control.[20] With these provisions, Arkin believes it is entirely possible that killer robots will be able to outperform human soldiers with respect to adherence to the laws of war – especially where they have been given a specifically defined mission in a restricted area of operation (such as guarding and protecting a perimeter). In brief, Arkin maintains that autonomous weapons, suitably designed with AI-enhancements that incorporate ethical and legal constraints, will make warfare safer for noncombatants, when employed in relatively narrow, well-defined situations.

Arkin is careful to concede that it is premature to determine whether effective compliance by future autonomous weapons will really be feasible. He recognizes there are profound technological challenges to be resolved, such as effective target discrimination and recognition. For this reason, he has favored a moratorium to ensure that the technology meets international standards before being considered for deployment (thus invoking the due care or precautionary provision). Nevertheless, while Arkin considers it too early to tell whether the venture with autonomous weapons will be successful, he remains optimistic.[21]

Arkin's most recent observations on this overall problem are clearly meant to defuse, if not refute, the case against further deployment of use of LAWS that we examined in earlier chapters. Critics, like Asaro, Sparrow, and Sharkey, whose views we considered there at length, largely remain unconvinced. In fact, the chief concerns in response to these more recent modifications of the pro-LAWS position are that, far from constituting a panacea, introducing AI in the battlespace of LAWS will introduce even more new vulnerabilities instead. We will, for example, most assuredly encounter mistakes and errors, including spectacular ones, for which the causal explanations and appropriate determination of liability will prove even more difficult and convoluted. The incidence of possible but unpredictable emergent behaviors, in particular, Sharkey finds to constitute a foreseeable but largely unpreventable risk that is simply not worth incurring.

Finally, another skeptical military ethicist, Don Scheid,[22] offers a wholly different line of concern regarding the proposed uses of AI to enable moral machines. Even simple compliance with black letter law, let alone with the rules involved in forms of moral reasoning (such as utilitarian calculus), is not as easily reducible to straightforward algorithms as might be thought (no matter how subtle or sophisticated these may be). This is true for many different reasons.

First, even forms of behavior that seem to be captured by straightforward principles expressible as rules nonetheless are highly general in nature. They often presuppose a vast background of tacit knowledge, a kind of cultural horizon that connects specific behaviors with other kinds of information in a manner that itself is difficult to anticipate. Decades ago, at the comparative dawn of the AI initiative, the renowned philosopher of mind, Daniel Dennett, described this as the frame problem.[23]

How do we determine what sort of knowledge and what scope or range of data, for example, is required to reliably program a machine to follow what seems to be even the simplest set of operational instructions? Do we need to include information within the data set for an AI algorithm that, for example, controls a refrigerator that opening its door to remove a bottle of beer will not set off a nuclear explosion? That possibility would never occur to a human being but presumably not because the human is preprogrammed with this information. It is rather that the human being's situational awareness and cultural horizon include information that would already exclude this possibility from consideration.

This problem is one of the reasons that AI systems are prone not only to error but also to spectacular errors that would never occur to programmers as likely or even conceivable prospects against which to guard. As we observed repeatedly in an earlier chapter: *machines reason, but they do not reason like human beings*. It is especially difficult to design algorithms and dependent databases to handle straightforward legal compliance, let alone engage in complex, culturally freighted moral reasoning, let alone anticipate how these algorithms might respond in specific contexts.

Indeed, this frame problem or dilemma of cultural horizons is a central reason why the behavior of intelligent machines is sometimes characterized as brittle, or resembling a state of narrow rigidity that, in a human, would be diagnosed as some degree of autism. While machines can perform amazing, almost savant-like feats of what appears to be reasoning, they can otherwise seem clueless and childlike, even block-headed (or stupid?) with respect to what humans might regard simply as other similar dimensions of performance or awareness. If an AI system should happen to stray far off the script for a specified task or problem, it can make astonishing errors or omissions of judgment or otherwise engage in utterly unpredictable and unexpected emergent behaviors. The latter phenomenon, which can prove dangerous or unintentionally destructive, becomes even more of a problem as we progress from modular to general or strong AI.

A related issue, as Scheid describes it, involves problems that a particular characteristic of rules themselves present for understanding and carrying out rule-governed behavior. Ethical rules, laws or codes, and principles are always general by their very nature. Being abstract, they also embody some level of ambiguity and vagueness, which can lead to problems in specific cases. For instance, a given rule or law will be subject to interpretation and even have different meanings in different contexts. Very often, two or more rules or principles that conflict with each other still seem to apply to the same case.

These two foregoing issues are ubiquitous when it comes to laws and legal compliance. The first is our ignorance or our aforementioned inability to anticipate every future contingency that might arise. We will not be able to anticipate exceptional situations. Hence, autonomous weapons cannot be preprogrammed for all possible contingencies. This means that once we set down a rule for an autonomous machine, we will have to build in exceptions to the rule only after novel situations arise. Releasing or launching a weapons system with such properties into the combat environment almost certainly bears the prospect of seeming negligent, if not reckless. Scheid defers to the renowned legal philosopher H.L.A. Hart on this difficulty, who writes:

> If the world in which we live were characterized only by a finite number of features, and these together with all the modes in which they could combine were known to us, then provision could be made in advance for every possibility. We could make rules, the application of which to particular cases never called for a further choice. Everything could be known, and . . . something could be done and specified in advance by rule. This would be a world fit for "mechanical" jurisprudence.[24]

Both Scheid and I agree in adding a further caveat to Hart's observation: namely, that this would also be a world perfectly fit for inflexible, rule-governed machines. The inherent complexity and ambiguity of the wider inhabited world, especially regarding ethics and law, is not easily reducible to or explainable in terms of such mechanical behavior.

The second problem is that even with the best and wisest of amended rules and exceptions, there must inevitably be a certain vagueness or open texture on the fringes. Describing this problem, Hart himself explains:

> All rules involve recognizing or classifying particular cases as instances of general terms, and in the case of everything which we are prepared to call a rule it is possible to distinguish clear central cases where it certainly applies and others where there are reasons for both asserting and denying that it applies. Nothing can eliminate this duality of a core of certainty and a penumbra of doubt when we are engaged in bringing particular situations under general rules. This imparts to all rules a fringe of vagueness or "open texture."

Once confronted with a case in the penumbra, a decision must be made as to whether or not the rule should apply. In the sphere and practice of law, such decisions are made in courts of law or legislatures, where all manners of pros and cons are considered, often bringing to bear a number of general and competing values.

These two problematic features of rules present formidable challenges for programmers and AI-based machines. Theoretically, Scheid observes, AI machines may be able to handle these problems (unforeseen contingencies and rule vagueness), possibly through the application of such things as meta rules and fuzzy logic.[25] But, he concludes:

> [I]f so, they will have to embody far more sophisticated AI systems than anything yet in existence. How autonomous weapons may be expected to handle these problems of interpreting and applying rules is anyone's guess.[26]

Notes

1 Cf. J.F. Allen, "AI Growing Up: The Changes and Opportunities," *AI Magazine* 19 (4) (1994): 13–23; Pei Wang, "On Defining Artificial Intelligence," *Journal of Artificial General Intelligence* 10 (2) (2019): 1–37. Also see (Lin et al. 2018).
2 EU High-Level Expert Group on Artificial Intelligence, "A Definition of AI: Main Capabilities and Disciplines" (2019), https://ec.europa.eu/digital-single-market/en/news/definitionartificial-intelligence-main-capabilities-and-scientific-disciplines [accessed 23 March 2022].
3 https://afresearchlab.com/technology/artificial-intelligence/#:~:text=Artificial%20Intelligence%20(AI)%20refers%20to,smart%20software%20behind%20autonomous%20physical [accessed 5 May 2022].
4 NATO, "Allied Joint Doctrine for Cyberspace Operations," AJP-3.20 (2020), www.gov.uk/government/publications/allied-joint-doctrine-for-cyberspace-operations-ajp-320 [accessed 13 May 2022].
5 N.J. Nilsson, *The Quest for Artificial Intelligence* (Cambridge: Cambridge University Press, 2010).
6 G. Apruzzese, M. Colajanni, L. Ferretti, A. Guido, and M. Marchetti, "10th International Conference on Cyber Conflict (CyCon)," *Tallinn* (2018): 371–390. https://doi.org/10.23919/CYCON.2018.8405026.
7 A. Gilli, M. Gilli, A.S. Leonard, and Z. Stanley-Lockman, "'NATO-Mation': Strategies for Leading in the Age of Artificial Intelligence," *NDC Research Paper 15*. NATO Defense College "NDC Research Papers Series" (2020).
8 D.S. Berman, A.L. Buczak, J.S. Chavis, and C.L. Corbett, *Information* 10 (4) (2019): 122, https://doi.org/10.3390/info10040122.
9 L. Vaccaro, G. Sansonetti, and A. Micarelli, *Computers* 10 (1) (2021): 11, https://doi.org/10.3390/computers10010011; J. Lowe-Power, A. Akram, et al., "The gem5 Simulator: Version 20.0+: A New Era for the Open-source Computer Architecture Simulator," *arXiv* preprint arXiv:2007.03152 (2020). https://arxiv.org/abs/2007.03152 [accessed 23 August 2022].
10 The preceding summary encapsulates the presentations, comments, and findings of an international team of AI and defense personnel, military and civilian, assembled for the annual McCain Conference at the U.S. Naval Academy in April 2022. Under Chatham House rules, no specific attributions or quotations are cited; however, a list of the participants and topics can be found at: www.usna.edu/Ethics/Research/McCain/RegistrationInformation.php [accessed 5 May 2022].
11 Ronald Arkin, "The Case for Ethical Autonomy in Unmanned Systems," *Journal of Military Ethics* 9 (4) (2010): 334.
12 Ronald Arkin, Point/Counterpoint section, "The Case for Banning Killer Robots," *Communications of the ACM* 58 (12) (December 2015): 4; "Lethal Autonomous Systems and the Plight of the Non-combatant," *AISB Quarterly* (137) (July 2013): 2.
13 Ronald E. Arkin, "Ethical Robots in Warfare," *IEEE Technology and Society Magazine* 28 (1) (Spring 2009): 29–30. (IEEE is Institute of Electrical and Electronic Engineers.)
14 Ibid., p. 4.
15 Ronald Arkin, "A Roboticist's Perspective on Lethal Autonomous Weapon Systems," in "Perspectives on Lethal Autonomous Weapon Systems," *UNODA Occasional Papers*, No. 30 (November 2017): 43. (UNODA is United Nations Office for Disarmament Affairs.)
16 Ronald E. Arkin, *Governing Lethal Behavior in Autonomous Robots* (Boca Raton, FL: CRC Press, 2009): 69.
17 Ibid., 185.
18 Ibid., 187.
19 Ronald C. Arkin and Patrick Ulam, "An Ethical Adaptor: Behavioral Modification Derived from Moral Emotions," *Technical Report GIT-GYU-09–04*.
20 Ronald Arkin, Point/Counterpoint section, "The Case for Banning Killer Robots," *Communications of the ACM* 58 (12) (December 2015): 5.

21 Ronald C. Arkin, *Governing Lethal Behavior in Autonomous Robots* (Boca Raton, FL: CRC Press, 2009): 211.
22 Don E. Scheid, *Ethics, Artificial Intelligence, and Military Weapons Technologies* (London: Routledge, forthcoming 2023).
23 Daniel C. Dennett, *Elbow Room: The Varieties of Freedom Worth Wanting,* 2nd ed. (Cambridge, MA: MIT Bradford Books, 2015). First published in 1984.
24 H.L.A. Hart, *The Concept of Law*, 2nd ed. (Oxford: Clarendon Press, 1994): 128.
25 For example, as in Nikos Tsourveloudis, et al., "Autonomous Navigation of Unmanned Vehicles: A Fuzzy Logic Perspective," *Journal of Cutting Edge Robotics* (2005), www.academia.edu/15518799/Autonomous_Navigation_of_Unmanned_Vehicles_A_Fuzzy_Logic_Perspective. See also Sefer Kurnaz, et al., "Fuzzy Logic Based Approach to Design of Flight Control and Navigation Tasks for Autonomous Unmanned Aerial Vehicles," *Journal of Intelligent and Robotic Systems* 54 (2009): 229–244, www.academia.edu/25112107/Fuzzy_Logic_Based_Approach_to_Design_of_Flight_Control_and_Navigation_Tasks_for_Autonomous_Unmanned_Aerial_Vehicles [accessed 3 April 2022] and Dan Necsulescu, et al., "Swarming Unmanned Aerial Vehicles: Concept Development and Experimentation," Technical Memorandum DRDC Ottawa TM-2003–176 (December 2003), www.academia.edu/18036303/Swarming_Unmanned_Aerial_Vehicles_Concept_Development_and_Experimentation_A_State_of_the_Art_Review_on_Flight_and_Mission_Control [accessed 14 April 2022].
26 Don Scheid, *Ethics, Artificial Intelligence, and Military Weapons Technologies* (London: Routledge, forthcoming 2023): chapter 5.

References

Allen, J.F. "AI Growing Up: The Changes and Opportunities," *AI Magazine* 19 (4) (1998): 13–23.

Air Force Research Laboratory. "Artificial Intelligence," https://afresearchlab.com/technology/artificial-intelligence/#:~:text=Artificial%20Intelligence%20(AI)%20refers%20to,smart%20software%20behind%20autonomous%20physical [accessed 23 August 2022].

Apruzzese, G.; Colajanni, M.; Ferretti, L.; Guido, A.; Marchetti, M. "10th International Conference on Cyber Conflict (CyCon)," *Tallinn* (2018): 371–390, https://doi.org/10.23919/CYCON.2018.8405026.

Arkin, Ronald E. "Ethical Robots in Warfare," *IEEE Technology and Society Magazine* 28 (1) (Spring 2009): 29–30.

Arkin, Ronald E. *Governing Lethal Behavior in Autonomous Robots* (Boca Raton, FL: CRC Press, 2009).

Arkin, Ronald. "The Case for Ethical Autonomy in Unmanned Systems," *Journal of Military Ethics* 9 (4) (2010).

Arkin, Ronald. "Lethal Autonomous Systems and the Plight of the Non-combatant," *AISB Quarterly* (137) (July 2013).

Arkin, Ronald. Point/Counterpoint section. "The Case for Banning Killer Robots," *Communications of the ACM* 58 (12) (December 2015).

Arkin, Ronald. "A Roboticist's Perspective on Lethal Autonomous Weapon Systems," In "Perspectives on Lethal Autonomous Weapon Systems," *UNODA Occasional Papers*, No. 30 (November 2017).

Arkin, Ronald M.; Ulam, Patrick. "An Ethical Adaptor: Behavioral Modification Derived from Moral Emotions," *Technical Report GIT-GYU-09–04*. 2009.

Berman, D.S.; Buczak, A.L.; Chavis, J.S.; Corbett, C.L. "A Survey of Deep Learning Methods for Cyber Security," *Information* 10 (4) (2019): 122, https://doi.org/10.3390/info10040122.

Dennett, Daniel C. *Elbow Room: The Varieties of Freedom Worth Wanting*. 2nd ed. (Cambridge, MA: MIT Bradford Books, 2015). First published in 1984.

EU High-Level Expert Group on Artificial Intelligence. "A Definition of AI: Main Capabilities and Disciplines" (2019), https://ec.europa.eu/digital-single-market/en/news/definitionartificial- intelligence-main-capabilities-and-scientific-disciplines.

Gilli, A.; Gilli, M.; Leonard, A.S.; Stanley-Lockman, Z. "'NATO-Mation': Strategies for Leading in the Age of Artificial Intelligence," *NDC Research Paper 15*. NATO Defense College "NDC Research Papers Series" (2020).

Hart, H.L.A. *The Concept of Law*. 2nd ed. (Oxford: Clarendon Press, 1994).

Kim, Bumsoo; Hubbard, Paul; Necsulescu, Dan. "Swarming Unmanned Aerial Vehicles: Concept Development and Experimentation," Technical Memorandum DRDC Ottawa TM-2003–176 (December 2003), www.academia.edu/18036303/Swarming_Unmanned_Aerial_Vehicles_Concept_Development_and_Experimentation_A_State_of_the_Art_Review_on_Flight_and_Mission_Control [accessed 14 April 2022].

Kurnaz, Sefer; Cetin, Omer; Kaynak, Okyay. "Fuzzy Logic Based Approach to Design of Flight Control and Navigation Tasks for Autonomous Unmanned Aerial Vehicles," *Journal of Intelligent and Robotic Systems* 54 (2009): 229–244, www.academia.edu/25112107/Fuzzy_Logic_Based_Approach_to_Design_of_Flight_Control_and_Navigation_Tasks_for_Autonomous_Unmanned_Aerial_Vehicles [accessed 3 April 2022].

Lin, Patrick, et al. *Robot Ethics 2.0: From Autonomous Cars to Artificial Intelligence*, co-edited with Ryan Jenkins and Keith Abney (New York: Oxford University Press, 2017).

Lopez, C. Todd. "Department of Defense Adopts 5 Principles of Artificial Intelligence Ethics," *OSD* (Washington, DC, 25 February 2020), https://www.defense.gov/News/News-Stories/Article/Article/2094085/dod-adopts-5-principles-of-artificial-intelli gence-ethics/ [accessed 23 August 2022].

Lowe-Power, Jason; Mutaal Ahmad, Abdul; Akram, Ayaz; et al. "The gem5 Simulator: Version 20.0+: A New Era for the Open-source Computer Architecture Simulator," *arXiv* preprint arXiv:2007.03152 (2020). https://arxiv.org/abs/2007.03152 [accessed 23 August 2022].

Lucas, George. *Military Ethics: What Everyone Needs to Know* (New York: Oxford University Press, 2016).

NATO. "Allied Joint Doctrine for Cyberspace Operations," AJP-3.20 (2020), www.gov.uk/government/publications/allied-joint-doctrine-for-cyberspace-operations-ajp-320 [accessed 13 May 2022].

Nilsson, N.J. *The Quest for Artificial Intelligence* (Cambridge: Cambridge University Press, 2010).

Riza, Shane. *Killing Without Heart: Limits on Robotic Warfare* (Washington, DC: Potomac Books, 2013).

Sharkey, Noel. "Why Robots Should Not Be Delegated the Decision to Kill," *Connection Science* 29 (2) (2017): 177–186.

Scharre, Paul. *Army of None* (New York: W.W. Norton, 2018).

Scheid, Don E. *Ethics, Artificial Intelligence, and Military Weapons Technologies* (London: Routledge, forthcoming 2023).

Surgeon General. *IV Operation Iraqi Freedom 05-07, Final Report* (Washington, DC: Surgeon General's Office, Mental Health Advisory Team (MHAT), 17 November 2006), https://ntrl.ntis.gov/NTRL/dashboard/searchResults/titleDetail/PB2010103335.xhtml [accessed 23 August 2022].

Tsourveloudis, Nikos C.; Doitsidis, Lefteris; Valavanis, Kimon P. "Autonomous Navigation of Unmanned Vehicles: A Fuzzy Logic Perspective," *Journal of Cutting Edge Robotics* (2005), www.academia.edu/15518799/Autonomous_Navigation_of_Unmanned_Vehicles_A_Fuzzy_Logic_Perspective.

Vaccaro, L. Sansonetti, G.; Micarelli, A. "An Empirical Review of Automated Machine Learning," *Computers* 10 (1) (2021): 11, https://doi.org/10.3390/computers10010011.

Vallor, Shannon. *Technology and the Virtues: A Philosophical Guide to a Future Worth Wanting* (New York: Oxford University Press, 2017).

Wallach, Wendell. *A Dangerous Master: How To Keep Technology from Slipping Beyond Our Control* (New York: Basic Books, 2015).

Wallach, Wendell; Allen, Colin. *Moral Machines: Teaching Robots Right from Wrong* (New York: Oxford University Press, 2008).

Wang, Pei. "On Defining Artificial Intelligence," *Journal of Artificial General Intelligence* 10 (2) (2019): 1–37.

6

ARTIFICIAL INTELLIGENCE AND CYBER OPERATIONS

Concern for recognizing and adhering to relevant ethical norms and standards in the development and eventual military uses of artificial intelligence (AI) in cyber operations is often voiced by national and military leaders in the United States, United Kingdom, Australia, and Europe. The U.S. Department of Defense's Joint Artificial Intelligence Center (JAIC), established in 2018, for example, lists leadership in military ethics and AI safety as among its five pillars of AI strategy.[1] What exactly such vague and generalized expressions of concern mean in practice, however, is often far from clear. And efforts to operationalize or otherwise use ethical norms in the development and use of AI-enhanced military technologies generally are not obviously apparent, let alone featured in the forefront of specific AI initiatives.

One study of ethics aimed at both AI lifecycle actors and end users, titled "Artificial Intelligence Ethics Guidelines for Developers and Users: Clarifying Their Content and Normative Implications,"[2] enumerates normative implications of existing AI ethics guidelines for developers and organizational users of AI generally. This chapter enumerates 11 principles, comprising a much larger list of specific guidelines, most of which are drawn from a general ethics overview by Jobin et al.[3] They are as follows.

1 *Transparency* in all facets of AI technology (data, algorithms, and decision-making) throughout the phases of development and use.
2 *Justice and fairness* guaranteed by developers and users so that AI does not discriminate against any groups or provide unfair outcomes.
3 *Nonmaleficence* to avoid AI harming human beings.
4 *Responsibility*: All AI actions and their consequences must always be traceable to a legal person.
5 *Privacy* should be respected and ensured by AI-supported systems and weapons.

DOI: 10.4324/9781003273912-7

6 *Beneficence:* AI use should be beneficial for humans.
7 *Freedom and autonomy:* AI use should strengthen democratic values and personal self-determination.
8 *Trust:* Developers and users of AI should demonstrate their trustworthiness and the reliability of their AI systems.
9 *Sustainability:* Development and use of AI technology should be environmentally sustainable;
10 *Dignity:* AI use should not violate fundamental human rights.
11 *Solidarity:* AI use should promote social welfare and security.

Obviously, not all such considerations were intended to apply specifically to military uses of AI but are meant to guide AI research and implementation more generally, to include domestic and commercial uses. In their totality, however, these principles encompass the range of unique moral concerns that increasing degrees of AI and AI-augmented systems introduce (whether we are considering a lethal autonomous weapons system, enhanced wargaming and strategic planning, or merely a home digital assistant).

One area in particular that seems especially well informed by this general inventory is the realm of AI-augmented cyber operations. To begin with, the list of the possible threat actors conducting AI adversarial attacks is the same for traditional cyberattacks; these actors vary from the unsophisticated (script kiddies)[4] to the sophisticated (state actors and state-paid actors), including cybercriminals, terrorists, and hacktivists, as well as malicious and non-malicious insiders.

The European Union's Agency for Cyber Security categorizes threats into eight main categories: (1) *nefarious activity/abuse*, namely malicious action to disrupt the functioning of AI systems; (2) *surveillance/interception/hijacking*, involving actions whose goal is to eavesdrop or otherwise control communications; (3) *physical attacks* intended to sabotage the components or infrastructure of the system; (4) *unintentional damages*, that is, accidental actions harming systems or persons; (5) *failures/malfunctions*, when a system itself does not work properly; (6) *outages*, that is, unexpected disruptions of service; (7) *disasters*, namely, natural catastrophes or larger accidents; and finally (8) *legal threats*, which occur when a third party uses applicable law, domestic or international, to constrain the cyber operations of an opponent.[5]

Adversarial input attacks and poisoning attacks[6] are examples of abuse. In input attacks, the input is manipulated in ways that may go unnoticed by the human eye, as, for instance, when tape is affixed to a road sign. Poisoning attacks, by contrast, target the design process of AI and the learning process itself. Poisoning can be done both to algorithms and to the massive data sets upon which machine learning is based. In addition to nefarious activity, Hartmann and Steup discuss techniques that can be used in eavesdropping on different neural networks and support-vector networks. The entry and exit points (not all applicable for each method) include input, labelling, preprocessing, feature extraction, classifiers, and weights. Noise generator and selector points are included simply to illustrate that AI methods are vulnerable both to actions with unintentionally destructive consequences and to deliberately malicious actions. When data sets are corrupted or algorithms are biased, the conclusions AI reaches will likewise be distorted or biased. And here lies the core of the problem: to what extent can we trust the results and decisions recommended by AI?

Cyberspace Operations

AI solutions vary in complexity, and the context where they are used sets unique demands regarding both the requirements for flawlessness of decisions and the degree of autonomy delegated to AI. This applies especially with respect to AI tools used in cyberspace. NATO, the United States, and allies (such as members of the "Five Eyes") currently use AI to shrink critical timelines for cyber-threat situational awareness. AI use in cyber operations enhances the capability to detect threats and malicious activities at a rate that is not humanly possible. Suspicious events, behaviors, and anomalies can be rapidly identified for cyber professionals and operators to further investigate and deploy mitigation strategies. This decreases the likelihood of adversaries gaining access to NATO and U.S. Department of Defense networks, infrastructure, and weapons systems.[7]

According to NATO's operational doctrine for cyberspace (NATO 2020, 2), cyberspace is not limited to, but at its core consists of, a computerized environment that is artificially constructed and constantly under development. NATO doctrine (NATO 2020, 3) divides cyberspace into three layers: physical (e.g., hardware), logical (e.g., firmware, protocols), and *cyber persona* (virtual identities, e.g., emails, net-profiles). The logical layer is always involved in *cyberspace operations*, but effects of those operations can also impact both the physical and cyber persona layers of cyberspace. Furthermore, NATO doctrine recognizes that cyberspace operations can affect human senses, decision-making, and behavior. Similarly, cyberspace operations can have an impact on other physical elements that are directly included within or connected to cyberspace. Activities outside of cyberspace that have an effect on cyberspace (e.g., the physical sabotage of hardware components), are not, however, considered cyberspace operations. In general, the basic principles applicable to NATO joint operations apply to cyberspace operations just as they do to operations in the kinetic domain (a separate document governs targeting in this domain: NATO 2019). However, the concept of time and reach can be somewhat different in different situations. Cyberspace operations doctrine (NATO 2020) lists some direct and indirect effects that cyberspace operations can have. The first five are effects that defensive operations normally have in one's own *communication and information systems* (CIS) while the remaining are effects that offensive operations can have on the other's (adversary's) network.

1 Secure against compromise of CIA (confidentiality, integrity and availability) of our own CIS, as well as the data they store.
2 Isolate the communication between adversaries and our own affected systems.

3 Contain the spread of the malicious activity.
4 Neutralize malicious activity permanently from our own CIS.
5 Recover quickly from the effects of malicious activity (network resilience).
6 Manipulate the integrity of an adversary's CIS.
7 Exfiltrate the information of adversaries through unauthorized access to their own CIS.
8 Degrade an asset of an adversary to a level below its normal capacity or performance.
9 Disrupt an asset of an adversary for an extended period of time.
10 Destroy an asset of the adversary.

From a legal perspective, cyber operations are expected to conform to international law (such as the United Nations Charter, laws of armed conflict, and human rights law) as well as to applicable domestic law (i.e., the laws of the nation carrying out cyberspace operations). A specific cyber operation plan should include a description of the rules of engagement and should define the standing authority and expected effects of cyberspace operations. Estimation of effects on dual-use objects (e.g., network infrastructure), other prospective collateral damage, and likelihood of attribution for the operation can be difficult to determine.

Instruments of international law, as mentioned earlier, are extrapolated to cyberspace operations in the Tallinn Manual 2.0 (2017) while treaties and legislation pertaining to conventional armed conflict were extrapolated to the cyber domain in the initial Tallinn Manual (2013).[8] The manuals are not represented as if they constituted binding international law, but like many other manuals (e.g., the 1994 *San Remo Manual* on International Law pertaining to Armed Conflicts at Sea),[9] they are intended to provide guidance in applying existing law to specific complex or novel situations. In this chapter, I omit discussion of specifics on who within the organization actually has final responsibility for conducting such operations, as well as which type of cyber operations are intended, as these specifics obviously vary from one state jurisdiction to another.

Some Examples of AI-Supported Cyberspace Measures

A useful listing of defensive and offensive cyberspace operations can be found in Truong, Diep, and Zelinka (2020).[10] On the defensive side of AI-based cyber applications, they list *malware detection* (PC malware, Android malware), *network intrusion* (intrusion detection, anomaly detection), *phishing/spam detection* (web phishing, mail phishing, spam on social media, spam mail), and other, similar measures (e.g., continuous monitoring of advanced persistent threats (APTs); identifying domain names generated by domain generation algorithms). For malicious use of AI, they list autonomous intelligent threats (strengthening malware and social engineering) and tools for attacking AI models (adversarial inputs, poisoning training data, and model extraction). Kaloudi and Li offer a similar survey,[11] but they focus chiefly on the offensive side with examples that they also map onto the cyber targeting chain that is often used when attack vector vulnerabilities are estimated. This chain contains three main phases: *planning* (reconnaissance and weaponization), *intrusion* (delivery, exploitation, and installation), and *execution* (command and control actions or C2).

There are also seven subphases. AI methods are used in the *reconnaissance* phase for selecting targets and learning targets' standard behavior. In the *weaponization* phase, AI can be thought to generate attack payloads, aid in password guessing or in launching brute force attacks, generate abnormal behavior, and detect new target vulnerabilities. In the *delivery* phase, AI programs can help conceal ongoing attacks (permitting them to remain undetectable by the victim) and conceal malicious intent. Automated methods establish means of distributing disruptive content in the *exploitation* phase. AI algorithms that can evolve and self-propagate malicious code are both used in the *installation* phase. Finally, in the C2 and action phase, AI activates the malicious code and harvests the outcomes of the operations. Kaloudi and Li also discuss using AI-based methods on the defensive side. In their framework, methods for behavioral and risk analysis are to be used in the *planning* phase. Methods that are suited to detect anomalies and offensive AI patterns are suited for the *intrusion* phase. In the *execution* phase, AI algorithms handle real-time response and configuration management.

Some AI methods used in real-time response against cyberattack fall within a grey zone between defensive and offensive tools. James Pattison defines (and advocates) *active cyber defense* as a situation in which the organization that is first targeted or attacked preemptively attacks or immediately retaliates by "hacking back."[12] Pattison's contrast appears to discriminate between offensive measures as a tactic of active defense (i.e., both repelling an initial attack and simultaneously taking up the initiative of retaliation within the initial attack framework) and the more conventional meaning of "offensive" as *initiating* the conflict (strategic offense). (I further analyze and endorse both Pattison's and Lin's advocacy of preventive cyber self-defense in Chapter 9.)

The definition of passive and active cyber defense depends to a large extent upon where the action occurs. When the cyber measures are initiating activity only inside the targeted organization's network, they are called passive defensive measures (e.g., firewalls). If the defensive activity extends beyond the targeted organization's network, it is classified as an active defensive measure. The disruptiveness and intrusion level of these methods varies. Examples of these are honeypots, botnet takeouts, and intrusion into the attackers' network to gain information or rescue stolen information.

Some measures that are used in defensive work (such as penetration testing within one's own network to detect and patch the security breaches found) can be used in another organization's network, making use of the same testing measures in an offensive cyberspace operation. It is also worthy of mention that the examples of AI-supported methods discussed in Kaloudi and Li (2020) and labeled as offensive operations can also be classified as *malicious uses* of AI, as they are, for example, in the European Union Agency for Cybersecurity (ENISA 2020).

Ethics and Cyber Operations Personnel

In keeping with the focus of the PRIO project, I want to focus particular attention on those who actually engage directly in carrying out AI-supported cyberspace operations. Each of the effects of cyberspace operations described earlier poses delicate, and sometimes, nonapparent ethical and legal dilemmas. Despite the considerable comparative advantages AI enhancement can provide in pursuing these objectives, its use as a tool within cyber operations has exacerbated three problems.

- *Inadvertent escalation*, insofar as AI-enabled autonomous interactions without humans in the loop are resistant to normal measures of supervision and control;
- *Proliferation*, insofar as AI reduces the demand for human personnel otherwise required for cyber operations, thereby decreasing the cost of these operations; and
- As these lowered costs, in turn, permit wider participation in cyber operations, that consequent proliferation of state and nonstate actors makes the *attribution* of cyber operations for purposes of defense and response proportionately more difficult.

Here, the term *proliferation* is invoked in the sense that arms control analysts use the term: that is, increasing the availability of offensive weapons (rather than necessarily or inevitably increasing the ease or the incidence of conducting those conflicts). That is to say, possession of effective offensive cyber capability by an increasing number of operators poses the grave risk of increasing their individual capacity to inflict ever-more-severe damage during an attack. Until recently, for example, only those few states that possessed large and dedicated cyber programs with many personnel working in collaboration were able to launch effective cyberattacks (like Stuxnet). By increasingly incorporating AI enhancement, however, now even small-scale actors can enter the game. An example of sophisticated cyber proliferation in this sense is found in the growing rate of ransom incidents in which municipalities and businesses have been locked out of their computer systems. The program being used for this purpose, WannaCry, was reportedly developed initially by the U.S. National Security Administration and was somehow exfiltrated and released on the dark web (perhaps by a disgruntled employee).[13] There it was obtained and used by cybercriminals until it was detected and removed. This weapon has unfortunately proliferated. The concern is that AI use may only exacerbate this problem.

On the other hand, it bears mention that current and future uses of AI do not represent only ethical dilemmas. One obvious upside of AI is to strengthen defensive cyber capabilities via earlier detection and appropriate defensive response while easing the strain and manual workload of the human defenders. Another ethical upside in the war context is the enhanced ability to bring force to bear on an adversary with less destructiveness. One party might opt to shut down rather than physically destroy an adversary's power grid, for example, allowing services to resume when the conflict has been resolved.

AI, Privacy, and Data Protection

The EU has adopted what is likely the most extensive and stringent privacy and security laws in the world at present, known as the General Data Protection Regulation (GDPR). Although drafted and adopted by the EU, GDPR imposes surprisingly extensive legal and ethical obligations on organizations and states throughout the world which might be involved in targeting the security of, or collecting data about, citizens in EU countries.[14] Inasmuch as cutting-edge, AI-enhanced cybersecurity systems are increasingly data-driven, they increasingly risk running afoul of data protection regimes such as the GDPR.[15] Proper deployment of such systems thus must include some consultation with competent professionals capable of mapping the complex domain of requirements and exceptions characteristic of these bodies of law respecting data privacy.

The GDPR, for example, applies to all companies, organizations, and government agencies that process personally identifiable information on individuals residing in the EU, regardless of where the entity is located.[16] To be sure, states involved in the realm of policing enjoy great latitude under the GDPR, such that when such actors collect data solely to prevent crimes or threats to public safety, the GDPR does not restrict their activities (see Article 23). To the extent that defensive military cybersecurity is somewhat akin to crime prevention (prevention of harm to citizenry), the armed forces of member and allied nations enjoy similar freedom from GDPR privacy restrictions. There are also specific exclusions that EU member states can apply in areas such as security and defense.[17]

Cybersecurity reporting requirements may also fall under GDPR exemptions or exceptions. In some situations, for example, member states require a wide range of entities (e.g., telecommunications and social media organizations) to share or distribute information to other entities (e.g., national police forces). Those entities required to engage in such information distribution remain exempt from the requirements of the GDPR *so long as sufficient safeguards for the data are in place.* Moreover, Article 23 of the GDPR authorizes an individual member state, "when necessary and proportionate," to restrict the scope of the obligations under GDPR Article 23 (2018). Nevertheless, private entities developing cybersecurity systems must otherwise be mindful of GDPR protections. The U.S. Department of Defense attorney Brandon W. Jackson has observed, for example,

> Autonomous cybersecurity systems are driven by data, and the European Union General Data Protection Regulation (GDPR) is an unavoidable moderator in this regard. The GDPR places significant restraints on the collection and use of data in Europe. Moreover, the extraterritorial nature of the regulation compounds the impact it has on global industries.[18]

While Jackson concludes that "today's AI-based cybersecurity systems are likely capable of complying with the GDPR," he also cautions that "absent a technical solution, maintaining compliance will becoming increasingly difficult as these

[AI-enabled] systems achieve greater autonomy" (Jackson 2020). These challenges will become more salient as AI components of cybersecurity systems become more important in the private sector. Moreover, although we may think we understand how moral rules apply in peacetime, what do we do when we find ourselves in a complex and wholly unfamiliar crisis, such as an armed conflict? What regulations might individuals or organizational sectors engaging in routine defensive cyber operations in times of peace be allowed, or even required, to override when routine levels of peacetime conflict suddenly ramp up during the outbreak of war?

Earlier, I purposely omitted discussion of who might be conducting cyberspace operations, as these assignments vary widely depending upon national context. However, from the ethical point of view, all who are engaged in defensive cyber operations should also consider the ethical dilemmas that can arise in switching from defensive to more aggressive offensive cyber operations. A civilian defensive cyberspace operator, for example, might be recruited by the military into an offensive cyber operation (much as, during World War II, civilians were called to duty as code breakers or to calculate bombing trajectories). This will certainly affect the legal and regulatory environment and confront individual operators with new ethical challenges.

Ethical Issues for Operators and End Users

For purposes of discussion, let us presume the end users about whom we are concerned constitute cyber operators functioning within a military hierarchy or chain of command (inasmuch as offensive cyber operations are usually carried out exclusively by properly authorized military forces). As the cyber operator inherits an occupation, we consider the two forms of occupational ethics that apply in this domain: military ethics and engineering ethics. From these perspectives, in turn, we attempt to derive appropriate moral and legal stances for individual operators to adopt in response to the 11 AI ethics guidelines set forth earlier in this chapter.

Transparency in AI-Supported Cyberspace Operations

Transparency can be understood in several different ways. Rather than attempt to offer an exhaustive catalog, it might help to think of undesirable and desirable transparencies, also including platforms other than cyber and AI-supported cyberspace operations.

In general, transparency in any domain and with respect to any weapons system or supporting technology or doctrine is something policymakers and their militaries are well advised to avoid. A similar logic applies to cyberspace operations, along with the specific tools and procedures that might be used in carrying them out (whether AI-supported or not) because these must remain organizational secrets. Undesirable transparency comes in several forms, the most important of which in our context being the undesirable revelation of information that should be kept out of the wrong hands. Law professor David Pozen has argued, for example, that as public institutions became subject to more and more policies of openness and accountability, demands for transparency became more and more threatening to the functioning and legitimacy of those institutions.[19] An even more direct threat is a real or potential adversary's (Red Team's) ability to discern enough about the "good" side's (Blue Team's) capabilities, training, and doctrines, alongside intentions to neutralize some or all advantages those would confer. For example, if the opposing Red Team knows Blue's catalog of zero-day exploits useful for disabling currently fielded AI, and it also knows under what circumstances each zero-day exploit would be deployed and revealed, the Red Team thereby acquires a decided advantage.

In both offensive and defensive operations, the capabilities of AI-supported cyberspace operations are rarely revealed intentionally. Occasionally, a nation might decide to send a message of national will or technological superiority to control Red Team's psychology and motivate them to act in certain ways. But this is relatively rare. The plan for a cyber operation must be issued in advance and approved by appropriate authorities, and this requires some level of transparency.[20] The plan should include a description of the rules of engagement, and it should define the standing authority and expected effects of cyberspace operations. The plan should also comply with applicable international law. Here, the two Tallinn manuals provide at least some guidance to end users in determining when, where, and how compliance with relevant international law will likely affect their anticipated operations (e.g., *Tallinn Manual* 2.0, 2017; Rule 103).

Transparency has another meaning in the realm of development as well as in *testing, evaluation, verification, and validation* (TEVV).[21] The essence of transparency here is that governments and their militaries should acquire and field only technologies with known (or at least knowable) effects under given sets of conditions. Similarly, industries and other organizations that develop systems that then pass TEVV regimens should emerge as open books: that is, there should be no unpleasant surprises once the systems are fielded. This sense of transparency could require a degree of flexibility with respect to strong AI. It is conceivable that some aspects of a system's or weapon's transitions through sense–think–act iterations will not be fully understood, even when the TEVV process reveals regularity sufficient to engender the confidence that a nation needs to field the system.

What has come to be called "explainable AI"[22] helps significantly to increase transparency between AI and its users. It incorporates four principles: explanation, meaning, accuracy, and the limits of applicable knowledge.[23] Following these principles in designing AI systems helps to ensure that they operate only within the context for which they are designed, such that the outputs are accompanied with machine reasoning that is understandable to the different user groups. Desirable transparency can also be presented to all sides as a shared acknowledgment of unsafe practices that all should avoid for their mutual benefit. As with nuclear weapons, states have agreed on some desirable safety practices. Efforts are ongoing to establish similar practices also for use of AI (e.g., the Global Partnership of Artificial Intelligence).[24]

We thus have two distinct kinds of transparency: one that pertains to *weapons developers* and the other that pertains to *end users* in the cyber battlespace. The first (developers) must demonstrate (be transparent about) the efficacy and safety of the systems they have designed. The second group (cyber operators) ordinarily aims at *surprise*. In this sense, transparency (vis-à-vis the enemy, at least) is inimical to their mission. Sometimes, however, cyber weapons are put to deterrent use: in that instance, a military will deliberately reveal details about its capabilities to dissuade an enemy from some line of action. In this context, transparency will be militarily appropriate. Moreover, apart from transparency toward enemies, military personnel who use AI-based cyber weaponry must, on demand, reveal to their superiors and others engaged in post-battle assessments what exactly happened when these weapons were deployed. In this sense, a strict obligation of transparency exists.

We might moreover observe that the transparency appropriate to the battlespace falls first and foremost within the purview of military ethics while the transparency incumbent on developers mainly pertains to engineering ethics. There are evidently areas of overlap: for instance, engineers have an ethical mandate, clearly recommended by their code of professional ethics, *not* to field weapons systems incorporating military decision algorithms (such as the U.S. Air Force's Arachnid) unless the TEVV process has ensured there will be no surprises once the AI-supported technologies are finally deployed. Cyber operators, likewise, must acquire a basic understanding of the safety constraints of the systems they use, constraints that pertain chiefly to engineering ethics. There will, of course, be something less than full transparency between state security organizations that conduct cyberspace operations and, say, the general public. The same applies for the individual users of AI. Trade and national security secrets (particularly offensive cyber capabilities) must never be disclosed to friends, family, or the public. In another sense, however, the engineering-based transparency between the AI-supported tool developer and the end users requires that the staff of the client security agency or organization understand how the AI technology they are using really works, such that their decision-making about its employment is fully informed. In this instance, transparency is desirable and even required.

Justice and Fairness in AI-Supported Cyber Operations

Concerns regarding justice and fairness often focus on implicit bias in databases that might result in unjust discrimination in operational outcomes. AI development depends on having sufficient data necessary to achieve optimal performance. As described in the previous chapter, we know that biased data sets can create problems in AI algorithms, such as the well-known discovery that some facial recognition programs have failed to recognize Black women more often than they have failed to recognize White men. This phenomenon has obvious ethical implications. One solution is to increase the amount of data available to the AI system as it learns how to perform its tasks with greater proficiency (optimization). The quest to acquire ever-increasing volumes of data can threaten individual privacy and corporate security and run afoul of the regulatory regimes described earlier that are in place to ensure that privacy.

Furthermore, while the problem of bias in data sets and among designers, testers, and operators is important, the general concerns for justice and fairness in a military setting might encompass even more. The sorts of calculations implied by the *in bello* principle of proportionality, and the kind of deontic work that underlies the principle of discrimination, require an underlying conception of justice. Lacking such a conception, how would one know what to count as good or bad in a proportionality calculation, and how would one judge the aptness of rules for determining who is a combatant and who is not as prerequisite to applying the principle of discrimination?

Consider the following three situations in which an AI-enhanced cyberspace operation might introduce even more complications than the human-controlled cyberspace operation is causing at present. The first one is the pace at which move–countermove stratagems are exercised. Already today, the need for countering a cyberattack in cyberspace can be too time-limited to leave room for ethical deliberations. Those considerations should be discussed and established well in advance within the rules of engagement prior to the conduct of specific cyber operations. This requirement is already clearly specified within NATO's cyberspace operational doctrine. Once AI-enhanced tools are introduced, however, cyber–cyber interactions can take place even faster, affording little or no chance of detecting errors before disaster occurs. This accelerated operational tempo of AI-enhanced cyberspace operations thus could result in an unanticipated outcome ranging from, say, an error in discrimination all the way to a grave war crime.

A second situation arises from our basic ignorance of *why* attacks and counterattacks unfold as they do. Suppose that an accidental but highly destructive attack occurs during the conduct of an AI-supported cyberspace operation. It may prove difficult, if not impossible, to reverse engineer from effect to algorithmic cause.[25] It is one thing to ask for lenience at the state level after providing a clear explanation of what transpired, and it is quite another only to be able to state helplessly, "We certainly never intended for those terrible tragedies to occur, and we haven't the least idea how or why they occurred." The latter suggests gross and culpable incompetence, reckless endangerment, or worse, criminal negligence on the part of cyber operators and design engineers.

The third situation arises from the ease of introducing what we might term multidimensional distancing in cyber operations. Much has been written about the moral dangers of standoff weapons. The principal concern in that instance is that as the spatial or temporal distance between a would-be shooter and her intended victim increases, the shooter is less likely to be deterred by the ordinary human instinct not to take another human life. In one possible cyber analogue, an AI-supported cyberspace operations can be psychologically tailored to, say, avoid provoking the qualms of legislatures, command authorities, and operators and thereby permit such agents to proceed thoughtlessly in approving or doing violence that normally would not be countenanced. In the cyber domain, and, especially with the aid of AI, tailoring a weapon to combine different types of such moral distancing would be relatively simple.

Nonmaleficence in AI-Supported Cyber Operations

It is tempting to say that with respect to nonmaleficence and benevolence, AI-supported cyber defense and offense are not significantly different from operations in other domains conducted with noncyber means. Indeed, there are many enlightening similarities and analogies among domains and weapons. The *Tallinn Manual* (2.0), for example, states that, similar to other dual-use objects encountered in conventional warfare, "cyber infrastructure used for both civilian and military purposes is a military objective" (Rule 101), and therefore it constitutes a legitimate military target. The manual, however, forbids the use of other stratagems, such as cyber booby traps associated with objects specified in the law of armed conflict (e.g., providing medical assistance, per Rule 106). The manual's team of experts offers a specific illustration of the latter, in which some form of malware is embedded in phony emails allegedly from legitimate medical personnel that might somehow result in physical illness (Rule 106, Explanation 4).

Just as with traditional warfare, offensive cyber operations can be used to harm civilian noncombatants. The harm can be indirect, affecting the systems noncombatants use, but it can also be direct (as in the previous illustration, through malware embedded in digital medical devices). Collateral damage is also possible with offensive cyberspace operation due to the connectivity of different systems and networks. Dual-use targets remain an issue of concern in cyber operations just as in conventional or kinetic operations. For example, disrupting traffic in networks that might be used for both military and civilian purposes will have an impact on civilian operations, as well as on the military.

An odd and interestingly unique property of cyber warfare, reminiscent of war in earlier historical eras, is that many defensive and offensive cyber weapons at present are conceivably *reusable* if captured or stolen and repurposed (like WannaCry) or are recovered after they are launched or fired, with the caveat that many are context specific. The Stuxnet/Olympic Games code was useful to penetrate an industrial control system featuring a specific model and array of Siemens centrifuges while demonstrating how to create a man-in-the-middle program to deceive their operations during the destruction of the centrifuge array. Owing to built-in design precautions, however (of the kind we are advocating here), reverse engineering and repurposing this particular weapon proved difficult, if not impossible. Other cyber weapons, absent such safeguards, might prove more vulnerable to malevolent reuse.

Defensive measures such as coded encryption algorithms are likewise reusable in certain contexts. The WannaCry software weapon constitutes a prime example. Aside from its use after having been stolen, it is unclear whether the same weapon, if it had first been used as apparently intended by the United States, would have been *recoverable*, and if so, whether it could subsequently have been repurposed and proven useful in the arsenals of adversaries, as it proved useful in the arsenals of criminals. The point is that once a nation develops an offensive cyber weapon, it is important that a blend of pessimism and humility motivates the designers to build defenses against any capture or reuse of their own innovation. If this proves to be impossible, the designers must seriously consider whether the weapon should be built at all. Similarly, once a nation finds a potent defensive cyber tool, it behooves it to envision possible offensive means to overcome it. In general, a nation cannot be sure its offensive and defensive weapons will not be stolen or otherwise turned against it by malicious users. Prudence, as well as law and moral considerations, suggests that nonnegligent designers anticipate and take precautions against such reuse. Likewise, when developing and fielding cyber defenses, we must think of our activities not only in terms of benevolent protections provided on our own and our allies' behalf but also on the harm these cyber defenses might cause if the adversary appropriates them through theft or inference (aided perhaps by observing the effects of multiple, probing attacks).

What does all this mean for the end user, the individual guy or gal who resides at what military personnel colloquially term the pointy end of the spear? Based on NATO's cyberspace operational doctrine, offensive operations are understandably not to be conducted without authorization at the highest decision-making level. Even so, it is customarily teams of cyberspace operators who will finally be tasked with actually carrying out these commands. They are therefore in a position not unlike that faced routinely by platoons of conventional combatants concerned with determining when it is ethically acceptable to attack or destroy an adversary. Other issues discussed earlier likewise fall finally to individual cyber operators (usually working in small teams), such as the responsibility for carefully developing, deploying, and storing (archiving) cyber weapons. The end user at the tactical level can also serve as a knowledgeable advisor to command, offering input on the risks, as well as benefits gained from using specific cyber tools. All these factors conspire to place a burden of responsibility on cyber end users (just as on conventional combatants) – a requisite Code of the Cyber Warrior[26] – requiring operators and end users to be knowledgeable about the ethical dilemmas attendant upon their own actions when carrying out the orders they might receive.

Responsibility in AI-Supported Cyber Operations

The final observation in the preceding discussion segues neatly into the topic of responsibility, and how responsibility and accountability are delegated or distributed in cyber operations.

Conventional military missions usually have a designated leader and commander who operates in turn with a well-defined chain of command. Cyber operations are no different in that respect, so that, as in conventional operations, ultimate responsibility for operational outcome and wider effects of specific cyber operations falls under international law to the mission commander. *Tallinn Manual* 2.0, Rule 85, specifically states the following:

(1) Commanders and other superiors are criminally responsible for ordering cyber operations that constitute war crimes;

(2) Commanders are also criminally responsible if they knew or, owing to the circumstances at the time, should have known their subordinates were committing, were about to commit, or had committed war crimes and failed to take all reasonable and available measures to prevent their commission or to punish those responsible.

To avoid criminal activities, NATO's doctrine specifically states that detailed discussion at higher decision levels, including legal experts, must take place in advance of executing an offensive cyberspace operation. Practically speaking, this means that the decisions to carry out the specified offensive operation will have been determined in the appropriate echelons of the chain of command well before the boots on the ground/fingers on the keyboard end user or cyber operations specialist proceeds to execute a specific offensive cyber operation. Nonetheless, accidents may yet occur, and ignorance of relevant software design or operational procedures can still bring about the unfortunate result that the end users actually conducting the cyber operations may be discovered to have acted wrongly. In these cases, it is for digital forensic investigation to bring forth the evidence and for the judicial system to use that evidence to prove guilt.[27]

What happens, however, if or when an AI-enhanced system *itself* haphazardly runs amok? Absent a thoughtful advance notion of collective or systemic responsibility (and liability), such accountability is likely to be assigned arbitrarily or by rote (as described earlier) to the highest ranking member of the military unit directly implicated in the damage caused by the AI-enhanced system. It might not make sense, or even seem altogether just, however, simply to assign blame to the ranking officer or commander when AI-enhanced cyber activities go awry. Yet, perhaps, the threat of assigning responsibility serves as a useful precaution, encouraging senior commanders to be certain they fully understand the operations and implications of specific cyber operations, or cause them, at least, to demand to crack open any black boxes or otherwise demand that the AI-enhanced systems they are ultimately responsible for using are themselves fully explainable as described earlier, knowing in advance that they themselves might ultimately be on the hook in the worst case.

An additional wrinkle regarding responsibility is compartmentalization. A familiar bureaucratic principle in defense and security operations requires, for example, that one have not only the *appropriate clearance* to be read in on any given highly classified topic but also the *demonstrable need to know*. This dual requirement leads naturally to the compartmentalization that stovepipes whole communities to keep the information they need more secure than it would otherwise be. Compartmentalization increases the risk of accidents whenever linkages between parts of an interlocking system are poorly understood by its individual operators, who focus solely on their specific tasks, thereby ignoring the ramifications for the overall system.[28]

A leader at any level of the command hierarchy will probably be too busy (and perhaps also lack the specific expertise) to evaluate the ethical aspects of any complex weapons system, cyber or not, such that assigning responsibility for technical failures to that leader would prove to be somewhat arbitrary in any case.

But if one factors in the black-box aspect of AI itself, together with the compartmentalization that is commonplace throughout the entire cyber operations realm, individual leadership responsibility for tech-based failures of discrimination or proportionality will seem increasingly implausible. The inevitable conclusion is that responsibility will often be systemic in nature rather than traceable to specific individuals (see Leveson 2011; n. 28). Responsibility for deploying and using AI that subsequently runs amok is not crystal clear and will most likely vary dramatically from case to case.

What does this factor mean for the end user? This problem likely transcends questions of professional military ethics related to command responsibility in cyber operations. It may also invoke the purely personal moral values and commitments of the operator herself. How willing is any given operator to utilize a tool whose functionality he or she is not entirely sure of? How much effort will that individual operator expend to learn and understand the specific cyber weapon or tool she is using? How much autonomy is the individual operator willing to delegate, in turn, to an AI-enhanced cyber weapon or system itself, especially knowing that it is the human operator (rather than the weapon) who will nonetheless be held responsible in the end for its proper functionality? Yet again, how willing is the individual operator likely to be to confess his or her own mistakes and culpable ignorance, or even to report incriminating activity by others, in cases where that operator has either authorized or used AI-supported tools even before official permission has been given or in contexts where the AI-supported tools perhaps were not intended to be used? Can we say with certainty whether the communities of concerned cyber operations specialists have worked through such issues sufficiently?

Privacy in AI-Supported Cyber Operations

When conducting defensive and offensive cyber operations, the full privacy of the user cannot be guaranteed. Both defensive and offensive cyber operations employ AI-enhanced tools for network and systems monitoring and analysis, but the sensitivity and level of detail vary. AI-supported tools obviously make the monitoring and analysis of information faster. The problem with guaranteeing individual identity or privacy during such operations is that everything will be stored, thereby offering the possibility of subsequent use of stored data for illegal purposes. As discussed under the category of transparency earlier, private information that a nation has stored on its own equipment can be used against it by any adversary if that information is exfiltrated or stolen. Also, such data can be misused by one's own operators when, for example, routine monitoring of the networks that one individual may be assigned to protect also affords a possibility for that individual to spy on her own colleagues. It is therefore both an operational and engineering-related question to determine what kind of information is relevant to monitor, store, and analyze in each operation.

Another hypothetical ethical dilemma arises when ongoing criminal activity is inadvertently discovered through routine monitoring and oversight but when reporting or acting on this discovery might also compromise an important primary mission. For example, when spying on adversaries' networks, a cyber operator might notice ongoing criminal activities engaged in by colleagues (e.g., trafficking in child pornography). What should the appropriate individual choice or organizational ethical decision be: to protect a child but blow the cover, or decide instead to ignore the discovery and continue the operation?

This, in turn, raises the additional specter of what has come to be called lawfare: using provisions of applicable law as weapons against an adversary.[29] *The New York Times* reported at the time that SolarWinds attackers, to avoid NSA scrutiny, had used U.S.-based servers to stage their operations. This effectively stymied NSA's investigation of the security breach owing to the prohibition of such domestic surveillance under statute 215 of the Patriot Act.[30] Come to think of it, why *wouldn't* a hostile actor twist any tool at hand, including the Fourth Amendment guaranteeing freedom of expression, into a useful weapon in the cyber arena?

Even further, intelligence expert Jim Baker worries about the vast amounts of information concerning the behavior of U.S. citizens that can be gleaned from newly emerging 5G networks, an ever-enlarging Internet of Things (IoT), and other similar sources.[31] Hostile powers could utilize the power and reach of AI to mine such data to gain the ability to understand, then predict, and finally manipulate behaviors in the United States to suit their ends. Presumably, a primitive version of this tactic was used in the Russian disinformation and voter manipulation efforts during the 2016 U.S. elections. Baker concludes, however, by pointing out that U.S. counterintelligence will be an obvious target: ominously, undermining the efforts of the security guardians by understanding them, predicting their next moves, and finally manipulating them through information operations.

Even though such information operations themselves are not strictly a focus of this chapter, the worries outlined by Baker are relevant for even the rank-and-file cyber operators to understand. Variation in internal laws and compliance of international rules between nations differentiates between the possibilities of methods used in defensive and offensive cyber operations. The European Union's GDPR (mentioned earlier) is an example, where there are major differences in compliance required between nations. How can a cyber incident or a conflict (or even war) be considered fully fair when opposing sides are constrained by law in different ways? Those final examples redound in turn upon the characters of individual operators. Just as we encounter in conventional armed conflict, how willing is one of these end users to adhere to legal restrictions applying to her or to the methods she uses, if the adversary is not likewise bound by them?

Beneficence in AI-Supported Cyber Operations

Even if it seems at times counterintuitive, moral considerations require that AI use should, on balance, promise at least to prove beneficial: it should be used for securing the common good, social good, and peace. In this instance, of course, the ethical dilemma is to define *whose* well-being warrants consideration. In cyberspace operations, as in conventional conflict, there is always "us" and "them": the Blue team versus the Red team, or the nation and its allies versus adversaries and competitors. An individual cyber operations specialist is quite likely to find herself belonging to several different legitimate groups of stakeholders involved in the resulting calculus of beneficence. She will be part of an organization, such as a cybersecurity unit, to be sure. But there might be internal conflict inside the organization itself dividing it into separate, competing teams, each of which also includes other individuals with disparate goals, each one worrying "What does this mean for me?" Also, an organization's goals might sometimes fail to align with its supervening nation's goals. Whose overall welfare then has the highest priority? And even more to the point: which standpoint enjoys the higher priority, the individual operator's own nation's welfare or interest, or the standpoint of international humanitarian law and the human rights of others, possibly including the enemy or adversary?

The use of AI decreases the manual workload in cyberspace operations, for instance, by analyzing net traffic and disclosing anomalies or scanning for system weaknesses, all of which benefit the individual operator. AI can also provide a vastly enhanced background for decision-making based on predictions (e.g., mapping prospects for possible collateral damage resulting from a planned strike), thereby allowing cyber operators to discern which offensive cyber operations would lessen the harm done to the enemy but still prove of maximum benefit to the attacker. In this fashion, for example, use of AI enhancements allows the requisite concern for beneficence to be looked at in comparison with reduction of maleficence to adversaries, thereby significantly improving compliance with the requirement of proportionality of means and ends during conflict.

Freedom and Autonomy in AI-Supported Cyber Operations

China's current efforts aimed at finding ethnic minorities and categorizing them as potential threats are an example of a large-scale use of AI-supported tools in a cyber domain in which individual freedom is severely threatened.[32] Methods and tools used in the cyber operations discussed in this chapter could, in theory, likewise be used in finding and categorizing people according to some other kind of threat assessment. The regulations and laws established through the GDPR set well-defined limits to the use of data collection for such purposes. First, the persons whose data would be collected must give their prior, informed consent. Second, access rights to the data are also limited – meaning, for example, that military units do not automatically have authorized access to the personal finance data or phone traffic data of civilians. Likewise, police units do not have access to individual health records without either prior permission or legal warrants.

Surveillance can also be carried out within an organization's own network, however, as well as blocking access to information flow. In some organizations, for example, social media sites are blocked during working hours via organizational tools whose use is perfectly legal. Similarly, as discussed with respect to terms of individual privacy, employee preferences can be cataloged and may even be used against them inside an organization. Hence, the risk of discrimination and of overriding individual freedom and autonomy exists internally.

From the standpoint of the individual cyber operator, as a result, two familiar ethical questions can arise. One is the same as in privacy discussions generally: namely, whether to use the confidential information of one's colleagues for one's own purposes. The second question is, what does working under the prospect of such constant surveillance do to the individuals surveilled?

Trust in AI-Supported Cyber Operations

Trust is closely related to the initial principle of transparency, inasmuch as both infuse individual, organizational, and state levels. Trust develops over time, a maxim that applies to both human relationships and relationships between humans and their technologies. We use smartphones for a variety of purposes, for example, and trust of the general public in the safety of this technology has largely been established. We may be aware of some downsides (for example, that the smartphone is constantly collecting data on us), but its utility in enabling our manifold daily routines and especially its instant connectability simply outweighs these well-known downsides.

Transparency regarding how AI functions is likewise one of the key points for maintaining public trust. However, there are other trust-related issues in using AI tools that pose ethical questions for end users to consider. One such question, related once again to transparency, is the degree to which end users credit the results yielded or produced through the use of specific AI applications. One might think that the higher the level of engineering education the user has, the more the consequent trust in the results of AI-assisted operations can be grounded confidently in expert knowledge rather than in mere faith. Perhaps, a person possessing a high degree of knowledge is better suited than others, for example, to challenge the results and decisions offered by AI.

Being a trustworthy person is also often cited as a chief virtue of a good person. What does trustworthiness mean in cyber operations? Is it a loyalty to your unit, to your people, to a state, or to humankind? Here there are once again several layers of significance to ponder, but at least two are important to identify: namely, being a whistleblower and being an insider threat. Where does one draw the line between staying loyal and remaining silent instead of becoming a whistleblower by bringing attention to ongoing misuse of a cyber tool? Or when does one decide to become an insider threat to one's organization or government, either to exact personal revenge or from having been influenced by others? In the example of the NSA, cyber operations technician Edward Snowden apparently (on his own account, at least) decided to become a whistleblower, while an as-yet-unnamed employee stole and freely distributed WannaCry on the dark web, presumably as some kind of punishment or revenge.

Sustainability, Dignity, and Solidarity in AI-Supported Cyber Operations

Obviously, cyber operations consume energy. It is difficult to determine the degree to which energy consumption increases or decreases with AI-supported cyber enhancements than without. Nonetheless, sustainability from the energy perspective is something that developers of AI-enhanced cyber tools, in principle at least, should be expected to factor into the design of their systems. Offensive cyberspace operations generally, of course, may have environmental effects. For example, disturbing the functionality of a dam can cause a flood. However, the use of cyberattacks for delivering disturbing effects need not destroy the targeted system itself. Rather, the goal can be to disable the targeted system for a particular time. In this sense, cyberattacks can prove less harmful to society than kinetic operations (bombing raids, for example) and in this sense are arguably more sustainable.

Respect for human dignity generally means respecting basic human rights and recognizing that each person has inherent value. In general, AI-supported tools should be used in such a way that dignity is preserved. Similarly, use of AI should promote social security and cohesion and not undermine solidarity. Cyberspace operations that we have focused on in this chapter do not target specific individuals directly. Neither are they used to create, manipulate, and spread false information. Those are instead means that pertain to information operations. However, the effect on dignity of the cyberspace operations we consider in this chapter can be indirect. AI-supported tools can be used, for example, to extract sensitive information from a database owned by an organization (e.g., a commercial company) that is to be harmed. If the data is subsequently leaked, thereby damaging the reputation of the company, its customers, whose personal data has now been publicly released, are the surrogate victims to be classified "collateral damage," as it were?

Similarly, social cohesion and solidarity might be indirectly affected by cyber operations. For example, offensive cyber operations can be used to degrade, disrupt, and destroy supply chains of the adversary. Even if the direct effect is on those supply chain systems, the indirect effect can fall upon civilian groups needing humanitarian help. Here again, the rules of engagement should also be discussed with and among the tactical-level end users of the AI, both from the military ethics/LOAC point of view and also (just as importantly) from a personal point of view. With which commands is the end user ultimately willing to comply? What can AI be trusted to decide alone, and where should a human be part of the decision-making process?

Conclusion

With the considerable assistance and input from my PRIO colleagues, I have attempted in this chapter to enumerate and describe many of the benefits, as well as some of the moral and legal challenges that end users in AI-enhanced cyber operations, both offensive and defensive, are likely to face. Many of these challenges have to do with individual and collective accountability for any negative or unintended consequences of AI-augmented cyber operations, coupled with the thorny problem of transparency and proper attribution of responsibility for those consequences. These dilemmas are particularly intractable when gauged asymmetrically: that is, between operators and their agencies who are tasked with conducting legally permissible and ethically responsible operations in cyber conflict, on the one hand, and those, on the other hand, who decline to become encumbered by any such scruples or intentions. It helps to restore the resulting apparent imbalance between parties to cyber conflicts if the ethical challenges can be identified in advance and legally compliant and morally responsible considerations baked into the strategies formulated in response. One thereby avoids the need to introduce legal and moral considerations on the fly as additional constraints to be imposed upon decision-making and time-sensitive action in the midst of conflict.

This chapter intends to initiate, if nothing else, a serious discussion about the important task of anticipating and developing strategic responses to cyberattacks and intrusions, responses that are reasonably guaranteed, in themselves, to uphold the values of our respective nations and allies, even while we are engaged in the complex and time-sensitive tasks of providing security for our citizens' lives and property in the cyber domain.

Notes

1 Joint Artificial Intelligence Center (JAIC) (2018), www.ai.mil/about.html.
2 M. Ryan and B.C. Stahl, "Artificial Intelligence Ethics Guidelines for Developers and Users: Clarifying their Content and Normative implications," *Journal of Information, Communication and Ethics in Society* (2020), https://doi.org/10.1108/JICES-12-2019-0138/full/html.
3 A. Jobin, M. Ienca, and E. Vayena, "The Global Landscape of AI Ethics Guidelines," *Nature Machine Intelligence* 1 (9) (2019): 389, https://doi.org/10.1038/s42256-019-0088-2.
4 "Script kiddie" is a derogatory term that computer hackers have coined to refer to amateur, but often quite dangerous, exploiters of internet security weaknesses.
5 ENISA ad hoc Working Group on Artificial Intelligence, AI CYBERSECURITY CHALLENGES-Threat Landscape for Artificial Intelligence (2020), www.enisa.europa.eu/publications/artificial-intelligence-cybersecurity-challenges.
6 M. Comiter, "Attacking Artificial Intelligence-AI's Security Vulnerability and What Policymakers Can Do About It," *Belfer Center for Science and International Affairs* (2019), www.belfercenter.org/publication/AttackingAI [accessed 12 May 2022]; K. Hartmann and C. Steup, "12th International Conference on Cyber Conflict (CyCon)," *Estonia* (2020): 327–349. https://doi.org/10.23919/CyCon49761.2020.9131724.
7 U.S. Joint Artificial Intelligence Center (JAIC), "Integrating AI and Cyber into the DoD" (2019), www.ai.mil/blog.html [accessed 12 May 2022].
8 Michael N. Schmitt, ed., *Tallinn Manual 1.0-On the International Law Applicable to Cyber Warfare* (Cambridge: Cambridge University Press, 2013); M.N. Schmitt and L. Vihul, eds., *Tallinn Manual 2.0 – On the International Law Applicable to Cyber Operations,* 2nd ed. (Cambridge: Cambridge University Press, 2017).
9 *San Remo Manual on International Law Applicable to Armed Conflicts at Sea* (12 June 1994), https://ihl-databases.icrc.org/ihl/INTRO/560 [accessed 14 May 2022].
10 T.C. Truong, Q.B. Diep, and I. Zelinka, "Artificial Intelligence in the Cyber Domain: Offense and Defense," *Symmetry* 12 (3) (2020): 410, https://doi.org/10.3390/sym12030410.

11 N. Kaloudi and J. Li, "The AI-Based Cyber Threat Landscape: A Survey," *ACM Computing Surveys* 53 (1) (2020), https://doi.org/10.1145/3372823.
12 J. Pattison, "From Defence to Offence: The Ethics of Private Cybersecurity," *European Journal of International Security* 5 (29) (2020): 233, https://doi.org/10.1017/eis.2020.6. For a definition and examination of "hacking back" as an active cyber defense measure, see Patrick Lin, "The Ethics of Hacking Back," a policy report prepared for the National Science Foundation by the Ethics and Emerging Sciences Group at California Polytechnic State University (San Luis Obispo, CA, 26 September 2016), www.academia.edu/33317069/Ethics_of_Hacking_Back [accessed 14 April 2022).
13 N. Harley, "North Korea behind WannaCry Attack Which Crippled the NHS after Stealing U.S. Cyber Weapons, Microsoft Chief Claims," *The Telegraph* (2017). See also B. Buchanan, *The Hacker and the State* (Cambridge, MA: Harvard University Press, 2020), https://doi.org/10.4159/9780674246010–004.
14 B. Wolford, "What Is GDPR, the EU's New Data Protection Law?" GDPR.EU (2019), https://gdpr.eu/what-is-gdpr/ [accessed 26 May 2021].
15 Tony Kontzer, "What Does the Near Future of Cyber Security Look Like?" RSA Conference Blog (2019), www.rsaconference.com/library/Blog/what-does-the-near-future-of-cyber-security-look-like-a-roomful-of-rsac-attendees [accessed 14 May 2022].
16 D. Kawamoto, "Will GDPR Rules Impact States and Localities?" *Government Technology* (2018), www.govtech.com/data/Will-GDPR-Rules-Impact-States-and-Localities.html [accessed 14 May 2022].
17 Council on Foreign Relations, "Control+Shift+Delete: The GDPR's Influence on National Security Posture," *Net Politics* (8 October 2019), www.cfr.org/search?keyword=gdpr-influence-nationalsecurity-posture [accessed 14 May 2022].
18 B.W. Jackson, "Cybersecurity, Privacy, and Artificial Intelligence: An Examination of Legal Issues Surrounding the European Union General Data Protection Regulation and Autonomous Network Defense," *Minnesota Journal of Law, Science & Technology* 21 (1) (2020): 169.
19 D.E. Pozen, "Transparency's Ideological Drift," *Yale Law Journal* 128 (2018): 100.
20 C.R. Kehler, H. Lin, and M. Sulmeyer, "Rules of Engagement for Cyberspace Operations: A View from the USA," *Journal of Cybersecurity* 3 (1) (2017), https://doi.org/10.1093/cybsec/tyx003.
21 See the Defense Innovation Marketplace guide to TEVV cybersecurity: https://defenseinnovationmarketplace.dtic.mil/wp-content/uploads/2018/02/OSD_ATEVV_STRAT_DIST_A_SIGNED.pdf See also MITRE, "Verification and Validation, Systems Engineering Guide" (2013), www.mitre.org/publications/systems-engineering-guide/enterprise-engineering/systems-engineering-for-mission-assurance [accessed 14 May 2022].
22 See DataRobot White Paper, "Trusted AI 101: A Guide to Building Trustworthy and Ethical AI Systems," www.datarobot.com/resources/trusted-ai-guide/?utm_medium=search&utm_source=google&utm_campaign=Content2021TRUSTAI101USNBrT0415GPS&utm_term=explanaible%20ai&utm_content=explanaibleai_variation_rsa&campaignid=12760455499&adgroupid=129394814636&adid=558672517802&gclid=CjwKCAjwve2TBhByEiwAaktM1IErqBqqQCr0d1MkK_XqWiKWjNIMOSlrpBkhQzWPK-5a03iEOK4srxoCpRwQAvD_BwE [accessed 12 May 2022] "Responsible AI," a related concept, refers to a normative commitment on the part of AI researchers and designers (military and civilian) only to use AI with good intentions to empower their organizations and impact the general public in a trustworthy manner. See: www.accenture.com/us-en/services/applied-intelligence/ai-ethics-governance#:~:text=Responsible%20AI%20is%20the%20practice,and%20scale%20AI%20with%20confidence.
23 P.J. Phillips, C.A. Hahn, P.C. Fontana, D.A. Broniatowski, and M.A. Przybock, "Four Principles of Explainable Artificial Intelligence," *NISTIR* 8312 (2020), https://doi.org/10.6028/NIST.IR.8312-draft.

24 Global partnership of artificial intelligence (GPAI), "Working Group on Responsible AI" (2020), https://gpai.ai/projects/responsible-ai/ [accessed 14 May 2022].
25 W. Knight, "The Dark Secret at the Heart of AI," *MIT Technology Review* (2017), www.technologyreview.com/2017/04/11/5113/the-dark-secret-at-the-heart-of-ai/ [accessed 14 May 2022].
26 See Matthew Beard, "Beyond Tallinn: The Code of the Cyber Warrior?" in *Binary Bullets: The Ethics of Cyberwarfare,* eds. Fritz Allhoff, Adam Henschke, and Bradley Jay Strawer (New York: Oxford University Press, 2016): 139–156.
27 Rebecca Crootof, "War Torts: Accountability for Autonomous Weapons," *University of Pennsylvania Law Review* 164 (6) (May 2016): 1347.
28 See N.G. Leveson, *Engineering a Safer World* (Cambridge, MA: MIT Press, 2011): 103–167, for an illustrative example of this kind of distributed responsibility that led to a friendly fire incident in Northern Iraq in 1994.
29 The term "lawfare" was first coined by U.S. Air Force adjutant general, Major General Charles J. Dunlap, Jr (now at Duke Law School) in 2001 to describe the misuse of IHL as a form of asymmetrical warfare. It has since developed various uses and definitions. See "Lawfare 101: A Primer," *Military Review* 97 (May–June 2017): 8–17. See also Orde F. Kittrie, *Lawfare* (New York: Oxford University Press, 2016).
30 David E. Sanger, N. Perlroth, and J.E. Barnes. "As Understanding of Russian Hacking Grows, So Does Alarm," *New York Times* (2021), www.nytimes.com/2021/01/02/us/politics/russian-hacking-government.html [accessed 14 May 2022].
31 J. Baker, "Counterintelligence Implications of Artificial Intelligence – Part III," Lawfare (10 October 2018), www.lawfareblog.com/counterintelligence-implications-artificial-intelligence-part-iii [accessed 14 May 2022].
32 See Human Rights Watch (HRW), "China: Big Data Fuels Crackdown in Minority Region" (2018), www.hrw.org/news/2018/02/26/china-big-data-fuels-crackdown-minority-region [accessed 14 May 2022].

References

Accenture. "Responsible AI: Scale AI With Confidence," www.accenture.com/us-en/services/applied-intelligence/ai-ethics-governance#:~:text=Responsible%20AI%20is%20the%20practice,and%20scale%20AI%20with%20confidence.

Baker, J. "Counterintelligence Implications of Artificial Intelligence – Part III," *Lawfare* (10 October 2018), www.lawfareblog.com/counterintelligence-implications-artificial-intelligence-part-iii [accessed 14 May 2022].

Beard, Matthew. "Beyond Tallinn: The Code of the Cyber Warrior?" in *Binary Bullets: The Ethics of Cyberwarfare*, ed. Fritz Allhoff, Adam Henschke, and Bradley Jay Strawer (New York: Oxford University Press, 2016): 139–156.

Buchanan, B. *The Hacker and the State* (Cambridge, MA: Harvard University Press, 2020), https://doi.org.10.4159/9780674246010–004.

Comiter, M. "Attacking Artificial Intelligence: AI's Security Vulnerability and What Policymakers Can Do About It," *Belfer Center for Science and International Affairs* (2019), www.belfercenter.org/publication/AttackingAI [accessed 12 May 2022].

Council on Foreign Relations. "Control+Shift+Delete: The GDPR's Influence on National Security Posture," *Net Politics* (8 October 2019), www.cfr.org/search?keyword=gdpr-influence-nationalsecurity-posture [accessed 14 May 2022].

Crootof, Rebecca. "War Torts: Accountability for Autonomous Weapons," *University of Pennsylvania Law Review* 164 (6) (May 2016).

DataRobot. White Paper. "Trusted AI 101: A Guide to Building Trustworthy and Ethical AI Systems," www.datarobot.com/resources/trusted-ai-guide/?utm_medium=search&utm_source=google&utm_campaign=Content2021TRUSTAI101USNBrT0415GPS&utm_

term=explanaible%20ai&utm_content=explanaibleai_variation_rsa&campaignid=12760455499&adgroupid=129394814636&adid=558672517802&gclid=CjwKCAjwve2TBhByEiwAaktM1IErqBqqQCr0d1MkK_XqWiKWjNIMOSlrpBkhQzWPK-5a03iEOK4srxoCpRwQAvD_BwE [accessed 12 May 2022].

Department of Defense. "Defense Innovation Marketplace Guide to TEVV Cybersecurity," https://defenseinnovationmarketplace.dtic.mil/wp-content/uploads/2018/02/OSD_ATEVV_STRAT_DIST_A_SIGNED.pdf.

Dunlap, Charles J., Jr. "Lawfare 101: A Primer," *Military Review* 97 (May–June 2017): 8–17.

ENISA ad hoc Working Group on Artificial Intelligence. "AI Cybersecurity Challenges: Threat Landscape for Artificial Intelligence" (2020), www.enisa.europa.eu/publications/artificial-intelligence-cybersecurity-challenges

GDPR. General Data Protection Act (European Union), Article 23, "Restrictions" (2018), https://gdpr-info.eu/art-23-gdpr/ [accessed 23 August 2022].

Global Partnership of Artificial Intelligence (GPAI), "Working Group on Responsible AI" (2020), https://gpai.ai/projects/responsible-ai/ [accessed 14 May 2022].

Harley, N. "North Korea behind WannaCry Attack Which Crippled the NHS After Stealing U.S. Cyber Weapons, Microsoft Chief Claims," *The Telegraph* (14 October 2017).

Hartmann, K.; Steup, C. "Hacking the AI: The Next Generation of Hijacked Systems," *12th International Conference on Cyber Conflict* (CyCon), Estonia (2020): 327–349, https://doi.org/10.23919/CyCon49761.2020.9131724.

Human Rights Watch. "China: Big Data Fuels Crackdown in Minority Region" (2018), www.hrw.org/news/2018/02/26/china-big-data-fuels-crackdown-minority-region [accessed 14 May 2022].

International Committee of the Red Cross. *San Remo Manual on International Law Applicable to Armed Conflicts at Sea* (12 June 1994), https://ihl-databases.icrc.org/ihl/INTRO/560 [accessed 14 May 2022].

Jackson, B.W. "Cybersecurity, Privacy, and Artificial Intelligence: An Examination of Legal Issues Surrounding the European Union General Data Protection Regulation and Autonomous Network Defense," *Minnesota Journal of Law, Science & Technology* 21 (1) (2020): 169.

Jobin, A.; Ienca, M.; Vayena, E. "The Global Landscape of AI Ethics Guidelines," *Nature Machine Intelligence* 1 (9) (2019): 389, https://doi.org/10.1038/s42256-019-0088-2

Joint Artificial Intelligence Center (JAIC) (2018), www.ai.mil/about.html.

Joint Artificial Intelligence Center (JAIC). "Integrating AI and Cyber into the DoD" (2019), www.ai.mil/blog.html [accessed 12 May 2022].

Kaloudi, N.; Li, J. "The AI-Based Cyber Threat Landscape: A Survey," *ACM Computing Surveys* 53 (1) (2020), https://doi.org/10.1145/3372823.

Kawamoto, D. "Will GDPR Rules Impact States and Localities?" *Government Technology* (2018), www.govtech.com/data/Will-GDPR-Rules-Impact-States-and-Localities.html [accessed 14 May 2022].

Kehler, C.R.; Lin, H.; Sulmeyer, M. "Rules of Engagement for Cyberspace Operations: A View From the USA," *Journal of Cybersecurity* 3 (1) (2017), https://doi.org/10.1093/cybsec/tyx003.

Kittrie, Orde F. *Lawfare* (New York: Oxford University Press, 2016).

Knight, W. "The Dark Secret at the Heart of AI," *MIT Technology Review* (2017), www.technologyreview.com/2017/04/11/5113/the-dark-secret-at-the-heart-of-ai/ [accessed 14 May 2022].

Kontzer, Tony. "What Does the Near Future of Cyber Security Look Like?" RSA Conference Blog (2019), www.rsaconference.com/library/Blog/what-does-the-near-future-of-cyber-security-look-like-a-roomful-of-rsac-attendees [accessed 14 May 2022].

Leveson, N.G. *Engineering a Safer World* (Cambridge, MA: MIT Press, 2011): 103–167.

Lin, Patrick. "The Ethics of Hacking Back," a policy report prepared for the National Science Foundation by the Ethics and Emerging Sciences Group at California Polytechnic State University (San Luis Obispo, CA, 26 September 2016), www.academia.edu/33317069/Ethics_of_Hacking_Back [accessed 14 April 2022].

MITRE. "Verification and Validation, Systems Engineering Guide" (2013), www.mitre.org/publications/systems-engineering-guide/enterprise-engineering/systems-engineering-for-mission-assurance [accessed 14 May 2022].

NATO. "Allied Joint Doctrine for the Conduct of Operations," AJP-3.19 (February 2019), https://www.gov.uk/government/publications/allied-joint-doctrine-for-the-conduct-of-operations-ajp-3b [accessed 23 August 2022].

NATO. "Allied Joint Doctrine for Cyberspace Operations," AJP-3.20 (2020), www.gov.uk/government/publications/allied-joint-doctrine-for-cyberspace-operations-ajp-320 [accessed 13 May 2022].

Pattison, J. "From Defence to Offence: The Ethics of Private Cybersecurity," *European Journal of International Security* 5 (29) (2020): 233, https://doi.org/10.1017/eis.2020.6.

Phillips, P.J.; Hahn, C.A.; Fontana, P.C.; Broniatowski, D.A.; Przybock, M.A. "Four Principles of Explainable Artificial Intelligence," *NISTIR* 8312 (2020), https://doi.org/10.6028/NIST.IR.8312-draft.

Pozen, D.E. "Transparency's Ideological Drift," *Yale Law Journal* 128 (2018): 100.

Ryan, M.; Stahl, B.C. "Artificial Intelligence Ethics Guidelines for Developers and Users: Clarifying Their Content and Normative Implications," *Journal of Information, Communication and Ethics in Society* 19 (1) (2020): 61–86, https://doi.org/10.1108/JICES-12-2019-0138/full/html.

Sanger, David E.; Perlroth, N.; Barnes, J.E. "As Understanding of Russian Hacking Grows, So Does Alarm," *New York Times* (2021), www.nytimes.com/2021/01/02/us/politics/russian-hacking-government.html [accessed 14 May 2022].

Schmitt, M.N., ed. *Tallinn Manual 1.0: On the International Law Applicable to Cyber Warfare* (Cambridge: Cambridge University Press, 2013).

Schmitt, M.N.; Vihul, L., eds. *Tallinn Manual 2.0: On the International Law Applicable to Cyber Operations*. 2nd ed. (Cambridge: Cambridge University Press, 2017).

Truong, T.C.; Diep, Q.B.; Zelinka, I. "Artificial Intelligence in the Cyber Domain: Offense and Defense," *Symmetry* 12 (3) (2020): 410, https://doi.org/10.3390/sym12030410.

Wolford, B. "What Is GDPR, the EU's New Data Protection Law?" GDPR.EU (2019), https://gdpr.eu/what-is-gdpr/ [accessed 26 May 2021].

7

THE DEVOLUTION OF NORMS IN CYBER WARFARE FROM STUXNET TO SOLARWINDS

How then should we begin to think about the kinds of background rules and regulatory principles that most if not all inhabitants of the cyber domain might wish to have?

The majority of defense and policy analysts at present cite cyber conflict (including cyber warfare) as an example – indeed, one of the principal examples – of grey zone conflict. This Pentagon/Defense Department designator strikes me as a broader and less well-defined category than the soft war/unarmed conflict classification (which I have utilized here).[1] The Russian Federation's initial occupation and subsequent annexation of the Crimean peninsula in Ukraine in 2014, for example, is also classified by Pentagon specialists as war in the grey zone. But those infamous little green men who fought alongside Russian separatists living in Ukraine were hardly unarmed, even if their green uniforms bore no identifying insignia. Nevertheless, with suitable caution, it seems clear that the different experts are talking about more or less the same kinds of low-intensity international conflict, and so despite the occasional ambiguity with this terminology on some other issues, there seems to be no question whatsoever that *cyber conflict resides at the center* of whatever that grey zone otherwise designates.

It may thus appear that there is a broad working consensus that at least some forms of cyber conflict, as soft war or unarmed conflict, are in certain respects *like* war,[2] but perhaps a different form of warfare, subject in principle to the same sorts of moral concerns and legal constraints as conventional and hybrid war. But that would not be entirely accurate. In fact, for well over a decade there has been a debate raging over whether or not there really is any such thing as genuine cyber *warfare*. Prof. Thomas Rid of the Johns Hopkins School for Advanced International Studies (SAIS) in Washington, DC, first published his famous works in 2012–2013 (while teaching at King's College, London) advancing the controversial claims that policy discussions concerning cyber "war" are nothing more than hyperinflated,

DOI: 10.4324/9781003273912-8

excessively metaphorical speech.[3] This claim is more than mere academic quibbling over terminology. Instead, this discussion bears directly on the problem we are considering in this book: namely, what kinds of laws (if any) and what kind of rules or principles or moral norms should apply to cyber conflict in particular (as well as, for that matter, to grey zone conflict more generally), especially when such conflict fails to rise to the equivalent of a conventional use of force?

Suppose we grant Prof. Rid his point that there is, strictly speaking, no such thing as cyber warfare and acknowledge (as we do here) that cyber conflict is a form of unarmed conflict that falls squarely within the grey zone. Certainly, we must then acknowledge that whatever else it is, has been, or will become, all cyber conflict that cannot be classified simply as random vandalism, vigilantism, or criminal behavior is *some form of state-sponsored espionage or covert action*. Usually, but not always, the distinction turns on the agents involved in carrying out malevolent cyber activities. If these are individuals or nonstate organizations, then their cyber activities, if harmful, constitute either vandalism or straightforward crime. If the vandalism is not simply perverse mischief but is aimed at some political purpose or influence, however ill-defined, then the agents are vigilantes. Incidents and agents of random vandalism are too numerous (and annoying) to mention. The shadowy and loosely organized group known as Anonymous engages in vigilantism – that is, vandalism and other kinds of illegal and destructive criminal activity aimed at making a political statement or advancing some political agenda (invariably including their presumed right to engage in such cyber operations freely with impunity and utter lack of accountability). By contrast, the so-called Silk Road was a straightforward criminal enterprise aimed at acquiring wealth for its developers through the marketing of illegal merchandise like drugs on the dark web rather than advancing any sort of political cause.

This leaves the considerable swath of state-sponsored cyber groups and their activities: the North Korean cyber warriors, the Internet Research Agency based in St. Petersburg (Russia), PLA Unit 61398 in Shanghai, the Cutting Sword of Justice in Iran – the list is extensive and, not to be forgotten, includes the agents who designed and deployed Stuxnet, Flame, Duqu, and other malware associated with Operation Olympic Games (thought most likely to be agents of the Israeli and/or American governments). The cyber operations themselves range from exfiltration of classified or proprietary commercial and defense data to destruction of property, severe degradation of military and security operational capacities, as well as ransomware attacks on a wide range of targets, to name but a few. Almost all such cyber operations are technically criminal activities involving trespass, theft, extortion, blackmail, and destruction of property (among many others).

These cyber operations, however, primarily constitute forms of espionage (intelligence, surveillance, and reconnaissance) and covert action, and since 2015, they have come to be labeled state-sponsored hacktivism (e.g., Lucas 2015, 2017) to distinguish them from more conventional criminal activities. Many individual incidents are offensive in nature, but quite a number are defensive, preemptive, retaliatory, or punitive – distinctions that matter from a legal or moral standpoint only if separated from their inherently criminal features and attributed to nation-states engaged in hostile, low-intensity conflict (and thus operating under a somewhat different legal regime).

In sum, there is no way of denying that at the very least, when we are not merely talking about crime and vandalism and conventional but malevolent cyber actions of those sorts, then we are certainly talking about the remaining kinds of cyber operations as being forms of espionage (or, as I prefer to call them, espionage on steroids). This connects the consideration of cyber conflict very closely, as a result, to whatever conclusions we may ultimately draw from the reflections elsewhere by others, such as Cécile Fabre,[4] primarily engaged in trying to think through what rules might apply, or what principles might be brought to bear, or what moral or legal norms might be emerging in the practice of espionage and intelligence gathering and covert action. That is to say, if there are any governing principles that define best practices (or the limits of acceptable practice) to which nations ought to be held *when engaging in espionage generally*, then we may expect that at least some of these same rules, principles, or norms will probably apply, by extension, to cyber operations as well.

The nascent and at present rather limited terrain of intelligence ethics might, however, not seem to be a very promising area to begin exploring in search of new insights for our cyber problem. But in entertaining that presumption, we may find ourselves gravely mistaken. Former CIA Deputy Director Michael Morell, however, speaking at the 2021 annual McCain Conference in Annapolis, highlighted the increasing emphasis within that agency on *ethics training* focused on enhanced recognition, understanding of, and compliance with that agency's guidelines on permissible practices regarding espionage and HUMINT (intelligence collection from human operatives) as well as covert operations.[5] As other contributors to that symposium went on to attest, even espionage practices can be guided by reflections on better and worse practices regarding the recruiting and use of intelligence assets, deception, limits on the use of false identities, election interference and regime change, and many routine practices in what otherwise seems a very morally murky realm of activity (see also Perry 2009).

Many readers, of course, will remain highly skeptical that any rules or constraints could be applied to such activities that take place at the farthest boundaries, if not entirely outside of, the normal rule of law – let alone would they ever come to believe that moral principles (such as trust, honesty, the right not to be harmed or killed wantonly, or have one's personal possessions and property confiscated or destroyed without justification) would find widespread allegiance in the espionage community. But, having read the profound challenges to such skepticism raised during the 2021 McCain Conference on this topic by thoughtful philosophers and even practitioners of these activities, I wonder if, by extension, some of the lessons learned in these deliberations concerning ethics and espionage might carry over into our consideration of the ethical dilemmas posed by cyber conflict as well.[6] So we have a good fertile field to till with these various related discussions, but at the same time, the question remains that faced us with all of those things as well: *can we really talk about ethics or the rule of law in the cyber domain?*

Suppose we begin by considering the incredible, exponential proliferation of incidents of cyber vandalism, criminal schemes, and vigilante operations that began on the then-newly created world wide web in the 1990s. Early in the new century, most of the nations that were active in the cyber domain agreed, at an international conference in Bucharest in 2001, on a set of *norms or rules* or principles, mostly extrapolations of existing international law that would guide the behavior of nations responding to criminal activities in the cyber domain. That agreement, the International Convention on Cyber Crime (also called the Bucharest Convention, or ICCC) specified how the constabulary forces of sovereign nations could cooperate with one another in fighting cybercrime. It also defined what nations are responsible for doing when an international cybercriminal operation like the Silk Road is discovered to be headquartered within their own borders.

According to this convention, when individual governments detect somebody like Ross Ulbright (who turned out to be managing the Silk Road transactions from a laptop while seated at a Starbucks in San Francisco) operating within their borders, their law enforcement agencies are enjoined to cooperate on apprehending the suspects and shutting down the criminal enterprise. In the infamous instance cited here, the FBI took the lead in Operation Onymous, assisted by information and support from other nations through police and intelligence agencies like Interpol and the European Union Agency for Law Enforcement Cooperation. Interestingly, this convention for the first time holds the governments of individual nations responsible and liable for criminal activities that originate within their own borders. Theoretically, the right of national sovereignty may be overridden if a host nation for an international cybercriminal enterprise is unable or unwilling to take action or cooperate with other nations to shut down the criminal activity.[7]

The Bucharest Convention thus marked a major advance to combat cybercrime early on in the history of cyber conflict. Unfortunately, that spirit of cooperation has not expanded or evolved much further since then to address the advanced persistent threat of conflict among and between nations and state actors in the cyber domain. In fact, at first glance we observe something like the opposite: a degradation or devolution of customary norms of behavior in the international arena with respect to cyber conflict. This is, after all, a domain in which the criminals initially, along with the vigilantes and the hackers, and now the nations who are actually transforming their international behavior to correspond, can seemingly (as I have often observed) do anything they please, to anyone they like, whenever they wish, with little fear of accountability or retribution.

Interestingly, instead of building exotic and highly disruptive cyber weapons of war as originally anticipated, we have witnessed nations (like China) who were originally expected to build and use exotic and destructive cyber weapons behaving more and more like individual vandals, vigilantes, and criminals instead! This is the surprising evolution (or, from a moral and legal perspective, devolution) entailed in the rise of state-sponsored hacktivism. There are many reasons for these developments, of course (Lucas 2017). But chief among them is the relative simplicity of developing and deploying such strategies (in lieu of expensive and time-consuming exotic cyber weapons like Stuxnet), coupled with the fact that the resulting disruptions, while often grave and serious, still fall below a hypothetical level of attribution and accountability that would likely trigger a kinetic response from the victim.

I have invoked the term *norms* several times in passing, a term quite familiar to scholars in the field of international law and international relations. Norm, however familiar it might seem, is nonetheless a very soft, vague, and illusive term with many meanings in different contexts. In a descriptive, behavioral sense, for example, norm can just mean something like normal or customary, such as simply how Smith and Jones usually behave, or what Smith and Jones (normally) do or tolerate being done to themselves or to one another.

A norm, however, can also be *an action-guiding principle*, intended to limit or constrain malevolent behavior, such as the Principle of Reciprocity (i.e., refrain from inflicting upon others any actions one would not wish to have inflicted upon oneself) or *lex taliones*, attempting to limit retaliation by a victim for any harm suffered to the proportionate inflicting of a like harm upon the perpetrator. Here, the norm functions more like a rule to be followed or a command to be obeyed (or to be disobeyed only at one's peril). Invocation of norms may frequently oscillate between these descriptive and regulatory (normative) functions. This is especially true with regard to international law, which is sometimes described as what (presumably civilized and law-abiding) nations and peoples customarily do or tolerate being done (*jus gentium*) while at other times it is characterized, in a far more regulatory or normative sense, as setting forth obligatory (or, at least, aspirational) standards of nation-state behavior within the community of nations (e.g., the U.N. "Universal Declaration on Human Rights," 1948).

This is, to say the least, a fascinating and complex topic interwoven in law, jurisprudence (legal philosophy), and moral philosophy (ethics) as well as in political theory, sociology, and even group psychology. I cannot hope to do it justice here, save to observe an interesting characteristic of regulatory norms in particular: they are not necessarily fixed or invariant, but they seem to arise or emerge in the course of human history and experience (as does their consequent influence upon conventional practices).[8] This, of course, is the point of this brief digression: to set the stage for an inquiry concerning current and emerging norms of responsible behavior within the cyber domain.

Of course, just as there is skepticism from Prof. Rid about the very existence of cyber war, there is even stronger skepticism from most of the participants and adversaries engaged in cyber operations at present about the possibility of there being any really meaningful norms or action guiding principles of behavior. Now and then frustrated leaders and even cyber victims in the international arena call for some kind of enhanced governance: perhaps, a conference or an international treaty similar to the CCC. Yet, prospects for sufficient cooperation among the major players to limit their own independence of action seem remote at best. The incentives for powerful individual players to constrain their own behavior for the sake of greater security are not currently apparent.

Instead (in a sense that will require our further attention and analysis), in the cyber domain, we dwell virtually in a lawless frontier, a state of nature, in which the most unscrupulous and effective cyber warriors do as they wish, and (to paraphrase the Greek historian Thucydides or the character Thrasymachus in Plato's *Republic*) the weaker and more vulnerable desperately seek the best bargain they can get. It is also interesting from the standpoint of those who work in moral and political philosophy that this current condition as it persists in the cyber domain is *not* some kind of thought experiment. We are not talking about a mythical condition in the ancient past before the origins of civilization. For all our talk of the virtual world, this fundamental situation is all too real! Indeed, inadvertently we find ourselves immersed in a kind of laboratory constituting individuals and their clusters and organizations in the very first genuine global state of nature we have ever authentically encountered. That in itself is remarkable in that the actors and agents in that world find themselves very much in the situation that the philosopher Thomas Hobbes described four centuries ago in the *Leviathan*: "a war of all against all." Again, this is all something that warrants more careful attention and analysis.

Interestingly (at least to theoreticians), it seems that we might finally get to observe how that theoretical or hypothetical condition works out for all of us in actual practice. It remains to be seen whether our real lives (in the cyber domain, at least) will turn out to be "nasty, brutish, and short" (as Hobbes describes) or whether, somehow, in the nick of time, some sort of transition out of that state of nature into something more stable and secure will occur. From Hobbes's account, we have some clues as to what that transition might look like or what form it might take. Perhaps, a massive hegemon – the United States or Russia or China, or some other powerful nation – will manage to gain an upper hand, exerting so much dominance over the cyber domain that they are able to dictate unilateral terms of peace and security to all the other inhabitants of that world. China certainly operates with that kind of power and impunity in the cyber domain within its own geographic borders.

That would be one possibility – a leviathan emerging to dominate the cyber domain. Or perhaps there could be something more like what Hobbes himself envisioned as a slightly more preferrable transition from the mythical, original position or state of nature: a transition to a law-governed civil society within cyberspace, defined by a tacit contract among government and the governed. The mystery in Hobbes's account was always *how* that transition was actually going to take place. What are the prospects, the incentives, when dealing with an enormous range of individual and small collective actors, each motivated by self-interest and utter antipathy (or at least benign indifference – what Hobbes himself termed universal diffidence) to finally defer to all the others by forfeiting a measure of their own freedom for the sake of the common good?

Hobbes himself was always a little vague about that, insisting that it must happen, it had to happen (and indeed, apparently it *had* happened at some points in human prehistory), without a clear hint of what the cause or motivation would be beyond the obvious misery for everyone to remain in that state of nature forever.

Indeed, the only thing Hobbes describes as something akin to a moral obligation in the state of nature is to *get out of it* – to quit it, as he says – as quickly as we can. So overwhelming is that obligation, as Hobbes describes it, that it confers upon society the right to override the freedom of individuals resisting that transition, even to take their lives if necessary.

So again, we might ask, where does this speculation leave us in the real world of cyber conflict? We could conceivably discover a consensus among the various inhabitants or participants in the cyber domain that we would like to be in a better, more stable relationship with one another than we are now – very much as many (but not all) nations agreed regarding cybercrime in the Bucharest Convention. The case for making or forcing this transition might be especially compelling in the United States, which recently discovered that its vital assets were severely compromised by what certainly appears to be, and pretty clearly was, a massive Russian cyberattack. The SolarWinds attack has been described ruefully by some U.S. espionage experts as perhaps the greatest single exfiltration of information and damage done to vital security and defense systems ever achieved. Its continuing revelations certainly constitute espionage and covert action on steroids.

No doubt we would like something better. But what is that arrangement likely to be beyond some form of retaliation in kind (which the U.S. cyber community presumably began to undertake early in 2021)? Even as President Biden imposed some economic sanctions and other forms of punishment on Russia, their government continued to protest and deny they were responsible, as all malevolent cyber perpetrators do: "We didn't do it. Somebody else did." And it is hard to move beyond that tiny level of uncertainty to marshal effective global sanctions or impose any other meaningful form of punishment or retaliation. Otherwise, as we noted, there's very little prospect for writing any new black letter law or formal treaties, unless (as some of the most pessimistic skeptics fear) such a massive and cataclysmic, apocalyptic event takes place within the cyber domain that it compels us in its aftermath of necessity to do that. The cost of that would be terrible indeed. So, absent that draconian incentive, what else is there to hope for instead?

Perhaps, instead, we should proceed more modestly, experientially, or *inductively*. One of the things I have been tracing over the course of the past several years is a kind of plot of the details of successive major malevolent cyber events so as to discern whether there is any kind of pattern or trajectory to these events. What, in fact, are state actors and agencies doing, or what do they seem to tolerate being done? Anything at all? Everything in general? Or are there empirical limits to what is deemed acceptable damage or injury?

Even if there is not anything positive that is discernable, are we collectively learning where such limits may lie, so as to lodge plausible complaints when those limits are exceeded or to provide objective and justifiable grounds for remonstrating? Is there, that is to say, anything like a gradual recognition of best practices and limits on acceptable practice? Specifically, if we plot time (chronology) of successive events on a horizontal X-axis and multiple parameters on a vertical Y-axis to track things like intensity, destructiveness or harm, target discrimination and collateral damage done, successful attribution, and so forth, would we discern any pattern of behavior? Would we detect any lessons being learned ("Wow! *That* didn't go as planned! Let's not try *that* again!").

I start my own plot with the first plausible incident of cyber war: the Estonian attacks in late April 2007, followed by working through Syrian air defense hacks by Israel later that year (2007), and on to similar disruptive cyberattacks by the Russian Federation against Georgia (2008), and then on to Stuxnet, Duqu and Operation Olympic Games (2010–2012). I consider the North Korean cyberattack on Sony Pictures in 2014, and the U.S. Office of Personnel Management (OPM) personnel records hacks discovered in the summer of 2015, and proceed on through time to the massive ransomware attack on Ukraine in 2017 (NotPetya), alongside the pirated WannaCry crypto worm allegedly used by North Korea on National Health Service hospitals in the United Kingdom (among many targets worldwide). One of the most frightening of these recent attacks occurred in late April 2020 threatening the integrity of Israel's desalination and water purification infrastructure – frightening because this was not simply a disruption of service or a data breach but an attack that threatened serious, real-world consequences. Thousands of civilians could have been poisoned, sickened, or even killed. SolarWinds (2021), by contrast, while thought to be an enormously damaging act of espionage, at least did not eventuate in actual human casualties . . . at least, yet!

There are myriad accounts on the Internet of individual cyberattacks, lists of the ten biggest or the ten worst. Cybersecurity experts have a much greater grasp on the range and extent of these events, but it is surprising how much detailed and, with due caution, accurate information there is on these events in the public domain. The list goes on, and I will want us to reexamine and add to it as necessary from a variety of possible perspectives in the next two chapters. Tracking these malevolent cyber operations is an exercise that many of us should engage in, partly to help determine the answer to a highly vexed and subjective set of questions. *Are there any patterns we can detect*, for one: or is this all just random, oscillating hodgepodge? To aid this public effort, I recommend doing something that most lists of cyber events fail to do: separate the operations carried out by agents of nation-states (the Syrian electronic army, the Iranian and North Korean cyber warriors, and so forth) from the criminal or vigilante acts perpetrated by individuals and nonstate organizations (as was apparently the case in the disruptive DarkSide ransomware attacks on the Colonial oil pipeline in the eastern United States in 2021).[9]

This is not because the criminal acts are less serious. Some of these are devastating, and often they attract wider attention. The point is rather that our question is about state behavior, responsibility, and accountability – and the prospects for reaching any kind of tentative agreement or consensus among nation-state adversaries about what would constitute widely accepted norms of responsible behavior in the cyber domain that might just succeed in setting some kinds of limits to the nature and scope of malevolent cyber operations to keep them from getting out of hand. Criminals are much less likely to recognize international limitations, given that their motives are almost entirely profit-driven and do not incorporate political considerations that might modify their behavior.[10] And in any case, as we noted, we now have the kind of international cooperation, consensus, and jurisdictional coordination to stymie them effectively.

In a similar but more plausible fashion, I believe we can discern forms of behavior that everyone, upon reflection, might agree are off limits. The attacks on civilian hospitals or water infrastructure, which could result in harm or death to thousands who are not properly in the line of fire for state purposes, are one area of prospective agreement and international cooperative sanctions. As Israel's chief of cybersecurity said of the attacks on his country: "The Iranians should be careful. They are just as vulnerable, if not more so, than we are." That is the kind of deterrent logic that, frankly, makes sense to otherwise bitter enemies. It is all about keeping things from escalating out of hand to no one's ultimate advantage or benefit.

Stuxnet, by contrast, is an example we need to return to again and again for the lessons it offers. First, this weapon received a great deal of credit at the time and since for being a very principled weapon: one of the most proportionate and discriminate weapons ever deployed, in fact. Now, of course, the victims/adversaries didn't share that view, but many others, including critics of Israel and the United States, nonetheless acknowledged that the weapon targeted only the legitimate military target at issue, did no discernable collateral damage, and, after some initial confusion and controversy, even acknowledged that it did not contribute meaningfully to proliferation of similar attacks. The biggest difficulty here is that such precision cyber weapons are difficult to design and build. It is much easier to steal some sophisticated ransomware or buy it on the dark web and launch it indiscriminately against the civilian population of an enemy nation.

This tension encapsulates our international dilemma: a few states have the capacity to build cyber weapons that are highly effective, but also discriminate and proportionate, and thus conform to existing norms of international behavior concerning warfare conducted by these alternative means. But even for such states, that effort is complex, time-consuming, and expensive. All states, by contrast, have access to much simpler, cheaper, and politically effective cyber weapons that do not incorporate any effort to distinguish between ordinary citizens and legitimate military targets. It appears from these varieties of behavior in the cyber domain that the recent pattern of behavior among nation-states is unfortunately that their cyber operations are becoming *increasingly reckless, indiscriminate, and destructive*. From that pattern we might induce that there has been of late a very disappointing *devolution* in norms of responsible state behavior within the cyber domain.

But let me conclude on a more hopeful note. Even if there is no discernable upward trajectory in the tracking of actual cyber operations toward responsible constraint, there are some patterns that seem to warn of impending problems – of political affairs spiraling out of control needlessly if they are not reigned in. The cyberattack on water purification systems and similar attacks upon essential, but largely nonmilitary, infrastructure (even by criminal gangs, let alone nation-states) seem another area (alongside hospitals and health care infrastructure) in which widespread agreement to voluntarily abstain in the future might be attainable. The motivators would include the usual mixture of moral sensibility and political prudence (as most norms do, initially). We don't want our citizens harmed or killed, and certainly not on a massive scale – and we don't want to suffer the reprisals that would assuredly be inflicted upon us if we did such things to them. So, our new cyber norm becomes something like:

- **Adversarial or rival states engaged in cyber conflict should endeavor to limit their attacks to military targets and refrain from directly attacking civilians and civilian objects.**

A separate issue is the extent of the damage cause by these attacks, in comparison with the military or political objectives behind them. Consider, once again, for example the hacking and massive exfiltration, ostensibly by PLA cyber operatives, of personnel files of U.S. federal employees (including military and intelligence personnel) from the records of the Office of Personnel Management in 2015. The number affected was quite large: over 20 million individuals. So far as we know, however, all of those individuals worked in some way with and for the U.S. government. Technically speaking (that is to say), all of those affected were legitimate military targets, not random civilian citizens.

What the Chinese have done with those data since, however, is not entirely clear and remains to be seen. Was this perhaps a demonstration of power, a warning: "We have the capacity to do this kind of thing, and you can't stop it, so you better watch your step." Or are they yet today plotting some kind of major attack, aimed particularly toward those whose personnel records revealed them to be important – perhaps covert operatives or major senior diplomatic officials who could be extorted or blackmailed in some way? At present, the OPM hack represents a massive attack on a legitimate target, the damage from which has, as yet, fallen within the bounds of reasonable proportionality, with collateral damage to any others limited or nonexistent. Or so it seems. This suggests (especially in comparison to other cyber operations we have cited) another familiar norm we might extrapolate successfully to cyber adversaries:

- **The effect of cyberattacks should bear reasonable proportion to the political or military goals for which they are initiated and should incorporate all steps to limit or avoid collateral damage (serious and senseless harm) to unintended targets.**

Stuxnet, once again, constituted a weapon aimed at military targets only. It did not harm or kill anyone else and damaged very little other than its intended target, even when it escaped into the wild. Instead, it went dormant until it self-destructed and removed itself from improperly infected computers. Operation Olympic Games, moreover, appeared to be a stand-in for an otherwise likely conventional attack against Iran's well-protected nuclear facility at Natanz, which would most likely have been extensively destructive on both sides. Many cyberattacks among and between adversarial nations appear to incorporate this additional consideration, a cyber norm that follows from the wider norm of proportionality mentioned earlier:

- **In pursuing a justifiable grievance, all things considered, a justifiable cyberattack against an adversary (when possible) should be the option of first resort, in lieu of a conventional use of kinetic force whenever the former would likely prove far less destructive physically than the latter.**

Perhaps, these are sufficient examples to illustrate the procedure of discerning emergent norms of responsible state behavior, even in the face of decidedly reckless and irresponsible behavior. For those familiar with discussions of justified war, the first two norms might seem merely to echo concerns raised in that discussion. But that is hardly surprising, in that proportionality of ends and the distinction and attempted protection of innocent parties from collateral harm are concerns that arise in a variety of contexts in which moral rules are being violated, exceptions requested, and harm done to others in due course (e.g., civil disobedience, whistleblowing, lying and truth-telling, and promise-breaking, to name but a few). The third norm, however, is relatively new, independent from specifics of past historical discussions and at present would pertain uniquely to cyber warfare, as opposed to conventional conflict. But it is obviously an extension or extrapolation of the customary norm of proportionality of means.

Might cyber opponents and adversaries be reasonably expected to acknowledge and conform their behavior to such norms? What are people, or rather nations and their cyber agents, doing in the cyber domain that might tip us off as to what we can hope for in the way of norms of responsible state behavior? Such an analysis points the way toward standards and principles of restraint by which we might at least in a provisional way hope to reinforce, establish, recognize, comply, and hold nations accountable for failure.

This, of course, is largely what has occurred in international law over the course of centuries. We hold people and nations now, in the twentieth and twenty-first centuries, to much higher and more stringent standards of conduct regarding the use of force, waging of conflict, and concurrent respect for human rights than at earlier historical periods. With the passage of time and building of precedent, our ability to reinforce these higher standards often strengthens through shaming, sanctions, public attention, and so forth, which is the hallmark of the enforcement of the international norms now enshrined in law.[11]

Notes

1 Michael Gross and Tamar Meisels discuss the range of moral and legal challenges arising in something they propose to call "soft war." If soft war in turn is taken as a synonym for unarmed conflict, then cyber is clearly a form of soft war. In their 2017 book on

the topic of soft war, in fact, Meisels and Gross devote all or portions of several chapters to the topic of cyber conflict. See *Soft War: The Ethics of Unarmed Conflict* (New York: Cambridge University Press, 2017).

2 As, for example, in the P.W. Singer and Emerson Brookings account of social media in *LikeWar: The Weaponization of Social Media* (New York: Houghton Mifflin Harcourt, 2018).

3 Thomas Rid, *Cyber War Will Not Take Place* (Oxford: Oxford University Press, 2013).

4 Cécile Fabre, *Spying Through a Glass Darkly: The Ethics of Espionage and Counter-Intelligence* (Oxford: Oxford University Press, 2022).

5 See Michael Morell, "The Ethics of Intelligence Gathering in the Grey Zone," 2021 McCain Conference, U.S. Naval Academy, www.youtube.com/watch?v=j346jFrqgzQ [accessed 14 May 2021].

6 See the full list of speakers and hear their presentations at: www.youtube.com/playlist?list=PLcuUHQsaiCX6RX9q9y3BrgB1rNzZsuqYa

7 It may seem tragically irrelevant in the midst of the collapse of the Afghan government 20 years later, but in 2001 the United States petitioned the Taliban to comply with this Convention and arrest or expel all Al Qaeda operatives from its borders. When the Taliban refused to do so, the United States then petitioned the U.N. Security Council for the right to intervene in that country itself to halt this criminal conspiracy. That right of intervention was acknowledged by the international community, marking the first time (and, to my knowledge, the only time) this new arrangement of holding a national government accountable for international criminal activities originating within its borders has been invoked. See David E. Graham, "Cyber Threats and the Law of War," *Journal of National Security Law* 4 (1) (2010): 87–102.

8 R. Axelrod, "An Evolutionary Approach to Norms," *American Political Science Review*, 80 (4) (1986): 1095–1111. J. Bendor and P. Swistak, "The Evolution of Norms," *American Journal of Sociology* 106 (6) (2001): 1493–1545.

9 Anthony M. Freed, "Inside the DarkSide Ransomware Attack on Colonial Pipeline," *Cyber Reason* (10 May 2021), www.cybereason.com/blog/inside-the-darkside-ransomware-attack-on-colonial-pipeline [accessed 14 May 2022].

10 Although, interestingly, following their highly damaging and disruptive attacks on the Colonial Pipeline and JB Foods in the United States, the (presumably) Russian-based criminal organization responsible for deploying the "DarkSide" ransomware actually admitted that some of their attacks, or the magnitude of them, might constitute unreasonably risky behavior from which they should abstain. According to *Newsweek Magazine*,

> [T]he hacker group issued an unusual apology for the attack later the same day, saying it would "introduce moderation" to "avoid social consequences in the future" and insisted that it was entirely profit-driven and "apolitical," in a statement posted to the dark web.
>
> See: www.newsweek.com/colonial-pipeline-hackers-darkside-apologize-say-goal-make-money-1590327 [accessed 4 September 2021]

11 Martha Finnemore, and Kathryn Sikkink, "International Norm Dynamics and Political Change," *International Organization* 52 (4) (1998): 887–917. I am grateful to Milton Regan, Jr., of the Georgetown University School of Law for pointing out this reference.

References

Axelrod, R. "An Evolutionary Approach to Norms," *American Political Science Review* 80 (4) (1986): 1095–1111.

Bendor, J; Swistak, P. "The Evolution of Norms," *American Journal of Sociology* 106 (6) (2001): 1493–545.

Fabre, Cécile. *Spying Through a Glass Darkly: The Ethics of Espionage and Counter-Intelligence* (Oxford: Oxford University Press, 2022).

Finnemore, Martha; Sikkink, Kathryn. "International Norm Dynamics and Political Change," *International Organization* 52 (4) (1998): 887–917.

Freed, Anthony M. "Inside the DarkSide Ransomware Attack on Colonial Pipeline," *Cyber Reason* (10 May 2021), www.cybereason.com/blog/inside-the-darkside-ransomware-attack-on-colonial-pipeline [accessed 14 May 2022].

Graham, David E. "Cyber Threats and the Law of War," *Journal of National Security Law* 4 (1) (2010): 87–102.

Gross, Michael L.; Meisels, Tamar. *Soft War: The Ethics of Unarmed Conflict* (New York: Cambridge University Press, 2017).

Lock, Samantha. "Colonial Pipeline Hackers, DarkSide, Apologize, Say Goal 'Is to Make Money'," *Newsweek* (11 May 2021), www.newsweek.com/colonial-pipeline-hackers-arkside-apologize-say-goal-make-money-1590327 [accessed 18 May 2022].

Lucas, George R., Jr. "Ethical Challenges of 'Disruptive Innovation': State-Sponsored Hacktivism and 'Soft' War," in *Evolution of Cyber Technologies and Operations to 2035*, ed. Misty Blower (New York: Springer International, 2015).

Lucas, George R., Jr. *Ethics and Cyber Warfare* (Oxford: Oxford University Press, 2017).

Morell, Michael. "The Ethics of Intelligence Gathering in the Grey Zone," 2021 McCain Conference, U.S. Naval Academy, www.youtube.com/watch?v=j346jFrqgzQ [accessed 14 May 2021].

NATO. "Allied Joint Doctrine for the Conduct of Operations," AJP-3.19 (February 2019), https://www.gov.uk/government/publications/allied-joint-doctrine-for-the-conduct-of-operations-ajp-3b [accessed 23 August 2022].

NATO. "Allied Joint Doctrine for Cyberspace Operations," AJP-3.20 (2020), www.gov.uk/government/publications/allied-joint-doctrine-for-cyberspace-operations-ajp-320 [accessed 13 May 2022].

Perry, David L. *Partly Cloudy: Ethics in War, Espionage and Covert Action* (Lanham, MD: Scarecrow Press, 2009).

Rid, Thomas. *Cyber War Will Not Take Place* (Oxford: Oxford University Press, 2013).

Singer, Peter W.; Brooking, Emerson T. *LikeWar: The Weaponization of Social Media* (Boston: Mariner Books, 2019).

8

PROSPECTS FOR PEACE IN THE CYBER DOMAIN

> In the nature of man, we find three principall causes of quarrel. First, Competition; Secondly, *Diffidence*; Thirdly, Glory. . . . Nature hath made men so equall, in the faculties of body and mind; as that though there bee found one man sometimes manifestly stronger in body, or of quicker mind then another; yet when all is reckoned together, the difference between man, and man, is not so considerable, as that one man can thereupon claim to himself any benefit, to which another may not pretend, as well as he. . . . For such is the nature of men, that howsoever they may acknowledge many others to be more witty, or more eloquent, or more learned; Yet they will hardly believe there be many so wise as themselves: . . . from this *diffidence* of one another, there is no way for any man to secure himself . . . till he see no other power great enough to endanger him.
>
> Thomas Hobbes, *Leviathan* (1651)[1]

Crying "Peace! Peace!" When There Is No Peace in the Cyber Domain

When we are not engrossed by (for example) the latest technologies available through the Internet of Things, it seems that our reflections concerning the cyber realm turn instead to the endless conflicts and prospects for virtual war in that domain. But what of the prospects for peace? To what extent is peace, rather than war, a desirable state in this domain? Even more to the point: how willing are the various agents who populate this domain to invest in efforts aimed at achieving the goal of peace rather than persisting in their present condition of seemingly endless and intractable strife?

As we noted in Chapter 7, nothing could seem more unpromising at first glance than attempting to discuss peace in the context of cyber conflict. Even apart from the moral conundrums of outright warfare, the cyber domain generally is often described as a lawless frontier or a state of nature, in which everyone seems capable

DOI: 10.4324/9781003273912-9

in principle of doing whatever they wish to whomever they please without fear of attribution, retribution, or accountability. When it comes to human behavior, and the treatment of one another, human behavior within the cyber domain might aptly be characterized, as we concluded as a war of all against all.

Let us pause to think about that familiar characterization more deeply. This grim and oft-cited generalization of our actual condition in the cyber domain at present is no more or less true than Hobbes's own original characterization of human beings themselves in a hypothetical state of nature. John Locke's subsequent benign account of that general condition (1689) was perhaps more accurate than that of Hobbes (if we can even speak about the comparative accuracy of hypothetical circumstances). For the most part, Locke contended, each of us minds her own business while almost everyone in that original position quietly pursues their own interests, *unless* someone or something provokes conflict.

Likewise, when we stop to consider it, the vast majority of actors in the cyber domain are relatively benign. They mind their own business, pursue their own ends, do not engage in deliberate mischief, let alone harm, do not wish their fellow citizens ill, and generally seek only to pursue the myriad benefits afforded by the cyber realm: access to information, goods and services, convenient financial transactions and data processing, and control over their array of devices from mobile phones to door locks, refrigerators and toasters, personal assistants like Alexa and Echo, and even swimming pools.

Beyond this (to employ some useful Aristotelian terminology), there are some natural virtues and commonly shared definitions of the Good in the cyber domain: anonymity, freedom, and choice, for example, along with a notable desire to avoid imposing any external constraints, restrictions, and regulations. These are things that cyber activists, in particular, like to champion and seemed determined to preserve against any encroachments upon them in the name of the rule of law (conveniently overlooking the numerous unfortunate occasions in which one individual's exercise of their claims to freedom and anonymity threaten the privacy of others).[2] Overall, however, we might characterize the cyber domain as colonized by libertarians and anarchists who, if they had their way, would continue to dwell in peace and pursue their private and collective interests without interference.

As with all relatively ungoverned frontiers, however, this natural tranquility is easily shattered by the malevolent behavior of even a few bad actors – and there are more than a few bad actors in the cyber domain. As a forthcoming book by Australian cybersecurity experts Seumas Miller and Terry Bossomaier portrays the matter,[3] the principal form of malevolent cyber activity is *criminal* in nature: theft, extortion, blackmail, vandalism, slander and disinformation (in the form of trolling and cyberbullying), and even prospects for homicide. Thus, we might conclude that the warfare in question within the cyber domain is of the metaphorical sort described by Hobbes, as opposed to the conventional activity described by Karl von Clausewitz. For the latter, war is an outgrowth of the natural conflict between clearly defined competing political policies of well-organized states, a natural if unfortunate outgrowth of a semblance of anarchy in international political relations. For Hobbes, in contrast, the condition of war is the natural condition of individual human agents (now to also include virtual individual agents in the cyber domain) apart from political institutions, dwelling in anarchy and absent any discernable supervening authority or rule of law. This, or perhaps its Lockean variant, thus seems an accurate and indisputable characterization of cyberspace, cyber citizens, and their resulting cyber conflict.

In contrast to the customary hypothetical invocations by modern political philosophers, however, as we discovered in the preceding chapter, cyber conflict at present does not constitute some hypothetical supposing or fictitious original position, affording a privileged vantage point for reasoning to adjudicate matters of fact. Rather, the cyber domain itself now confronts us with the first truly actual and authentic instance of such state or condition. A state of nature, accurately characterized by Hobbes's *bellum omnium contra omnes* (or else, Locke's peaceable libertarianism) is no more and no less what the cyber realm itself is.

And again, as we noted in Chapter 7, the cyber realm, with its many examples of conflict and lack of structure, also unintentionally provides us with the first authentic laboratory in which to examine the chief challenges and puzzles at the center of classic social contract theory. In the case of Hobbes, we asked: how do civil society, social order, and the rule of law ever manage to emerge from such a condition of primordial anarchy? If everything amounts to constant struggle and competition, for example, the most powerful (in the classical theory) or the most clever, innovative, and unscrupulous (in the case of cyber) hold the advantage. Why should they relinquish their advantage in either case? Remember that the underlying (if implicit) question in the *Leviathan* is: what, in this miserable, fallen world of ceaseless conflict, are the prospects for peace? And if it is peace, security, safety, as guaranteed through the rule of law that is the ultimate goal of the *Leviathan*, how is that goal to be attained?

When, in particular, we invoke Hobbes descriptively in this fashion, we are obliged to consider the normative dimension in his investigations that is quite often overlooked by descriptive political theorists. This alleged normative dimension is admittedly a rather thin moral conception offered up by a philosopher famed for his rejection of morality in virtually all other respects – *but it is a moral conception nonetheless*. It is the obligation incumbent upon all who dwell within this state of nature (as Hobbes editorializes) "to quit it with the utmost dispatch." Confronted with our natural condition, he argues, we are not permitted merely to wallow in it but to (somehow) transform it into something more stable and secure. On Hobbes's largely realist or amoral account, in point of fact, the sole action that would represent a genuinely moral or ethical decision beyond narrow self-interest would be the enlightened (but still self-interested) decision on the part of almost everyone to quit the State of Nature and enter into some sort of social contract that, in turn, would provide security through the stern imposition of law and order.

But if this caveat is to amount to anything more than a question-begging sleight of hand, we need to come to terms with (if not solve) what might be termed the realist paradox in Hobbes's account. For, in the cyber domain at least – and utterly unlike Hobbes's fictional individuals languishing unpleasantly in a hypothetical state of nature – we discover in the virtual world of cyberspace that law and order, let alone legal institutions like police, judges, and courts, are precisely what the rank-and-file individual actors and nonstate organizations (like Anonymous) *assiduously wish to avoid*. Hobbes's own solution to the problem of anarchy is likewise not one that any self-respecting cyber citizen would care to embrace: namely, that a well-regulated civil society will only be achieved through the forceful imposition of authoritarian rule. We have witnessed how nations like China currently attempt the Hobbesian formula in the cyber domain, with limited success. But that approach is not only anathema to democratic and rights-respecting societies – it would represent a fundamental betrayal of what we called earlier the natural virtues and limited natural rights valued by denizens of the cyber domain: liberty, anonymity, privacy, and behavior largely free from interference by others. There are no boundaries and no governments in cyberspace, and cyber citizens profess themselves unwilling to countenance or yield to such impositions, whatever Hobbes's theory may require and despite whatever the PRC or other authoritarian governments may attempt.[4]

I characterized Hobbes's theory itself as question-begging because a famous and seemingly incorrigible problem in the *Leviathan* itself is that the transition from anarchy to civil society is never really adequately explained. On the one hand, Hobbes appears to argue that the transition will occur pretty much as a matter of course, when inhabitants see their own self-interests optimized by sacrificing some of their freedom and rights in exchange for authoritarian-sponsored state security. But, at the same time, Hobbes recognizes that there is no guarantee that this benign transition will automatically occur. Some inhabitants, the most malevolent in particular, will be resistant. The truly powerful, the strongest in the state of nature (unlike those found to be comparatively weaker and more vulnerable), will never willingly yield their personal authority to the rule of law, simply because it can never be, or be seen to be, in their own individual self-interest to do so.

This is the original Hobbesian version of the reality paradox mentioned earlier: namely, to achieve what would clearly be in the self-interests of all, some act of force must be utilized to override the narrowly conceived self-interests of bullies and tyrants in the state of nature. Who, in the state of nature, will consent (let alone possess the wherewithal) to dispatch the troublesome tyrants and bullies? Just as importantly, how may the rest of us retain confidence that any individual volunteer who is willing to do so will do so without simply assuming their place? The moral imperative – the only moral imperative that Hobbes acknowledges – is that this transition to civil society be made. But apparently it cannot be made. Or at least, there is no clear path, no ironclad guarantee, that the necessary transition either can or will take place.

Emergent Norms for Cyber Conflict

When we turn to cyber conflict from the perspective of international relations, the malevolent actors are primarily rogue nations, terrorists, and nonstate actors (alongside organized crime). The reigning theory of conflict in international relations generally is Rousseau's metaphorical extension of Hobbes from individuals to states: the theory of international anarchy or political realism. There is one significant difference, however, between Hobbes and Rousseau on this condition of international anarchy. Although the state of nature for individuals in Hobbes's account is usually understood as a hypothetical thought experiment (rather than an attempt at a genuine historical or evolutionary account), in the case of international relations, by contrast, that condition of ceaseless conflict and strife among nations (as Rousseau first observed) is precisely what is actual and ongoing.

Conflict among and between international entities on this account naturally arises as a result of an inevitable competition and collision of interests among discrete states, with no corresponding permanent institutional arrangements available to resolve the conflict beyond the individual competing nations and their relative power to resist one another's encroachments. In addition, borrowing from Hobbes's account of the amoral state of nature among hypothetical individuals prior to the establishment of a firm rule of law, virtually all political theorists and international relations experts assume this condition of conflict among nations to be *immune* to the institutions of morality in the customary sense: namely, deliberation and action guided by moral virtues; an overriding sense of duty or obligation to enhance the individual well-being of others; recognition of and respect for basic human rights; and efforts to foster the common good.

However we characterize conventional state relationships, the current status of relations and conflicts among nations and individuals within the cyber domain also fits this model perfectly: a lawless frontier, devoid (we might think) of impulses toward virtue or concerns for the wider common good. It is a commons in which the advantage seems to accrue to whomever is willing to do anything they wish to anyone they please whenever they like, without fear of accountability or retribution. This seems, perhaps even more than in conventional domains of political rivalry, to constitute a genuine war of all against all, as I remarked earlier.

As we saw in Chapter 7, while at work on my own study of cyber warfare several years ago,[5] I noted some curious and quite puzzling trends that ran sharply counter to expectations. Experts and pundits had long predicted the escalation of effects-based cyber warfare and the proliferation of cyber weapons like the Stuxnet virus. The major fear was the enhanced ability of rogue states and terrorists to destroy dams, disrupt national power grids, and interfere with transportation and commerce in a manner that would, in their devastation, destruction, and loss of human life, rival conventional full-scale armed conflict. Those predictions preceded the discovery of Stuxnet, but that discovery (despite apparent U.S. and Israeli involvement in the development of that particular weapon as part of Operation Olympic Games) was taken as a harbinger of things to come: a future cyber Pearl Harbor[6] or cyber Armageddon.

I began to notice, however, that by and large, this was *not* the trajectory that international cyber conflict appeared to be following over that same period. Instead of individuals and nonstate actors becoming more and more empowered to emulate the large-scale destructiveness of nation-states, as predicted, those states instead were increasingly behaving collectively more and more like individuals and non-state organizations in the cyber domain. That is, the states, too, began engaging in identity theft, extortion, disinformation, election tampering, and other cyber tactics that turned out to be easier and cheaper to develop and deploy while proving less easy to attribute or deter (let alone retaliate against). Most notably, such tactics proved themselves capable of achieving nearly as much if not more political bang for the buck than effects-based cyber weapons (which, like Stuxnet itself, were large, complex, expensive, time-consuming, and all but beyond the capabilities of most nations).

In a defense security studies article published in 2015,[7] I labeled these curious disruptive military tactics state-sponsored hacktivism and predicted at the time that it was rapidly becoming the preferred form of cyber conflict or warfare. We should consider it a legitimate new form of warfare, I argued, based upon political motives and effects. State-sponsored hacktivism, for example, perfectly fitted Clausewitz's famous definition of warfare as politics pursued by other means. We were thus confronted with not one but two legitimate forms of cyber warfare: one waged conventionally by large, resource- and technology-rich nations seeking to emulate kinetic effects-based weaponry; the second by clever, unscrupulous but somewhat less well-resourced rogue states designed to achieve the overall equivalent political effects of conventional conflict. I did not maintain that this was a complete or perfect characterization, instead pleading only (with no idea what lay around the corner) that we simply consider it: that is, allow ourselves to consider the possibility that we might have been largely mistaken in our prior prevailing assumptions about the form(s) that cyber conflict waged by the militaries of other nations might eventually take. We might simply be looking in the wrong direction or (so to speak) over the wrong shoulder.

At about that time, almost as if on cue, cyber operators in the Russian Federation attempted to hack the 2016 U.S. presidential election. Almost simultaneously, the North Koreans proceeded to download the WannaCry software (stolen from the U.S. National Security Agency) from the dark web and used it to attack civilian infrastructure (mainly banks and hospitals) in European nations that had supported the U.S. boycotts launched against the North Korean nuclear weapons program. While our cybersecurity attentions were focused elsewhere, state-sponsored hacktivism had become the devastating tactic of choice among rogue nations, all while we had been guilty of clinging to our blind political and tactical prejudices in the face of overwhelming contradictory evidence. We (the United States, the United Kingdom, and our allies) had been taken in, caught flat-footed, utterly by surprise.

At the same time, readers (of whom there were not very many) and critics had been mystified by my earlier warnings regarding state-sponsored hacktivism. No one, it seems, could make any sense of what I was talking about. My editor at Oxford even refused me permission to use my original subtitle for the book: Ethics and the Rise of State-Sponsored Hacktivism. This analysis had instead to be buried in the book chapters. I managed, after a fashion, to garner a measure of revenge. When the book was finally published in the immediate aftermath of the American presidential election in January of 2017, I thanked my publisher's publicity and marketing team in jest: Vladimir Putin, restauranteur Yevgeny Prigozhin, the FSB, PLA Shanghai Unit 61384 (who had stolen my personnel files a few years earlier, along with those of some 20 million other U.S. government employees), and the North Korean cyber warriors, who had by then scored some significant triumphs at our expense. State-sponsored hacktivism had indeed, by that time, become the norm.

This is hardly something to gloat over – and in any case, where is the ethics discussion in all this? The central examination in my book was not devoted to straightforward mechanical application of conventional moral theory and reasoning (utilitarian, deontological, virtue theory, the ethics of care, and so forth) to specific puzzles but to something else entirely: namely, a careful examination of what, in the international relations community, is termed the emergence of norms of responsible state behavior. This, I argued, was vastly more fundamental than conventional analytic ethics. Such accounts are not principally about deontology, utility, and colliding trolley cars. They consist instead in a kind of historical moral inquiry that lies at the heart of moral philosophy itself, from Aristotle, Hobbes, Rousseau, and Kant to Rawls and Habermas – and the book's principal intellectual guide, the Aristotelian philosopher Alasdair MacIntyre.

The great puzzle for philosophers is, of course, how norms can be meaningfully said to emerge? Not just where do they come from, or how do they catch on, but how can such a historical process be validated, given the difference between normative and descriptive guidance and discourse? Perhaps, my willingness to take on this age-old question and place it at the heart of contemporary discussions of cyber conflict is why few have bothered to read the book. Who in the defense and cybersecurity communities cares about all that abstract, theoretical jabberwocky? Leaders and members of those communities want rather to discuss all the latest buzz concerning advanced persistent threats or the zero-day software vulnerabilities intertwined within the Internet of Things. Moral philosophers and ethicists, for their part, seek perennially to offer their moral analysis in terms of utility, duty, virtue, . . . and those infamous and seemingly ever-present colliding trolley cars – merely substituting, perhaps, driverless robotic cars for the trolleys and then wondering whether the autonomous vehicle should be programmed to permit the death of its own passenger while maneuvering to save the lives of five pedestrians.

All those concerns are fully legitimate, to a limited extent, but do not seem to cast any useful light on the overall problem of seeking peace and stability within the cyber domain. I found it necessary instead to examine the history and conceptual foundations of just war theory as an important example of the morality of exceptions or exceptionalism (i.e., how do we justify sometimes having to do things we are normally prohibited from doing?). I then applied these results to the international relations approach to emergent norms itself, as in fact dating back to Aristotle, and his discussion of the cultivation of moral norms and guiding principles within a community of practice, characterized by a shared notion of the good. Kant, Rawls, and Habermas were invoked to explain how, in turn, a community of common practice governed solely by individual self-interest may nevertheless evolve into one characterized by the very kinds of recognition of common moral values that Hobbes, as well, had implicitly invoked to explain the transition from a nasty, brutish state of nature to a well-ordered commonwealth – precisely the kind of thing we are trying to discern now within the cyber domain. Kant called this evolutionary learning process the Cunning of Nature while the decidedly Aristotelian philosopher, Hegel, borrowed and tweaked Kant's original conception under the title the Cunning of History. These, too, are important questions in their own right, possibly even as important as what happens when trolley cars (or driverless cars) collide. It seemed apparent, however, that the resolution of our underlying reality paradox lay in these broad historical reflections rather than in the diagnosis of a specific set of hypothetical moral puzzles.

Finally, in applying this historical, experiential methodology to the recent history of cyber conflict from Estonia (2007) to the present day, I proceeded to illustrate and summarize a number of norms of responsible cyber behavior that, indeed, seem to have emerged and caught on – and others that seem reasonably likely to do so, given a bit more time and experience. Even the turn away from catastrophic destruction by means of kinetic, effects-based cyber warfare (as shrilly predicted by Richard Clarke and others) and toward state-sponsored hacktivism instead as the preferred mode of international conflict likewise showed the emergence of these norms of reasonable restraint – doing far less genuine harm, while achieving similar political effects – not because we are nice but because we are clever, like Kant's race of devils, who famously stand at the threshold of genuine morality.

This last development in the case of cyber war is, for example, the intuitive, unconscious application by these clever devils of a kind of proportionality criterion, something we term in military ethics the economy of force, in which a clever and mischievous cyberattack is to be preferred to a more destructive alternative, when available – again, not because anyone is trying to play nice but because such an attack is more likely to succeed and attain its political aims without provoking a harsh response. But such attacks, contrary to the earliest events in Estonia (we then proceed to reason), really should be pursued only in support of a legitimate cause and not directed against nonmilitary targets (I'm not happy about the PLA stealing my personnel files, but I am – or was, after all – a federal employee, not a private citizen). And so, the evolutionary emergence of moral norms by means of Kant's Cunning of Nature (or Hegel's Cunning of History) thus appeared to be underway. Even a race of devils can be brought to simulate the outward conditions and constraints of law and morality – if only they are reasonable devils.

The Hobbesian Paradox *Redux*

Once again, critics may view this account of emergent norms as being nearly as thin and implausible a conception of morality as that of Hobbes's original attempt to encourage rogues and villains to embrace the rule of law. I cannot quarrel with this finding: morality is clearly treading on thin ice within the cold reaches of cyberspace. But what is the alternative?

We would need to countenance an act of monumentally immoral proportions in response to the moral outrage most of us might feel at being held perpetual hostages in cyberspace: our property, security, even our personal identities – as well as our public institutions and civil discourse and political decision-making – incorrigibly at risk to hijacking, theft, and corruption by unscrupulous persons, organizations, and rogue nations.[8] This seems unacceptable, and so some act of intervention, *forceful* intervention, must be contemplated and ultimately attempted. But by whom and upon what authority? Are all nations compelled to reassert national borders and build virtual firewalls around them to keep out intruders (and to keep their own citizens and inhabitants in line)? Is this the price of peace and cybersecurity? This seems also unacceptable.

Either we acknowledge and nurture the fragile norms that manage to sprout and grow in the thin moral soil of cyberspace, or else we will eventually be forced to colonize and tyrannize this new domain, extracting its legal order and compliance at the expense of its most promising virtues. So, let us consider, one last time, whether there are measures we could undertake to help foster this supposed emergence of norms of responsible state behavior. Perhaps, a sterner approach will be required.

Notes

1 Thomas Hobbes, *Leviathan*, Part I, Ch XIII [61]. "Penguin Classics Edition," ed. C.B. Macpherson (New York: Penguin Press, 1968): 183–185.
2 See G.R. Lucas, "Privacy, Anonymity and Cyber Security," *Amsterdam Law Forum* 5 (2) (Spring 2013): 107–114.
3 Seumas Miller and Terry Bossomaier, *Ethics & Cyber Security* (Oxford: Oxford University Press, forthcoming 2023).
4 It bears mention that China, for its part, has accused the United States and Western allies of attempting to impose its own form of hegemony on the "commons" that is the cyber domain, in exercises like the Tallinn Manual on International Law applicable to that domain. The official view is that cyberspace is a commons in which all actors (individuals, collectivities, and nations) may act without restriction. That international view, however, is inconsistent with their domestic practice. See David E. Sanger, "Differences on Cybertheft Complicate China Talks," *New York Times* (10 July 2013), www.nytimes.com/2013/07/11/world/asia/differences-on-cybertheft-complicate-china-talks.html [accessed 14 May 2022].
5 G.R. Lucas Jr., *Ethics & Cyber Warfare* (Oxford: Oxford University Press, 2017).
6 This phrase stems from a characterization of the threat by the then-Secretary of Defense Leon Panetta in 2011. Though challenged and disputed, it has endured in public discourse about cyber operations and so-called advanced persistent threats ever since. See Jason Ryan, "CIA Director Leon Panetta Warns of Possible Cyber – Pearl Harbor," *ABC News* (10 February 2011), https://abcnews.go.com/News/cia-director-leon-panetta-warns-cyber-pearl-harbor/story?id=12888905 [accessed 6 May 2022].
7 G.R. Lucas, "Ethical Challenges of 'Disruptive Innovation': State Sponsored Hacktivism and 'Soft' War," in *Evolution of Cyber Technologies and Operations to 2035*, ed. Misty Blowers (Basel: Springer International, 2015). "Advances in Information Security, Vol. 63," pp. 175–184.

8 For example, as described in Peter Warren Singer and Emerson T. Brooking, *LikeWar: The Weaponization of Social Media* (New York: Houghton Mifflin Harcourt, 2018).

References

Hobbes, Thomas. *Leviathan*, Part I, Ch XIII [61]. Penguin Classics Edition, ed. C.B. Macpherson (New York: Penguin Press, 1968 [1651]): 183–185.

Locke, John. *Second Treatise of Government*. Ed. C.B. Macpherson (Indianapolis, IN: Hackett Publishers, 1980 [1689]).

Lucas, George R., Jr. "Privacy, Anonymity and Cyber Security," *Amsterdam Law Forum* 5 (2) (Spring 2013): 107–114.

Lucas, George R., Jr. "Ethical Challenges of 'Disruptive Innovation': State Sponsored Hacktivism and 'Soft' War," in *Evolution of Cyber Technologies and Operations to 2035*, ed. Misty Blowers (Basel: Springer International Publishers, 2015).

Lucas, George R., Jr. *Ethics & Cyber Warfare* (Oxford: Oxford University Press, 2017).

Miller, Seumas; Bossomaier, Terry. *Ethics & Cyber Security* (Oxford: Oxford University Press, forthcoming 2023).

Ryan, James. "CIA Director Leon Panetta Warns of Possible Cyber-Pearl Harbor," *ABC News* (10 February 2011), https://abcnews.go.com/News/cia-director-leon-panetta-warns-cyber-pearl-harbor/story?id=12888905 [accessed 6 May 2022].

Sanger, David E. "Differences on Cybertheft Complicate China Talks," *New York Times* (10 July 2013), www.nytimes.com/2013/07/11/world/asia/differences-on-cybertheft-complicate-china-talks.html [accessed 14 May 2022].

Singer, Peter Warren; Brooking, Emerson T. *LikeWar: The Weaponization of Social Media* (New York: Houghton Mifflin Harcourt, 2018).

9

CYBER SURVEILLANCE AS PREVENTIVE SELF-DEFENSE

Heretofore, my summary of competing assessments of cyber war and weapons has ranged from denunciations of their widespread and indiscriminate destructiveness and deliberate targeting of civilian infrastructure, all the way to appraisals of cyber warfare as a morally preferable, less destructive alternative to conventional warfare. In this final chapter on this topic, I want to make a case for distinguishing permissible from impermissible forms of cyber conflict and from wholly impermissible large-scale criminal enterprises (including commercial and state-sponsored espionage) in the cyber realm. This case, in turn, will offer a more robust path toward encouraging responsible state behavior and deterring irresponsible behavior among individual and state actors in cyberspace. My strategy in this chapter, with reference to past cases of cyber conflict, is to argue in sum that an act of cyber warfare is permissible if it aims primarily at harming military (rather than civilian) infrastructure; degrades an adversary's ability to undertake highly destructive offensive kinetic operations; harms no civilians and/or destroys little or no civilian infrastructure in the process; and is undertaken as what I term a *penultimate last resort* in the sense that all reasonable alternatives short of attack have been attempted to no avail, and further delay would only make the situation worse.[1]

Assessing the Threat Trajectory

Despite the unexpected return of conventional kinetic conflict on a massive scale in Eastern Europe, ours still remains preeminently the age of cyber anxiety. Pundits opine, especially in developed, highly industrialized countries, on the global vulnerabilities to cyberattacks or to acts of cyberterrorism. Cybersecurity and fending off cybercrime remain a constant obsession and an ongoing concern. The potentially indiscriminate and uncontrollable aspects of cyber weapons, once unleashed in acts of terrorism or warfare, is the subject of grim and frightening prognostication.[2] In

DOI: 10.4324/9781003273912-10

many respects, the fear of uncontrolled proliferation and widespread destruction from cyber warfare has come to occupy a place in the public mind very similar to the current fear of terrorist attacks or even more to the threat of uncontrolled nuclear destruction that haunted public consciousness during the decades of the Cold War (and that has once again been resurrected during the Russian invasion of Ukraine). The situation of the United States and its allies in Western Europe vis-à-vis potential adversaries (like China or the Russian Federation) has, indeed, been portrayed as analogous to the nuclear Cold War: a proliferation and virtual arms race in the cyber arena, with only a presumed balance of destruction holding adversaries at bay.

Apart from the Convention on Cybercrime sponsored by the Council of Europe in 2001,[3] however, we see in our preceding accounts that not much progress has been made in the field of governance. That is, we seem not much closer now than we were some years earlier on discussions of the most likely ethical constraints on cyber conflict, or on the content of feasible treaties, or on the formulation of bright-line statutes in international humanitarian law that might serve to limit or regulate some of the most fearful or destructive prospects attendant upon cyber weapons development or permissible cyber tactics and strategy.

For example, among the earliest detailed treatments of the ethics of cyber warfare was the analysis of Randall Dipert, a philosopher at the University of Buffalo, writing in the December 2010 issue of the *Journal of Military Ethics*.[4] From the perspective of domestic and international law, an extensive survey was initially offered by Steven G. Bradbury in his keynote address for the annual *Harvard National Security Journal* symposium, "The Developing Legal Framework for Defensive and Offensive Cyber Operations."[5] Dipert, in his own article, lamented the relative lack of attention given to the ethics of cyber war at that time, and he cited a modest body of prior work in this field undertaken largely by computer scientists: Martin Libicki (RAND Corporation, now at the Center for Cyber Security at the U.S. Naval Academy), Herbert Lin (AAS, now on the faculty at Stanford),[6] and two colleagues at the Naval Postgraduate School, Neil Rowe and John Arquilla (incorrectly cited as Arguilla).

Rowe primarily discussed the status of cyber warfare and weapons with reference to current statutes of the law of armed conflict. He complained quite appropriately at the time that many of the strategies and weapons for cyber conflict under development then and since constitute potential violations of prevailing international humanitarian law (LOAC), in that many still deliberately target and aim to inflict widespread damage and suffering, and even injury and death, on civilian personnel and infrastructure.[7] Meanwhile, it was John Arquilla who coined the phrase "cyber warfare" itself while at the RAND Corporation in the 1990s.[8] Arquilla also wrote what is likely the very first and most original and pathbreaking article on ethics and information warfare.[9] Like Dipert, Arquilla discussed principally the ethical issues, as opposed to the legal status, of cyber conflict and filtered its principal strategies and tactics as understood at the time rather uncritically through the lens of traditional just war theory. I will return to his early and prescient observations in conclusion.

Dipert's 2010 account of the ethics of cyber warfare, while certainly not the first, was surely the most complete and up-to-date ethical account at the time from the standpoint of the status of the technology of cyber conflict, and it was also the most thorough and fully informed analysis from the standpoint of philosophy, ethics, and particularly just war theory. In keeping with what many other analysts concluded over the previous two decades with respect to the topics of terrorism, counterinsurgency, and irregular warfare, Dipert concluded likewise in the case of cyber conflict that the tactics and weapons of cyber warfare are such as to render traditional law and morality obsolete or, at least, largely inapplicable. His overall conclusion was that cyber conflict is so utterly unlike conventional war, and its weapons and tactics so novel and unprecedented that an entirely new regime of governance was called for. He thus echoed, and indeed fanned the flames of, public anxiety over this mode of conflict.

I do not doubt the gravity of the threat, nor do I dispute the seriousness of the concerns that Randall Dipert raised at the time. I continue to think, even now, however, that this topic suffered from a certain amount of confusion, hysteria, and threat inflation.[10] Subsequently, of course, challenges such as Dipert's helped inaugurate a determined effort to defend the sufficiency and applicability of international law, resulting in the two so-called Tallinn Manuals devoted to interpreting and applying existing legal regimes pertaining to conventional armed conflict, espionage, and other contested areas of international relations to cyber warfare in particular and to cyber operations more broadly (Tallinn 2.0).[11] I offered a detailed critique at that time of what I termed the Tallinn procedure or methodology (which I found to be deeply flawed) and the resulting utility of the manuals for resolving the kinds of questions and disputes that might routinely be expected to arise in the conduct of cyber operations, including adversarial conflict (I found them of marginal value).[12] There is no reason to rehearse these specific critiques, save to say that they inadvertently helped bolster Dipert's original assessment that (just as we discovered with robotics and LAWS in earlier chapters) cyber conflict remains anomalous and seriously under addressed in international law.

Hence, it is unfortunately still true that cyber conflict is, like robotics and artificial intelligence, a substantial challenge to our conventional thinking about war and armed conflict, and it certainly calls for disciplined and careful analysis and for some constructive efforts to meet the challenge of effective governance in the near future. The fear that we might unwittingly or inadvertently unleash a widespread and unrestrained, and highly destructive, conflict in the cyber arena, in particular, as an act of war remains a very real concern. Public discussions still often fail to distinguish, or even attempt to distinguish with sufficient care, among the many different kinds of cyber conflict and the manner in which extant law and current conceptions of morality would prove applicable to each. Proposing to do so was one of the chief positive achievements of the Tallinn deliberations, after which we are more careful to distinguish among

- what might be called cyber *vandalism* (a hacker breaking into, and lurking in defense information systems);

- acts of cyber*crime* (in which data are damaged or stolen, or services denied, for personal or corporate gain);
- cyber espionage (what might be accurately described as acts of cyber vandalism and cybercrime carried out by states or commercial corporations);
- cyber*terrorism* (in which all of the foregoing things, and also damage and destruction to physical infrastructure are inflicted by aggrieved nonstate agents to sow fear and confusion and to inflict widespread physical suffering upon random victims); and
- genuine acts of cyber *warfare*, in which the latter sorts of things (physical damage, causing death, destruction, and widespread physical suffering) are done deliberately, to specified adversaries, in pursuit of political objectives or conflict resolution by states, governments, and their military and intelligence forces.[13]

The general threat of cyberterrorism has been vastly overblown. Unlike irregular warfare and conventional acts of terrorism generally, genuine cyber *warfare* turns out to be very expensive and labor-intensive, and it therefore remains a highly state-centric enterprise. Terrorists can engage in vandalism and crime and have used the Internet to great advantage for the purposes of conventional propaganda and disinformation. But they cannot easily develop true cyber weapons or engage in acts of cyber warfare – nor have they yet been detected as doing so, or even trying to do so. To be blunt: neither my hypothetical 14-year-old hacker in your next-door neighbor's upstairs bedroom nor the two- or three-person ISIS cell plotting from a tiny third-floor flat in Hamburg is going to bring down the Glen Canyon and Hoover Dams. That fact offers occasion for modest hope, as we shall observe.

Justified Forms of Cyber Conflict

For the moment, I want to make a case that *there are acceptable forms of cyber conflict and cyber warfare* that can be justified from the standpoint of just war theory but that are either unaddressed or incompletely addressed in the Tallinn Manuals. Indeed, such cyber conflict (as Neil Rowe has allowed) may in some instances be preferable to conventional war and even to alternative forms of conflict resolution (such as economic sanctions), if properly conducted.[14] It should be possible for the international community on the basis of shared experience to distinguish between morally justified and unjustified forms of cyber conflict. I believe on balance, moreover, that when doing so we will be able to discern that those cyber strikes that have been conducted within the current constraints of law and morality (e.g., with respect to the prevailing principles of the law of armed conflict) have also, to date, proved more effective than other attacks (like the Iranian attempt in late 2019 to disrupt Israeli water purification systems) that potentially represent the commission of war crimes.

Consider again our paradigmatic cyberattacks of military significance. The first one entailed – indeed, relied almost exclusively on – the indiscriminate and disproportionate targeting of civilian infrastructure. Two of the initial paradigmatic attacks were presumably unleashed by the Russian Federation against nearby adversaries in Estonia (in April 2007) and once again in Georgia (in July and August 2008). The first instance, as we recall, was basically a distributed denial of service (DDOS), overwhelming and shutting down virtually all Internet-based services in a sophisticated country dominated by paperless government and heavily reliant upon Internet financial transactions.[15] A DDOS attack began around 20 July 2008 in Georgia, when botnets from all over the world began blasting Georgian computer services and networks with enormous amounts of useless data, much of which were eventually traced back to the Russian Business Network (RBN), an organized crime unit of Russian mafia. This was a prelude to conventional bombing and perhaps also intended as a prelude to full-scale cyber war (that, as it happened, was not carried out). The attribution of cyberattacks was, at that time, a formidable problem, and no official source in Russia ever acknowledged complicity in either case. What is significant, however, is that both strikes were acts of preemptive aggression, in that both were apparently responses to ordinary political actions by the eventual victim or target state that did not rise to the accepted level of *casus belli* in international law. Even more significantly, the Estonian strikes relied almost exclusively on targeting civilians and civilian infrastructure while the prelude attack in Georgia targeted primarily government offices and military defense systems, effectively shutting down coordination between the government and its military in Georgia. In neither case was extensive permanent or long-term damage done, nor injuries sustained, nor were lives directly lost as a result.

Even 15 or more years later, it remains difficult to gauge the effectiveness of the Estonian attacks, which certainly seemed to constitute some sort of retaliation for the government's decision to move a Russian war memorial statue from the center of the capital to a less prominent military cemetery, and to be further undertaken in support of the massive demonstrations and arrests of Russians living in Estonia that followed. The tensions gradually subsided. If, as is now suspected, these Estonian attacks were instead intended more as an initial proof of concept exercise, we might conclude that they were successful. Recent reconsiderations by Estonian cybersecurity experts of those early cyber operations in light of the Russian Federation's invasion of Ukraine, for example, suggest that these scripted parts of a well-developed strategic initiative to test the utility of cyberattacks on the defenses of former Warsaw Pact countries, as part of a long-term effort to return some, if not all beyond Ukraine itself, to Russian control.[16]

The Georgian attacks, by contrast, constituted more of a prelude or warm-up for conventional armed intervention: the first time, according to a subsequent NATO Cyber Defense study, that a conventional attack was deliberately preceded by a cyberattack,[17] which apparently served to prepare the way for Russia's subsequent conventional armed intervention in South Ossetia. Both attacks, from a political perspective, caused a great deal of resentment and inflamed hostilities, making a political solution to either conflict relatively unlikely. Both, of course, were nothing in comparison to what is transpiring in Ukraine, but it now seems highly likely that both were preparatory campaigns leading up to the Crimean annexation, the Donbas territorial disputes, and of course the 2022 invasion. Subsequent cyber operations (e.g., Petya ransomware in 2017), which seemed somewhat more random at the time, must now be absorbed within that narrative trajectory to include the 15 February 2022 DDoS attacks on Ukrainian government, defense, and major banking sites. In short, the Georgian cyberattacks, closely studied at the time, likely had as much or more to do with rehearsing for the coming Ukrainian military operations as they did with protecting Ossetian separatists in Georgia itself.

In light of the widespread and witheringly indiscriminate attack on civilians and civilian institutions, Estonia requested at the time that NATO recognize a violation of sovereignty, so as to trigger Article 5, the collective self-defense provision of the NATO treaty. Interestingly, that suggestion was rejected at the time on the grounds that "a cyber attack is not a clear military action."[18] In the second case, somewhat in contrast, the preparatory cyberattack on government offices and military installations assuredly aided the success of the conventional intervention and occupation. In neither of these known cases did the cyber strategy address, alter, or otherwise remedy or resolve the underlying political conflict. I have been inclined ever since to describe the indiscriminate and disproportionate attack on Estonia as an unjust cyberattack, in that it both lacked a sufficiently grave just cause (*casus belli*) and directly targeted civilians and civilian institutions indiscriminately and disproportionately in violation of the international law of armed conflict. By contrast, the cyberattack on Georgia might, at the time at least, be plausibly described as part of a legitimate political disagreement between two sovereign nations over control of territory deemed important to both. Such a claim would conventionally be taken to be a legitimate cause for the use of force when attempts at diplomatic solutions are unsuccessful. Moreover, the cyberattack was aimed primarily at disabling the opposing government's military capacities of command and control. No explicitly civilian infrastructure (nor civilians themselves) was deliberately targeted. This seemed at the time to constitute a justifiable use of cyber weapons in accordance with the constraints of LOAC as conventionally understood (although once again the Russian Federation's subsequent attacks on Ukrainian vital civilian infrastructure since the 2014 annexation of Crimea cast grave doubt on that benign analysis).

In Operation Orchard, Israel apparently likewise preceded its devastating F-15 air strikes against a secret Syrian nuclear facility near Dayr az-Zawr on 6 September 2007, with a full-scale cyberattack that managed to completely disable Syria's extensive Russian-made antiaircraft defense system, though once again the details are murky, and formal attribution has never been made or acknowledged. In this case, as in the Georgia case, the preemptive cyber strikes were directed entirely against military targets: radar and air defense systems, much as a conventional attack might have been, enabling Israeli fighters to penetrate deeply into Syrian airspace with little resistance. Unlike the conventional attacks that followed (in which several persons, allegedly including a number of North Koreans, were killed), however, the cyberattack attained the military objective of rendering defensive forces helpless, without widespread destruction of property or loss of life on either side.[19]

Especially because it was clearly a preemptive cyber (and conventional) attack, the extent of its justification depends heavily on the nature and imminence of the threat of harm (which was likely considerable) and the extent to which appropriate diplomatic means were first tried and exhausted. On the basis of the historical and political considerations at stake in otherwise permitting Syria and North Korea to engage in a clandestine violation of the international nuclear nonproliferation treaty, one might at the time have been inclined to judge that this focused attack on an adversary's illicit military installation was justified.

What might we conclude from this reconsideration of the original foregoing paradigmatic cases? In contrast to the more recent incidents we will shortly consider, the details of these by-now-classical cases are now reasonably well established in the public (nonclassified) record. Together, they provide an important set of evaluations that warrant review with respect to some of the core criteria of just war theory. Specifically, I want to invoke the key criteria of just cause and last resort with respect to the justification of war (*jus ad bellum*), together with proportionality and discrimination (or, in international law, the principle of distinction), as these latter two criteria are understood with respect to the conduct of hostilities and specific applications of force (*jus in bello*).

From the perspective of *jus ad bellum*, I would like to argue that the first of the two (presumed) Russian cyberattacks lacked a sufficient just cause and were not undertaken in any meaningful sense as a last resort. I believe we could verify and agree on that assessment even before these two attacks were absorbed in the now-emerging larger context of Russian strategic intentions for former Warsaw Pact member nations that fell out of their sway after 1989. In addition, from the perspective of the just conduct of hostilities (*jus in bello*), the first of the two Russian attacks was utterly indiscriminate and was likewise disproportionate in its threat of harm, at least, when compared either to the harm Russia or Russian citizens allegedly were suffering or to any legitimate military objective that might have otherwise been under consideration.

In light of the 2022 conventional invasion of Ukraine, we are obliged to recall that the Russian government has a long history of making too ready, indiscriminate, and disproportionate resort to force even when they have a putatively legitimate objective, whether in domestic or international situations (recall the October 2002 siege of a Moscow theater by Chechen rebels).[20] The Estonian attack seems to illustrate this tendency while the subsequent attack in Georgia could be said to have exercised some restraint. The same is true, by comparison, in the (presumed) Israeli preemptive military cyberattack on Syria, preceding its conventional strike against their nuclear facilities. A conventional strike had been continuously threatened in the event that Syria pursued development of a nuclear weapons program. There was arguably adequate justification leading up to the conventional attack and thus also justification for the preparatory cyberattack. Importantly, both the cyber and conventional military actions were undertaken only after reasonable diplomatic efforts (including embargoes of illegal shipments of materials from North Korea) had failed to halt the Syrian collaboration with North Korean agents. The targets of cyber strikes were entirely military, and the overall damage inflicted as a result was rather minimal and arguably proportional to the harm threatened, the wrong done, and the military objective in question.

If I am right, this suggests (in contrast to conclusions drawn by other observers) that not all cyber conflict escapes the analytical framework of classical or conventional just war theory, and vice versa, that consideration of just war doctrine may effectively guide the conduct of cyber war, even as it attempts to do for conventional and irregular warfare. In the latter case, one of the most controversial topics in this century has been the attempted resurrection and justification of preventive war, undertaken against an enemy who has as yet done no actual harm but represents a future threat of harm. Classical just war doctrine rejects the legitimacy of a cause for war that does not involve the actual (rather than merely threatened) infliction of harm through an act of aggression. And yet this has not seemed to many of us to address adequately, for example, the menace of rogue states or the dilemma of terrorists' ongoing *preparations* for attacks that have the aspects of an international criminal conspiracy not yet fully consummated.

The Legal and Moral Justification for Anticipatory Cyberattacks

As intriguing, widely cited, and closely studied as these paradigmatic cases have been,[21] three illustrations from more than a decade ago hardly suffice to illuminate either a recurring pattern or an evolution of customary behavior in a fluid environment such as cyber conflict. What happens, for example, when we move on to the U.S. Office of Personnel Management hack by the People's Liberation Army (2015), the North Korean attack on Sony Pictures, the Russian assault on the 2016 and 2020 American presidential elections, as well as to the discovery of SolarWinds, the theft of WannaCry, NotPetya, Cozy Bear, Holiday Bear, and other present or emergent advanced persistent threats in the cyber realm? Can we meaningfully discern any emergent trends or patterns of customary behavior in what otherwise seems a random and dismal chronological array of cyberattacks? Perhaps, even more importantly, *would it really matter*, and do any of the principal adversaries or stakeholders *even seem to care*?

In response, allow me to offer a sober, albeit purely personal and subjective summary assessment of the overall tenor of our PRIO project focus group discussions with cyber strategists and cyber operations experts during the past few years.[22] Personnel from Western European countries on the whole strike me as most concerned with legal compliance and moral rectitude in defining and carrying out what for them are primarily defensive cyber operations, attempting to shield their respective nations and the European Union generally from assaults stemming from advanced persistent threats. Representatives from the Five Eyes nations principally involved with cooperating with one another in sharing signal intelligence, establishing sound cybersecurity, and responding constantly to advanced persistent threats from adversaries like Russia and China, by contrast, tend to worry less about legal constraints and obstacles (like the European General Data Protection Regulation) than in upholding the core values of their respective nations and security services while protecting democratic regimes and vital commercial services (finance, energy, international trade) from disruption and damage. For these security services, the lines between what constitutes purely defensive and responsive cyber operations and offensive (or anticipatory) operations is less well defined while they rely for guidance less on the Tallinn Manuals than they do the very specific domestic legal constraints (such as the U.S. Patriot Act and presidential directives) defining and authorizing their sphere of operations. It perhaps goes without saying that the remaining principal state actors in the cyber domain – Russia, China, North Korea, and Iran, for example – are largely untroubled by such concerns (legal or moral, domestic or international).

In fairness, it may be noted that none of these participants or stakeholders in the cyber domain was invited to contribute to what I earlier described as the Tallinn process, and they vociferously objected afterwards that this entire arrangement simply mirrored the defects of international law generally as a one-sided concept invoking purely "Western" values and imposed as a kind of cultural hegemony upon the rest of the world. They justify their own unrestrained or unrestricted operations as an equitable response to this perceived imbalance of power, intended at least to level the playing field in the cyber domain. In practice, however, it has often been difficult to distinguish the resultant policy and operational activities of the cybersecurity forces of these nations from the activities of nonstate criminal organizations and individual actors. In fact, the Russian Federal Security Service (FSB) and foreign intelligence service (SVR) routinely make use of the work of known cybercriminals to carry out their own espionage and surveillance activities.[23]

The whole concept of emergent norms of responsible state behavior is focused precisely upon our ability to determine what constitutes responsible (as distinct from irresponsible) behavior. In these multiple subsequent cyberattacks and conflicts, however, one might cynically and callously conclude that European cybersecurity operators excessively wring their hands over what international law permits them to do, while the United States and its allies in the Five Eyes adopt a more tough-minded approach of act now and quibble later. The Russians, Chinese, North Koreans, and Iranians just don't care, and they do as they please, insofar as they can get away with it, limited at most by fear of detection and counterattack. Ukrainians, Malaysians, and others with fairly robust and sophisticated cyber capabilities can effectively ward off adversarial attacks with their own expertise but are otherwise left on their own to seek the best bargain they can get. That sounds familiar, and it does not sound promising regarding prospects for good governance in the future. Even worse, cybersecurity experts involved in strategic war gaming and simulated competition report that these perspectives on law and ethics invariably lead to the more unrestrained or unscrupulous competitors in these war games inevitably prevailing. In sum, they say, while the West worries about law and morality, the adversaries simply pick our pockets and eat our lunch. Or so conventional wisdom would have it.[24]

It might cheer us up to give one final nod to Operation Olympic Games, which after all constituted an anticipatory attack. Yet, recall that the New York Times in January of 2011 described Stuxnet, in particular, as "the most sophisticated cyber weapon ever deployed."[25] To this day, no nation or coalition has ever come forward to claim credit, or accept blame, for having engaged in what has gradually come to be identified as an act of preventive warfare.[26] Suspicion subsequently fell heavily upon those who stood to gain the most from the attack and perhaps on those who continue to smile the most broadly, but withhold comment, when the event is cited. The details are by now all too familiar to most readers, so let me simply summarize the key points of this act of what must be classified as anticipatory or preventive war.

The Stuxnet[27] virus was a cyber worm of unknown origin, apparently developed and released in a number of countries in 2009. By July 2010, it was known to have infected computers all over the world, seeming at first to pose an ominous and generalized threat to programmable logic controllers (PLCs), small computers that control everything from measuring filling for sandwich cookies to changing traffic lights, water flow valves on municipal systems . . . and the rate of spin of nuclear centrifuges. It gradually became apparent that nearly 60% of infected systems were located in Iran (although others were found in India, Pakistan, Indonesia, and Azerbaijan, as well as the United States and Europe), and so after some initial confusion, Stuxnet was assumed to be a cyber weapon targeted at Iran, which had subsequently failed in its primary purpose and run amok, spreading uncontrollably to unintended targets all over the world and thus demonstrating how indiscriminate and destructive cyber weapons were likely to be.[28] This was the assessment of Stuxnet offered, for example, in a footnote in Prof. Dipert's original pathbreaking essay on the ethics of cyber warfare at the time (Dipert 2010, 407, n. 3).[29]

What seemed a reasonable assessment at the time, however, turned out to be woefully inaccurate. Unlike most malware, Stuxnet did no discernable harm to infected computers and networks that did not meet specific configuration requirements. As one of the world's leading cyber forensic experts remarked at the time: "The attackers took great care to make sure that only their designated targets were hit. . . . It was a marksman's job."[30] While the worm apparently proved to be promiscuous, it had the additional feature of rendering itself inert if Siemens software was not found on infected computers. Importantly, its software contained safeguards to prevent each infected computer from spreading the worm to more than three others. Finally, all copies of the virus were apparently set to erase themselves on 24 June 2012 and apparently did so. No examples of this malware have been detected anywhere since that date.

Why Siemens software? The virus attacked and destroyed nuclear centrifuges manufactured by Siemens, overriding the proprietary software and overloading the centrifuges themselves until they self-destructed. It did so cleverly, in the manner of the Hollywood film *Ocean's Thirteen*, by running a second subroutine (known as a man in the middle) that disguised the damage in progress from operators and overseers until it was far too late to reverse the damage done. One line of code restricted this damage, however, only to an array or cascade of centrifuges of a specific size (to be precise: an array of exactly 984 centrifuges). Thus, unless one happened around the years 2010 to 2012 to be running a large array of exactly 984 Siemens centrifuges simultaneously, there was nothing whatsoever to fear from this worm, then or since.

This is a far cry from our subsequent experiences with malware like WannaCry and NotPetya! Stuxnet itself was an extremely sophisticated and highly discriminate weapon: estimates are that it must have been months, if not years, in development, with large teams of experts and access to highly restricted and classified information and equipment. This is not something a terrorist group or even likely a well-organized and funded criminal organization could have undertaken (and certainly not my much-invoked and maligned lone 14-year-old hacker!). The investment of time and resources and expertise were simply beyond any but a well-positioned state or coalition to effect. The damage was done exclusively to a cascade of centrifuges that had been illegally obtained on the black market and operated in an otherwise highly protected laboratory site at Natanz, in Iran, in explicit violation of the 1970 nuclear nonproliferation treaty.

The damage sustained within Iran to its clandestine and internationally denounced nuclear program was subsequently deemed substantial and thought to have put its nuclear weapons development program offtrack for several years. To be sure, scarcely a year later, that initial optimism had vanished when a report from the International Nuclear Regulatory Commission, released in November 2011, appeared to show the nuclear weapons program back on track and fully recovered from the cyber damage to its cascade of nuclear centrifuges. The Iranian nuclear weapons program remains a controversial threat over a decade later.

In keeping with our discussions of previous cyber conflicts: there was a good and justifiable reason at the time, reluctantly sanctioned in the international community, to undertake military action against Iran's nuclear weapons program. Famously, diplomatic efforts and other nonmilitary measures had been undertaken for years without success. The threat these illegal actions posed was serious, but it was then (and still is) *future* harm, threatened rather than as-yet inflicted, so this was clearly a *preventive* or anticipatory attack. The target was wholly military, and damage was entirely confined to the targets identified. There was no collateral damage of any meaningful or significant sort to lives or property: civilian personnel and infrastructure were apparently neither targeted nor affected. Most importantly, when compared against Operation Babylon, the conventional Israeli air raid against Iraq's nuclear program at Osirik on 7 June 1981, this cyber strike involved far less damage, harm, and risk of either for all concerned.[31]

Still there were concerns raised at the time that the promiscuous spread of the worm had eventually made this destructive weapon available to users all over the world, who might tweak it and release other versions.[32] This concern about Stuxnet as an open source weapon available for downloading by anyone, however, demonstrated a fundamental misunderstanding of the nature of individual cyber weapons. They are not at all like nuclear warheads or RPGs, simply obtainable and reusable by anyone. Rather, they are by and large one-off weapons: once they are used, their structure and function becomes readily apparent to security experts, antivirus and security protections are quickly developed, and the original weapon is seldom reused or usefully replicable. Subsequent claims of phantom sightings of Stuxnet-like viruses deployed by rogue hackers for malevolent purposes turned out either to be entirely false or else misidentifications of other Olympic Games viruses, like Flame and Duqu. There was not then, nor has there ever been since, an actual, verifiable reengineered clone of Stuxnet used for malevolent ends.

The Case for Preventive Cyber Self-Defense

In his original article "The Ethics of Information Warfare" (1999), John Arquilla outlined what I take to be an argument for permissible preventive cyberattack. Though obviously not as familiar with the broader range of classical just war doctrine as Dipert and subsequent just war and ethics experts, Arquilla nonetheless homed in on precisely the most relevant features of morally justified conflict: a grave and morally sufficient reason or just cause for war, a record of prior good faith attempts to resolve the conflict short of armed attack that made such war a necessary last resort, and, in the targeting and tactics, a focus solely on threatening and strategic military targets, with the likely prospect of confining harm almost entirely to those targets, and entailing no risk to, let alone deliberate targeting of, civilian personnel or infrastructure. Under such severe constraints, Arquilla concluded at that time, a cyber strike might be morally justified (1999, 392–393, n. 204).

I believe it is past time to acknowledge that this earlier conclusion was entirely correct. Tallinn manual casuistry notwithstanding, there are occasions in which such an offensive cyberattack, while strictly illegal, might be morally justified, even though it might constitute a preventive attack.[33] Stuxnet itself conformed almost perfectly to Arquilla's original constraints – so closely, in fact, as to raise suspicion that its perpetrators had read his article and followed his own outline of the relevant moral constraints virtually to the letter. I have myself been inclined to agree that the circumstances at the time warranted such a preemptive attack, and that, as designed and carried out, Stuxnet was an effective and morally justified military cyberattack. Just as importantly, that incident demonstrated that the use of cyber weapons in a situation we now classify as *jus ad vim* can be an effective alternative to conventional war, when less drastic forms of conflict resolution have been tried in good faith and have failed. And, contrary to the fears of Dipert and others at the time, such weapons and tactics can be designed to be effective, to discriminate, and to inflict proportionate damage on their targets – far more so than conventional attacks.[34]

Finally, I mentioned in passing earlier that this sophisticated weapon, and effective cyber weapons and strategy generally, were still expensive, skilled, labor-intensive, and therefore state-centric enterprises. It remains the case at present that no terrorist could, or has, attempted anything like this. An effective weapon of cyber warfare like Stuxnet, at least at present, simply outstrips the intellectual, organizational, and personnel capacities of even the most well-funded and well-organized terrorist organization, as well as those of even the most sophisticated international criminal enterprises. If one is going to bring down hydroelectric generators, nuclear centrifuges, and air traffic control systems, then one needs direct access to such devices or systems and the software that operates them, as well as an intimate knowledge of their operations. That irksome 14-year-old neighbor, in particular, who skipped (and subsequently flunked) physics and engineering classes to concentrate on his social networking skills lacks the requisite knowledge, as well as the access to the relevant hardware. If he succeeds in hacking into a defense department computer, he won't have a clue of what to do there, other than the cyber equivalent of spray-painting artistic graffiti on subway cars. Centrifuges and hydroelectric generators, for their part, do not fit neatly into terrorist apartments in Hamburg, or (sadly) even into the most well-equipped public high school laboratory.[35]

That is moderately encouraging news. In addition, I believe our experience of states as entities with political interests, unlike the usual case of terrorists and non-state actors, makes these activities amenable to good governance. In the Stuxnet case, we have an example of what good governance could license. In the other instances, we have examples of less justifiable actions (such as the indiscriminate and wanton targeting of civilians and civilian infrastructure) that might reasonably be renounced by all sides without any discernable loss of political advantage.

Thus, even if the prospects for genuine peace in the cyber domain remain dim for the present, I do believe we can now discern some principles of good practice with surprising normative force emerging through the foregoing examples of recent cyber operations, both good and bad, sufficient to move ahead with such discussions and the formulations of relevant treaties and protocols, and to put to rest some of the more extreme, hysterical, and unfounded fears about cyber conflict. Outlawing indiscriminate destruction and deliberate civilian targeting would constitute a good beginning, and the foregoing cases show that such measures would not rob states of their abilities to conduct political conflict effectively within the accepted bounds of law and morality.

Notes

1 These comments are derived from a presentation I made at a UNESCO-sponsored conference on cyber conflict organized and hosted by Luciano Floridi and Mariarosario Taddeo at the University of Hertfordshire (U.K.) in 2011. Similar cases for the moral permissibility of preventive or preemptive cyber conflict have been offered by James Pattison, "From Defence to Offence: The Ethics of Private Cybersecurity," *European Journal of International Security* 5 (29) (2020): 233, https://doi.org/10.1017/eis.2020.6.

2 Former U.S. National Security Adviser Richard A. Clarke dramatically outlines the terrifying contours of an imagined full-scale cyberattack on the United States at the conclusion of chapter 2 of *Cyber War: The Next Threat to National Security and What to Do About It*, coauthored with Robert K. Knake (New York: HarperCollins, 2010): 64–68. This popular account of cyber vulnerability engages in all of the equivocation, confusing hyperbole, and threat inflation that I attempt to describe later.

3 Council of Europe, "Convention on Cybercrime" (Budapest, 23 November 2001), http://conventions.coe.int/Treaty/EN/Treaties/html/185.htm.

4 Randall R. Dipert, "The Ethics of Cyberwarfare," *Journal of Military Ethics* 9 (4) (December 2010): 384–410. I wish to pay special tribute to his pioneering contributions to this issue and mourn his untimely and tragic loss.

5 Stephen G. Bradbury, "The Developing Legal Framework for Defensive and Offensive Cyber Operations," *Harvard National Security Journal* 2 (2), https://harvardnsj.org/wp-content/uploads/sites/13/2011/02/Vol-2-Bradbury.pdf. But see also: G. Darnton, "Information Warfare and the Laws of War," in *Cyberwar, Netwar, and the Revolution in Military Affairs*, eds. E. Halpin, P. Trovorrow, D. Webb, and S. Wright (Houndsmill, UK: Palgrave Macmillan, 2006): 139–156; Duncan B. Hollis, "New Tools, New Rules: International Law and Information Operations," in *The Message of War: Information, Influence and Perception in Armed Conflict*, eds. G. David and T. McKeldin, Temple University Legal Studies Research Paper No. 2007–15 (2008); Scott J. Shackelford, "From Nuclear War to Net War: Analogizing Cyber Attacks in International Law," *Berkeley Journal of International Law* 27 (1) (2008): 191–251; Matthew C. Waxman, "Cyber-Attacks and the Use of Force," *Yale Journal of International Law* 36 (2011): 421–459. The most detailed examination of this topic was undertaken by a working group at the NATO Cyber Security Defence Center Excellence (CCDCOE) in Tallinn, Estonia, published in two volumes edited by Michael Schmitt, the first dealing with international law applicable to cyber warfare (*The Tallinn Manual* [Cambridge: Cambridge University Press, 2013]), and *Tallinn 2.0*, adding a legal analysis of the more common cyber incidents that states encounter on a day-to-day basis and that fall below the thresholds of the use of force or armed conflict (Cambridge University Press, 2017).

6 For example, Martin C. Libicki, *Cyberdeterrence and Cyberwar* (Santa Monica, CA: Rand Corporation, 2009); *Conquest in Cyberspace: National Security and Information Warfare* (New York: Cambridge University Press, 2007); Herbert S. Lin, et al., *Technology, Policy, Law, and Ethics Regarding U.S. Acquisition and Use of Cyberattack Capabilities* (Washington, DC: National Research Council/American Academy of Sciences, 2009).

7 Neil C. Rowe, "War Crimes from Cyberweapons," *Journal of Information Warfare* 6 (3) (2007): 15–25; "Ethics of Cyber War Attacks," in *Cyber Warfare and Cyber Terrorism*, eds. Lech J. Janczewski and Andrew M. Colarik (Hershey, PA: Information Science Reference, 2008): 105–111; "The Ethics of Cyberweapons in Warfare," *Journal of Techoethics* 1 (1) (2010): 20–31. "Challenges of Civilian Distinction in Cyberwarfare," in *Ethics and Policies for Cyber Operations* (New York: Springer, 2017).

8 See his interview for PBS "Frontline" (4 March 2003), www.pbs.org/wgbh/pages/frontline/shows/cyberwar/interviews/arquilla.html [accessed 6 May 2022].

9 John Arquilla, "Ethics and Information Warfare," in *The Changing Role of Information in Warfare*, eds. Z. Khalilzad, J. White, and A. Marsall (Santa Monica, CA: RAND Corporation, 1999): 379–401. More recently, see "Conflict, Security, and Computer Ethics," in *The Cambridge Handbook of Information and Computer Ethics*, ed. Luciano Floridi (New York: Cambridge University Press, 2010): 133–149.

10 See, for example, the treatments of this topic at the time and since by highly respected journalists: James Fallows, "Cyber Warriors," *The Atlantic Monthly* (March 2010): 58–63; Seymour M. Hersh, "The Online Threat," *The New Yorker* (1 November 2010), both of whom echo the concerns of Clarke and Knake, cited earlier (n.1). A very thoroughly documented and persuasively written article by Thomas Rid of Kings College (London) subsequently appeared in the *Journal of Strategic Studies* (5 October 2011), forcefully arguing similar points about conceptual equivocation and threat inflation in the discussion of cyber war: see "Cyber War Will Not Take Place," *Journal of Strategic Studies*, https://doi.org/10.1080/01402390.2011.608939.

Rid went even further than I, claiming then and since that cyber "warfare," properly speaking, has never occurred and likely will not occur, and that what is being discussed (and "hyped") under that heading are actually Internet versions of sabotage, espionage, and subversion.

11 Michael N. Schmitt, ed., *Tallinn Manual 1.0-On the International Law Applicable to Cyber Warfare* (Cambridge University Press, 2013); M.N. Schmitt and L. Vihul, eds., *Tallinn Manual 2.0 – On the International Law Applicable to Cyber Operations,* 2nd ed. (Cambridge: Cambridge University Press, 2017).

12 On the failures of the first Tallinn Manual, see Lucas 2017, 76–78. In general, the manual's contributors were found to be narrowly unrepresentative, and the first manual itself "constituting a series of answers to questions that no one was asking." One legal staff member at the ICRC in Geneva in a 2015 conference described the first Tallinn manual as a "massive failure." Subsequently, when asking cyber operations specialists in the United States (e.g., the NSA) and elsewhere about the manual(s), the general comment was "We never use it."

13 Thomas Rid (n. 10) defines cyber war as a "potentially lethal, instrumental, and political act of force conducted through malicious code." What requires further explication is the nature of harm that can be suffered in a cyberattack, and whether forms of such harm that are nonlethal are still of sufficient gravity to warrant classification as acts of war (given that acts of sabotage are currently understood to constitute acts of war).

14 See Neil C. Rowe, "The Ethics of Cyberweapons in Warfare," *Journal of Techoethics* 1 (1) (2010): 20–31; "Towards Reversible Cyberattacks," in *Proceedings of the 9th European Conference on Information Warfare and Security* (Thessaloniki, Greece, July 2010), http://faculty.nps.edu/ncrowe/rowe_eciw10.htm [accessed 6 May 2022].

15 An excellent summary of the circumstances leading up to the attack on Estonia and its consequences can be found in Episode 2, Season 1 of the PBS program "Wired Science" from shortly after the incident in 2007, titled, "Technology: World War 2.0" at http://xfinitytv.comcast.net/tv/Wired-Science/95583/770190466/Technology%3A-World-War-2.0/videos?skipTo=189&cmpid=FCST_hero_tv. See also Charles Clover, "Kremlin-Backed Group behind Estonia Cyber Blitz," *Financial Times* (London, 11 March 2009), and Tim Espiner, "Estonia's Cyberattacks: Lessons Learned a Year On," *ZD NET UK* (1 May 2008). For an analysis of the attack against Georgia, see E. Tikk, K. Kaska, K. Rünnimeri, M. Kert, A-M. Talihärm, and L. Vihui, "Cyber Attacks Against Georgia: Legal Lessons Identified" (Tallinn, EE: NATO Cooperative Cyber Defence Centre of Excellence, 2008); and the United States Cyber Consequences Unit (US-CCU), "Overview by the US-CCU of the Cyber Campaign against Georgia in August of 2008," US-CCU Special Report (August 2009), www.usccu.org.

16 Gert Auväärt, Deputy Director of Estonia's Information System Authority (RIA), has observed that "Estonia's cyber threat level has risen following Russia's invasion of Ukraine and the cyber warfare efforts accompanying it." See: "Is the World Ready for a Cyberwar?" *e-Estonia* (Tallinn, 13 April 2022), https://e-estonia.com/is-the-world-ready-for-a-cyberwar/ [accessed 6 May 2022].

17 E. Tikk, K. Kaska, K. Rünnimeri, M. Kert, A-M. Talihärm, and L. Vihui, "Cyber Attacks Against Georgia: Legal Lessons Identified" (Tallinn, EE: NATO Cooperative Cyber Defence Centre of Excellence, 2008): 5. The apparent Israeli attack on a Syrian nuclear facility in the fall of 2007, however, predates this event and likewise constituted the coordination of cyber and conventional weapons.

18 Major Arie J. Schaap, "Cyber Warfare Operations: Development and Use under International Law," *Air Force Law Review* 64 (121) (2009): 144–145. Quoted in Steven G. Bradbury, "The Developing Legal Framework for Defensive and Offensive Cyber Operations," *Harvard National Security Journal* 2 (2) (2012).

19 Uzi Mahnaimi and Sarah Baster, "Israelis Seized Nuclear Material in Syrian Raid," *The Sunday Times* (London, 23 September 2007), www.timesonline.co.uk/tol/news/world/middle_east/article2512380.ece [accessed 15 July 2011]. For a summary of the cyber war elements of this strike, see David A. Fulghum, Robert Wall, and Amy Butler, "Israel Shows Electronic Prowess," *Aviation Week* (25 November 2007), www.aviationweek.com/aw/generic/story.jsp?id=news/aw112607p2.xml&headline=Israel%20Shows%20Electronic%20Prowess&channel=defense [accessed 15 July 2011]. See also "Cyberwarfare

Technology: Is Too Much Secrecy Bad?" *Airforce-technology.com* (9 April 2008), www.airforce-technology.com/features/feature1708/ [accessed 15 July 2011].

20 23 October 2002, on which the Russian security forces' "disastrous response" resulted in the death of all 39 Chechen attackers and 129 of the estimated 800 hostages taken. See Rebecca Leung, "Terror in Moscow," *CBS News "60 Minutes"* (11 February 2009), www.cbsnews.com/stories/2003/10/24/60minutes/main579840.shtml [accessed 15 July 2011].

21 Important contemporary discussions of cyber warfare ethics continue to rely heavily on these cases. See the numerous discussions of them by several contributors to Michael Skerker and David Wetham, eds., *Cyber Warfare Ethics* (Havant, UK: Howgate Publishers, 2021).

22 These remarks also reflect the summary findings that Professor David Whetham (Kings College, London) and I provided at the conclusion of a symposium of internationally distinguished and truly remarkable subject matter experts in cybersecurity and conflict in *Cyber Warfare Ethics,* eds. Michael Skerker and David Whetham (Havant, UK: Howgate Publishing, 2021).

23 See Michael Schwirtz and Joseph Goldstein, "Russian Espionage Piggybacks on a Cyber Criminal's Hacking," *New York Times* (12 March 2017), www.nytimes.com/2017/03/12/world/europe/russia-hacker-evgeniy-bogachev.html [accessed 9 May 2022]. The Five Eyes have issued a joint cybersecurity advisory warning of further such collaborative criminal and espionage activities by the FSB and SVR in retaliation against nations providing support to Ukraine during the 2022 Russian invasion. See Alert (AA22–110A): "Russian State-Sponsored and Criminal Cyber Threats to Critical Infrastructure," Cyber Security and Infrastructure Security Agency (9 May 2022), www.cisa.gov/uscert/ncas/alerts/aa22-110a [accessed 9 May 2022]. Most recently, these include DragonFly and/or BerserkBear, which reportedly

> targeted entities in Western Europe and North America including state, local, tribal, and territorial (SLTT) organizations, as well as Energy, Transportation Systems, and Defense Industrial Base (DIB) Sector organizations . . . [as well as] Water and Wastewater Systems Sector and other critical infrastructure facilities.

24 This attitude concerning impediments posed by ethical concerns, alongside technical incompetence, appears to have been one of the main factors in the resignation of a top Pentagon official working on artificial intelligence and cybersecurity in September, 2021. See www.reddit.com/r/sysadmin/comments/q613ah/a_pentagon_official_said_he_resigned_because_us/ [accessed 9 May 2022].

25 William J. Borad, John Markoff, and David E. Sanger, "Israeli Test on Worm Called Crucial in Iran Nuclear Delay," *New York Times* (15 January 2011), www.nytimes.com/2011/01/16/world/middleeast/16stuxnet.html?_r=1.

26 Michael J. Gross described this as "A Declaration of Cyber-War," *Vanity Fair,* www.vanityfair.com/culture/features/2011/04/stuxnet-201104 [accessed 3 March 2011]. For an equally thorough, but more recent, account of the entire Stuxnet affair, see also Kim Zetter, "How Digital Detectives Deciphered Stuxnet, the Most Menacing Malware in History," *Wired Magazine* (11 July 2011), www.wired.com/threatlevel/2011/07/how-digital-detectives-deciphered-stuxnet/all/1 [accessed 15 July 2011].

27 This nickname for the worm was coined by Microsoft security experts, an amalgam of two files found in the virus's code.

28 A study of the spread of Stuxnet was undertaken by a number of international computer security firms, including Symantec Corporation. Their report, "W32.Stuxnet Dosssier," compiled by noted computer security experts Nicholas Falliere, Liam O Murchu, and Eric Chien, and released in February 2011, showed that the main countries affected during the early days of the infection were Iran, Indonesia, and India: www.symantec.com/content/en/us/enterprise/media/security_response/whitepapers/w32_stuxnet_dossier.pdf.

Country	Infected Computers
Iran	58.85%
Indonesia	18.22%
India	8.31%
Azerbaijan	2.57%
United States	1.56%
Pakistan	1.28%
Others	9.2%

29 Computer expert Neil Rowe likewise offered this summary assessment of Stuxnet, that it had "run amok," and so proved both indiscriminate and disproportionate, in violation of the principles of just war and international humanitarian law: Neil C. Rowe, "War Crimes from Cyberweapons," *Journal of Information Warfare* 6 (3) (2007).

30 Comment of Ralph Langner, a computer security expert in Hamburg, Germany, quoted in *the New York Times* article cited earlier: *New York Times* (15 January 2011), www.nytimes.com/2011/01/16/world/middleeast/16stuxnet.html?_r=1.

31 See Peter Lee's similar analysis in the framework of justified preventive cyber war in "Ethics of Military Cyber Surveillance," *Cyber Warfare Ethics*, eds. Michael Skerker and David Wetham (Havant, UK: Howgate Publishers, Ltd., 2022): 110–128.

32 This concern is voiced explicitly in the online infographic documentary, "Stuxnet: Anatomy of a Computer Virus" by Patrick Clair (2011), http://vimeo.com/25118844. See also Ralph Langner's cybersecurity blog: "What Stuxnet Is All about," *The Last Line of Cyber Defense* (10 January 2011); "A Declaration of Bankruptcy for US Critical Infrastructure Protection," *The Last Line of Cyber Defense* (3 June 2011).

33 Here I concur from the standpoint of military cybersecurity with the observations of James Pattison regarding inclusion of the private sector in establishing a framework for preventive cyber self-defense. See James Pattison, "From Defence to Offence: The Ethics of Private Cybersecurity," *European Journal of International Security* 5 (2) (2020): 233–254.

34 *Jus ad vim* is a category of use of force that stops short of full-scale war but aims to compel an adversary to accede to the attacker's demand. See Michael Gross, "*Jus ad vim*: Sub-threshold Cyber Warfare," in *Cyber Warfare Ethics*, eds. Skerker and Wetham (Havant, UK: Howgate Publishers Ltd., 2022): 27–43. The term was coined by Michael Walzer in *Just and Unjust Wars* (New York: Basic Books, 1977): xv–xvi. See also Brandt S. Ford, "*Jus ad vim* and the Just Use of Lethal Force-Short-of-War," in *Routledge Handbook of Ethics and War*, eds. Fritz Allhoff, Nicholas Evans, and Adam Henschke (Oxford: Routledge, 2013).

35 N.B.: The "air traffic control scenario," in which one or more terrorists or nations identified as APTs "causes aircraft to collide or fall from the sky" is a more plausible and ominous case from the standpoint of both terrorism and even "vandalism," but it would at minimum require the leadership or assistance of a disaffected air traffic controller with years of experience and fairly robust security clearances.

References

Arquilla, John. "Ethics and Information Warfare," in *The Changing Role of Information in Warfare*, eds. Z. Khalilzad, J. White, and A. Marsall (Santa Monica, CA: RAND Corporation, 1999): 379–401.

Arquilla, John. Interview for PBS "Frontline" (4 March 2003), www.pbs.org/wgbh/pages/frontline/shows/cyberwar/interviews/arquilla.html [accessed 6 May 2022].

Arquilla, John. "Conflict, Security, and Computer Ethics," in *The Cambridge Handbook of Information and Computer Ethics*, ed. Luciano Floridi (New York: Cambridge University Press, 2010): 133–149.

Auväärt, Gert. "Is the World Ready for a Cyberwar?" *e-Estonia* (Tallinn, 13 April 2022), https://e-estonia.com/is-the-world-ready-for-a-cyberwar/ [accessed 6 May 2022]

Borad, William J.; Markoff, John; Sanger, David E. "Israeli Test on Worm Called Crucial in Iran Nuclear Delay," *New York Times* (15 January 2011), www.nytimes.com/2011/01/16/world/middleeast/16stuxnet.html?_r=1.

Bradbury, Stephen G. "The Developing Legal Framework for Defensive and Offensive Cyber Operations," *Harvard National Security Journal* 2 (2), https://harvardnsj.org/wp-content/uploads/sites/13/2011/02/Vol-2-Bradbury.pdf.

Clair, Patrick. "Stuxnet: Anatomy of a Computer Virus" (2011), http://vimeo.com/25118844.

Clarke, Richard A; Knake, Robert K. *Cyber War: The Next Threat to National Security and What to Do About It* (New York: HarperCollins, 2010): 64–68.

Clover, Charles. "Kremlin-backed Group behind Estonia Cyber Blitz," *Financial Times* (London, 11 March 2009).

CMS Admin. "Cyberwarfare Technology: Is too Much Secrecy Bad?" *Airforce-technology.com* (9 April 2008), www.airforce-technology.com/features/feature1708/ [accessed 15 July 2011].

Council of Europe, "Convention on Cybercrime" (Budapest, 23 November 2001), http://conventions.coe.int/Treaty/EN/Treaties/html/185.htm.

Cyber Security and Infrastructure Security Agency. Alert (AA22–110A). "Russian State-Sponsored and Criminal Cyber Threats to Critical Infrastructure" (9 May 2022), www.cisa.gov/uscert/ncas/alerts/aa22-110a [accessed 9 May 2022].

Darnton, G. "Information Warfare and the Laws of War," in *Cyberwar, Netwar, and the Revolution in Military Affairs*, eds. E. Halpin, P. Trovorrow, D. Webb, and S. Wright (Houndsmill, UK: Palgrave Macmillan, 2006): 139–156.

Dipert, Randall R. "The Ethics of Cyberwarfare," *Journal of Military Ethics* 9 (4) (December 2010): 384–410.

Espiner, Tim. "Estonia's Cyberattacks: Lessons Learned a Year On," *ZD NET UK* (1 May 2008).

Falliere, Nicholas; Murchu, Liam O.; Chien, Eric; Symantec Corporation. "W32.Stuxnet Dosssier" (February 2011), www.symantec.com/content/en/us/enterprise/media/security_response/whitepapers/w32_stuxnet_dossier.pdf.

Fallows, James. "Cyber Warriors," *The Atlantic Monthly* (March 2010): 58–63.

Ford, Brandt S. "Jus ad vim and the Just Use of Lethal Force-Short-of-War," in *Routledge Handbook of Ethics and War*, ed. Fritz Allhoff, Nicholas Evans, and Adam Henschke (Oxford: Routledge, 2013).

Fulghum, David A.; Wall, Robert; Butler, Amy. "Israel Shows Electronic Prowess," *Aviation Week* (25 November 2007), www.aviationweek.com/aw/generic/story.jsp?id=news/aw112607p2.xml&headline=Israel%20Shows%20Electronic%20Prowess&channel=defense [accessed 15 July 2011].

Gross, Michael J. "A Declaration of Cyber-War," *Vanity Fair* (2 March 2011), www.vanityfair.com/news/2011/03/stuxnet-201104.

Gross, Michael. "*Jus ad vim*: Sub-threshold Cyber Warfare," in *Cyber Warfare Ethics*, eds. Michael Skerker and David Wetham (Havant, UK: Howgate Publishers Ltd., 2022): 27–43.

Hersh, Seymour M. "The Online Threat," *The New Yorker* (1 November 2010).

Hollis, Duncan B. "New Tools, New Rules: International Law and Information Operations," in *The Message of War: Information, Influence and Perception in Armed Conflict*, eds. G. David and T. McKeldin. Temple University Legal Studies Research Paper No. 2007–15 (2008).

Langner, Ralph. "What Stuxnet Is All About," *The Last Line of Cyber Defense* (10 January 2011)
Langner, Ralph. "A Declaration of Bankruptcy for US Critical Infrastructure Protection," *The Last Line of Cyber Defense* (3 June 2011).
Lee, Peter. "Ethics of Military Cyber Surveillance," in *Cyber Warfare Ethics*, eds. Michael Skerker and David Wetham (Havant, UK: Howgate Publishers, 2022): 110–128.
Leung, Rebecca. "Terror in Moscow," *CBS News "60 Minutes"* (11 February 2009), www.cbsnews.com/stories/2003/10/24/60minutes/main579840.shtml [accessed 15 July 2011].
Libicki, Martin C. *Conquest in Cyberspace: National Security and Information Warfare* (New York: Cambridge University Press, 2007).
Libicki, Martin C. *Cyberdeterrence and Cyberwar* (Santa Monica, CA: Rand Corporation, 2009).
Lin, Herbert S., et al. *Technology, Policy, Law, and Ethics Regarding U.S. Acquisition and Use of Cyberattack Capabilities* (Washington, DC: National Research Council/American Academy of Sciences, 2009).
Lucas, George R., Jr. *Ethics and Cyber Warfare* (Oxford: Oxford University Press, 2017).
Mahnaimi, Uzi; Sarah Baster, Sarah. "Israelis Seized Nuclear Material in Syrian Raid," *The Sunday Times* (London, 23 September 2007), www.timesonline.co.uk/tol/news/world/middle_east/article2512380.ece [accessed 15 July 2011].
Owens, William A.; Dam, Kenneth W. Dam; Lin, Herbert S., eds. *Technology, Policy, Law, and Ethics Regarding U.S. Acquisition and Use of Cyberattack Capabilities* (Washington, DC: National Research Council/American Academy of Sciences, 2009).
Pattison, James. "From Defence to Offence: The Ethics of Private Cybersecurity," *European Journal of International Security* 5 (2) (2020): 233–254, https://doi.org/10.1017/eis.2020.6.
Public Broadcasting System. "Technology: World War 2.0," *Wired Science*, season 1, episode 2, http://xfinitytv.comcast.net/tv/Wired-Science/95583/770190466/Technology%3A-World-War-2.0/videos?skipTo=189&cmpid=FCST_hero_tv.
Rid, Thomas. "Cyber War Will Not Take Place," *Journal of Strategic Studies*, https://doi.org/10.1080/01402390.2011.608939.
Rowe, Neil C. "War Crimes from Cyberweapons," *Journal of Information Warfare* 6 (3) (2007): 15–25.
Rowe, Neil C. "Ethics of Cyberwar Attacks," in *Cyber Warfare and Cyber Terrorism*, eds. Lech J. Janczewski and Andrew M. Colarik (Hershey, PA: Information Science Reference, 2008): 105–111.
Rowe, Neil C. "The Ethics of Cyberweapons in Warfare," *Journal of Techoethics* 1 (1) (2010): 20–31.
Rowe, Neil C. "Towards Reversible Cyberattacks," in *Proceedings of the 9th European Conference on Information Warfare and Security* (Thessaloniki, Greece, July 2010), http://faculty.nps.edu/ncrowe/rowe_eciw10.htm [accessed 6 May 2022].
Rowe, Neil C. "Challenges of Civilian Distinction in Cyberwarfare," in *Ethics and Policies for Cyber Operations* (New York: Springer, 2017).
Schaap, Arie J. "Cyber Warfare Operations: Development and Use Under International Law," *Air Force Law Review* 64 (121) (2009): 144–145.
Schmitt, M.N., ed. *Tallinn Manual 1.0-On the International Law Applicable to Cyber Warfare* (Cambridge: Cambridge University Press, 2013).
Schmitt, M.N.; Vihul, L., eds. *Tallinn Manual 2.0 – On the International Law Applicable to Cyber Operations*. 2nd ed. (Cambridge: Cambridge University Press, 2017).
Schwirtz, Michael; Goldstein, Joseph. "Russian Espionage Piggybacks on a Cyber Criminal's Hacking," *New York Times* (12 March 2017), www.nytimes.com/2017/03/12/world/europe/russia-hacker-evgeniy-bogachev.html [accessed 9 May 2022].

Shackelford, Scott J. "From Nuclear War to Net War: Analogizing Cyber Attacks in International Law," *Berkeley Journal of International Law* 27 (1) (2008): 191–251.

Skerker, Michael; Wetham, David, eds. *Cyber Warfare Ethics* (Havant, UK: Howgate Publishers Ltd., 2021).

Tikk, E. Kaska, K.; Rünnimeri, K.; Kert, M.; Talihärm, A-M.; Vihui, L. "Cyber Attacks Against Georgia: Legal Lessons Identified" (Tallinn, EE: NATO Cooperative Cyber Defence Centre of Excellence, 2008).

u/heebro. [Nicholas Chaillan Says U.S. Cybersecurity Is Inferior to China's.], www.reddit.com/r/sysadmin/comments/q613ah/a_pentagon_official_said_he_resigned_because_us/ [accessed 9 May 2022].

United States Cyber Consequences Unit (US-CCU). "Overview by the US-CCU of the Cyber Campaign against Georgia in August of 2008," US-CCU Special Report (August 2009), www.usccu.org.

Walzer, Michael. *Just and Unjust Wars* (New York: Basic Books, 1977).

Waxman, Matthew C. "Cyber-Attacks and the Use of Force," *Yale Journal of International Law* 36 (2011): 421–459.

Zetter, Kim. "How Digital Detectives Deciphered Stuxnet, the Most Menacing Malware in History," *Wired Magazine* (11 July 2011), www.wired.com/threatlevel/2011/07/how-digital-detectives-deciphered-stuxnet/all/1 [accessed 15 July 2011].

10

LAW AND ETHICS FOR DEFENSE INDUSTRIES AND ENGINEERS

Concatenated Technologies

In late May, our small car wound along a two-lane highway climbing into the pristine evergreen-covered highlands north of Oslo, toward the small village of Raufoss. Two colleagues from the Peace Research Institute in Oslo, Henrik and Greg, had invited me to join them on a site visit to Nammo [short for "Nordic Ammunition Company"], a large Norwegian/Finnish aerospace and weapons manufacturer engaged in supplying armaments, rocket propulsion systems, and ordnance for the U.S. Department of Defense and numerous other allied military services around the world.[1] Nammo, for example, manufactures all the ordnance (guns, ammunition, and rocket engines for Sidewinder missiles) for the F-35 fighter jet. Almost alone among its peers and competitors, this production facility has its own enormous weapons proving ground right in its backyard, so to speak, enabling the company to develop and test and re-design and re-test in rapid sequence to deliver innovative weapons systems in a very short time. The local villagers, familiar with the important role this company has played in European defense for over a century, don't seem to mind the occasional noise.

The CEO of the company had expressed profound legal and moral concerns regarding the role of the company in the proposed development of new weapons systems incorporating artificial intelligence that he hoped we would help him and his leading engineers to address. Their general unease was similar to that encountered by U.S. defense policy expert, Paul Scharre, during his own service in the Pentagon (Scharre 2018). What led him (Scharre later reported) to undertake a leading role in formulating DoD Directive 3000.09 was that policymakers and weapons experts were constantly asking him, "can we do this?"[2] Their persistent questions were not in the slightest directed toward technological feasibility, but almost always constituted requests for legal and moral guidance: "*Can* we do this

DOI: 10.4324/9781003273912-11

[i.e., are we *legally permitted* to undertake this new project]?" And "*can* we do this" [meaning, is it *ethical* for us to undertake this new project]?"

The Nammo CEO and senior engineers invited our PRIO team to visit because they had basically the same sorts of questions on their side of the pond. This was interesting (and we were happy to help) inasmuch as engineers and CEOs of major defense contractors aren't usually thought to harbor such reservations. "Can we do it?" is always supposed to be a question of technological capability. If the answer is, "yes, we can!" then the assumption is that this is "our business," and if "we" don't design it and build it (whatever "it" may be) then someone else will (perhaps engineers working for the enemy or adversary).

From Nammo's perspective, however, the problems were less with specific weapons or types of technology, but with the potential for *combining* several different components into brand-new systems, with considerably enhanced destructive capabilities. The CEO referred to this as "*concatenation*," the stringing of different things together, as is frequently done in chemical reactions – sometimes with unique or unanticipated results. One of Nammo's featured systems, for example, is the M72 shoulder-fired anti-tank weapon, a rival of the U.S.-built "Javelin" missile system. In the search for effective and available weapons for NATO to provide to Ukraine, for example, their M72 would potentially play an important new role.

Most readers of this book will have already heard of the Javelin. It is an anti-tank missile system that has played a well-documented role in helping the Ukrainian Army resist the current ongoing Russian invasion. It fires a full-fledged rocket, with self-contained propulsion, fuel supply, and a "fire-and-forget" guidance system (autopilot), making it capable of considerable downrange accuracy up to 2.5 km. The weapon is intricate, expensive, and comparatively heavy (even though considerably lighter than its predecessors). It requires two people to carry, assemble, and fire it: the gunner, and the ammunition bearer. Mastering the use of the Javelin requires approximately two weeks of special training. And the U.S. may be running dangerously low on its available supply of these weapons, having already shipped over one-third of those available in its current arsenal to Ukraine.

By comparison, Nammo's M72, weighing about three kilos, can be easily carried, loaded, and fired by a single combatant. Its unusual feature is that it is "recoilless," meaning that there is no painful kickback or dangerous "blowback" of hot gasses from the small rocket-powered armor-penetrating projectile that it fires. It has a much shorter range than the Javelin, and lacking an internal guidance system, must be aimed and fired by the gunner like a rifle. The launch tube is fully reloadable and re-useable, so the system is considerably cheaper and requires less maintenance than the Javelin, and it is much, much easier to master. I experienced its relative ease of use directly: after a few minutes of orientation and explanation, I aimed and fired the M72 myself, twice hitting the prescribed target not far from its center ("bulls-eye"), at a range of about 120 meters. Greg, the younger of my two Norwegian colleagues (and the director of our PRIO project), did even better, putting his two shots nearly on top of one another, even closer to the bulls-eye. Henrik, a former Norwegian army conscript, did not fare so well, pulling both shots off to the left of the target – but that was likely intentional, as he had just come off five years of service on the Nobel Peace Prize committee. Greg, however, had no prior military experience to explain his accuracy. In fact, he had been a student in several of my graduate philosophy courses when we were both at Emory University 20–30 years earlier. We were insufferably proud of ourselves (though I didn't like being shown up by a former student!) and both of us felt prepared to deploy at once to Ukraine (which is where the M72 itself was eventually headed).

Here was the problem confronting the Nammo engineers. Because of its comparatively short range, the M72 as designed posed a serious risk for its user, requiring an approach to a pending target (an enemy tank) on the order of 300–500 meters, in order to aim and fire. The operators themselves become relatively vulnerable targets. Because it was both lightweight and recoilless, however, the M72 could easily be strapped to a small drone and flown over the target by the gunner from a considerably greater range (rivaling that of the Javelin). We witnessed several drone flights and M72 firings that illustrated the range and power of this new, "concatenated" weapon. No other weapon on the market with that considerable destructive power could be incorporated into and launched from a drone. And the drone required was merely a "hobbyist's" version: a small, remotely piloted aircraft that anyone could buy "off the shelf" online or from a local store without restriction. In terms of the dangers of arms proliferation, this posed a serious problem in and of itself, should a few of these M72s find their way into the hands of insurgents, terrorists, or criminals.[3]

In addition, however, it was fully within the competence of Nammo's engineers (or those of any other well-established aerospace and defense contractor, for that matter) to install some modifications in the drone: for instance, AI-enhanced navigational guidance and target-recognition software in lieu of the camera and remote controls required for human operation. Presto, just like that, these additional modifications produce a fully-autonomous lethal weapon – or even a swarm of such weapons, each carrying up to four loaded M72s – that could easily be launched into enemy territory and allowed to hunt, target, and destroy enemy forces without further meaningful human intervention or control.

Could they do this? Of course, at least from the standpoint of technology. It was far less of an engineering challenge (as a result of this peculiar and unique concatenation of products) than most of the other systems and engineering design dilemmas we have considered previously in this book. Would they be permitted legally to do this? Since all the components had previously been certified as legally permissible weapons and systems in their own right, it was not clear that this combination would automatically be illegal. But what of the moral questions we have considered throughout this book? Are there any principles that would apply, boundaries we should observe, or other constraints we should consider? Is this a reckless or criminally negligent combination of existing technologies? Would it represent a threat to human dignity if a swarm of these lethally-armed anti-tank drones attacked and destroyed a number of targets in the invading Russian army in the midst of its "special military operation?" Could such a conceivable autonomous robot armada be said notwithstanding to remain under "meaningful human control?"

Ethical Defense Engineering

The Nammo engineers had several other, somewhat more conventional ethical concerns. The Americans, they reported, were pressing them to replace the small tungsten slugs used for armor and bunker-piercing, encased in the tips of the artillery shells Nammo manufactures for the F-35's forward-firing cannon, with slugs made of depleted uranium (DU). The relative mechanical and cost advantages of replacing tungsten with "DU" is well-documented,[4] but the disadvantages of doing so are primarily threats of subsequent environmental contamination and potential risks to human health. The controversy over the relative risks of the two substances used in armaments are not fully resolved, but for a company committed otherwise to sustainability and human rights, it was a deeply troubling request. The CEO stated flatly that DU would never be substituted for tungsten in Nammo ordnance so long as he remained in charge.

It seemed to our site visit team that these are precisely the right questions to frame in the face of these unexpected turns of events, such as those resulting from the concatenation of familiar and readily-available technologies. Nammo engineers and their CEO were right to be concerned, and to exercise caution, and seek guidance as they proceeded to address an otherwise valid and urgent human need from Ukrainian victims. And frankly, it is impressive that they were concerned, and sensitive to the problems their work was engendering. They are not alone in harboring these concerns, as we have had ample occasion to observe. But what is most impressive is that so many involved and engaged designers and defense research engineers are increasingly accepting responsibility for their own efforts and leading the way toward forging acceptable answers to these questions, rather than simply ignoring them (as they have frequently been accused of doing). Even were critics opposed to their basic mission of arms manufacture, one could not possibly accuse the employees of this company of being "ethically illiterate" or "morally insensitive" to the questions their efforts raise.

Again, and on the whole, this seems to be a good thing. From the emergence and increasing use of remotely piloted vehicles to the advent of cyber war and conflict, we have seen time and again how the development of new and exotic military technologies has provoked fierce and divisive public debate regarding the ethical challenges posed by such technologies. For my own part, I have increasingly come to believe that the language of morality and ethics itself is serving us poorly in this context, often serving to further confuse, rather than to clarify or enlighten, us on how best to cope with the continuing development and deployment of seemingly exotic new military technologies.

There are numerous reasons for this unfortunate state of affairs. Segments of the public involved in these discussions harbor distinctive and incompatible – and sometimes conceptually confused and unclear – notions of what ethics entails.

From individual and culturally determined intuitions (including divergent religious traditions) regarding right conduct, through the achievement of beneficial outcomes, all the way to equating ethics with simple legal compliance, this results in frequent and virtually hopeless equivocation. In other contexts, I have termed this the problem of *folk morality* to call attention to its stubborn pervasiveness in public discourse, despite every conceivable attempt by scholars and experts to marshal evidence and arguments that decisively refute, correct, or recalibrate its principal components.[5]

There is an additional problem that ethicists have largely brought upon themselves. The greater majority of us appear to the wider public to be techno-pessimists who always object to the risks inherent in innovation and novelty. Obviously (as my colleague David Luban at Georgetown University rightly observes), a moral philosophy that *never* says "no" doesn't offer much of a rigorous standard for right conduct. But, of course, a community that almost always says "no" risks being dismissed as irrelevant and unhelpful. This is the kind of delicate line that ethicists retained to work for technology companies like Google, Amazon, and Facebook are obliged to walk almost daily: how do they constructively address otherwise unreflective, thoughtless, and excessively risk-prone innovation by their colleagues without simply losing all credibility? As we have noted repeatedly, those persons concerned with ethical conduct and the preservation of distinctive human values in the midst of disruptive technological innovation and deployment can sometimes seem to scientists and engineers (not to mention military personnel) instead as little more than technologically and scientifically illiterate alarmists and fearmongers who seem to wish only to impede the beneficial progress of science and technology. This is an enormous impediment to our joint efforts in fostering the requisite interaction between these collaborating disciplines otherwise concerned to promote safe, reliable, and socially responsible technological development.

Returning to the specific topic at hand: why then insist on invoking fear and mistrust, and posing allegedly moral objections to the development and use of remotely operated systems, for example, *instead of defining clear engineering design specifications* and *operational outcomes* that incorporate the main ethical concerns? Instead of simply saying "*no!,*" why not require engineers and the military to design, build, and operate to these exacting standards, if they are able, and otherwise to desist, until they succeed? Why engage in a science-fiction debate over the future prospects for artificial machine intelligence that would incorporate analogues of human moral cognition, when what is required, as we have witnessed in this book, is far more feasible and less exotic: namely, machines that function reliably, safely, and fully in compliance with applicable international laws – such as the law of armed conflict (LOAC) when operating in wartime?[6] Why insist without evidence or proof that the advent of cyber conflict and increasing reliance on artificial intelligence represent game changers that will usher in new modes of unrestricted warfare, in which all the known laws and moral principles of armed conflict will threaten to be rendered obsolete (as Randall Dipert originally prophesied), when what is required is merely appropriate analogical reasoning to determine how the known constraints extrapolate to these novel conditions?[7]

In this book, I have proposed initial outlines of a framework for identifying and fostering productive debate over the acceptable ethical boundaries regarding novel technologies. First, I surveyed the state of discourse surrounding the ethics of autonomous weapons systems and cyber warfare. Next, I discussed how attempting to codify the emerging consensus on ethical boundaries for a given technology can focus the conversation on unsettled areas more effectively than vague moral discourse. I then suggested some baseline voluntary principles (soft law) for the development and operation of autonomous systems and invited discussion on their accuracy and degree of comprehensiveness. I now want to suggest in conclusion how this methodology and many of these individual precepts apply toward the regulation and governance of other military technologies as well.

In the preceding chapters, I identified three prominent threads of discussion that served to illustrate the ethical debate over use and development of novel technologies: first, the original Arkin–Sharkey debate over the proposed benefits and liabilities of machine morality as part of the larger, seemingly relentless drive toward developing ever-greater degrees of autonomy in lethally armed remotely operated systems[8]; second, the efforts on the part of members of the International Committee on Robot Arms Control (ICRAC, now led by Peter Asaro, Jürgen Altmann, and Noel Sharkey) to outlaw the future development of autonomous lethally armed remotely operated systems under international law[9]; third, areas of emerging consensus or agreement among the contending stakeholders regarding the role of ethics in cyber warfare. This third debate centers on the development of cyber weapons and tactics, both those aimed indiscriminately at civilian personnel and objects, such as vital civil infrastructure, as well as highly discriminate cyber weapons like Stuxnet and Flame, which may be used in a preemptive or preventive fashion against perceived threats that have as yet resulted in no actual harm inflicted by the recipient of the cyberattack.[10]

These three examples certainly did not exhaust all the features of the wider debate over emerging military technologies, by any means. The increasing array of so-called nonlethal weapons, for example, involves questions about the use of such weapons on noncombatants, as well as the potential of such weapons to expand the rules of engagement for use of force, rather than lessening the destruction or loss of life as compared to the current regime.[11] Prospects for military uses of nanotechnology raised specters of weapons and systems that might cause widespread and catastrophic collateral or environmental destruction.[12] Efforts to use biological, neurological, and pharmaceutical techniques to enhance the capabilities of human combatants themselves raise a host of ethical questions: including informed consent for their use, determining the likely long-term health prospects for enhanced individuals following their military service, and the potentially undesirable social conflicts and transformations (civilian blowback) that such techniques might inadvertently bring about.[13] For the present, however, I will stick to the earlier three illustrations since, collectively, they encompass a great deal of the public debate over military technology, and the lessons learned in response have a wider applicability to these other areas and topics as well.

First, the prospects for machine models of moral cognition constitute a fascinating, but still futuristic, and highly speculative enterprise. The goal of developing working computational models of reasoning, including moral reasoning, is hardly impossible, but the effort required will be formidable, as we have seen.[14] *That entire effort may also be misguided.* Morality and moral deliberation, which would first require development of machine consciousness and self-consciousness to attain anything like choice or autonomy (let alone free will), are thus likely to remain firmly in the domain of human experience for the foreseeable future.

In any event, discussions of ethics and morality pertaining to remotely operated systems at present turn out to be largely irrelevant. We neither want nor need our remotely operated systems to be ethical, let alone more ethical or more humane than human agents. As we discovered earlier, we merely need them to be safe and reliable, to fulfil their programmable purposes without error or accident, and to have that programming designed to comply fully with relevant international law (LOAC) and specific rules of engagement. With regard to legal compliance, machines should be able to pass what we described as the Arkin test: autonomous remotely operated systems must be demonstrably capable of meeting or exceeding behavioral benchmarks set by human agents performing similar tasks under similar circumstances.

Second, proposals at this juncture to outlaw research, development, design, and manufacture of autonomous weapons systems seem at once premature, ill-timed, ill-informed – classic examples of poor governance. Such proposals do not reflect the concerns of the majority of stakeholders who would be affected; they misstate and would attempt to overregulate relevant behaviors.[15] Ultimately, such regulatory statutes would prove unacceptable to and unenforceable against many of the relevant parties (especially among nations or organizations with little current regard for international law) and would thus serve merely to further undermine respect for the rule of law in international relations. Machines themselves (lacking the requisite features of folk psychology, such as beliefs, intentions, and desires) by definition cannot commit war crimes nor could a machine be held accountable for its actions. The entire debate over an alleged responsibility gap in war machines, as well as concern for their potential violation of human dignity, constitutes an enormous red herring. Instead, a regulatory and criminal system, respecting relative legal jurisdictions, already exists to hold accountable individuals and organizations who might engage in reckless and/or criminally negligent behavior in the design, manufacture, and end use of remotely operated systems of any sort.[16]

Finally, it is well to observe that, in contrast to robotics (which has spawned tremendous ethical debate but little in the way of jurisprudence), discussions of the cyber domain have been carried out almost entirely within the jurisdiction of international law, with very sparse comment from ethicists until late in the last decade. Some have found the threat of a grave cyber-Armageddon of the sort predicted by Clarke and Knake (2010) and Brenner (2011) somewhat exaggerated and have even denied that the genuine equivalent of armed conflict has or could likely occur within this domain: no one has yet been killed, or objects harmed or destroyed, in a cyber conflict. As we have observed in these discussions, what has transpired instead is an increase in low-intensity conflict, such as crime, espionage, and sabotage, which blur the line between such conflict and war, resulting in cumulative harm greater or more concrete than damage caused by conventional war.[19] However, several recent conflicts, at least one of which (Stuxnet) did cross the boundary defining an act of war, have suggested the emergence of increasingly shared norms by which such conflict can be assessed and perhaps constrained.

The preceding comment illustrates an approach to understanding and governing the future development and use of exotic military technologies initially advocated by Professor Gary Marchant, Braden Allenby, and their colleagues originally at Arizona State University's Consortium on Emerging Technologies, Military Operations, and National Security:[17] namely, that instead of continuing efforts toward proposing unenforceable treaties or ineffectual bright line statutes of black letter international law, what is required is a form of governance known as *soft law*. Prof. Marchant and his coauthors (n. 16) invited those engaged in the development and use of such technologies, in the course of their activities, to reflect upon and observe what appear to them to be the boundaries of acceptable and unacceptable conduct and to codify these by consensus and agreement as the principles of best practice in their fields.

In addition, as we have observed in several of the areas outlined earlier, emergent norms regarding ethics, legal jurisdiction, and compliance – and, perhaps most importantly, appropriate degrees of consent and accountability for all the stakeholders – that together constitute the hallmarks of good governance, already have been largely established. What is urgently needed at this juncture is a clear summary of the results of the discussions and debates (as contained in the numerous citations earlier) that would, in turn, codify what we seem to have proposed or agreed upon in these matters, as distinguished from what requires still further deliberation and attention.

In the case of the debate over autonomous systems, for example, I would summarize the past several years of contentious debate in the following principles and precepts defining good or best practices, and just as importantly, demarcating the limits of acceptable versus unacceptable practice. I have already outlined this task in the realm of cyber conflict in Chapter 7,[18] based upon reactions to the several internationally acknowledged examples of cyber conflict that have recently occurred, from Estonia (2007) to Stuxnet and beyond. The point of such exercises is not to presume or preempt proper legislative authority but instead to focus future discussions upon whether such precepts are correctly stated (and if not, to modify them accordingly) and the extent to which they are in fact widely held and to identify areas of omission that must still be addressed. This seems to me a far more constructive enterprise at this point than further futile hand-wringing over the vague ambiguities of moral discourse.

Rather than engaging in a headstrong and ill-informed rush to proposing unenforceable treaties or legislating more ineffectual bright line statutes of black letter international law, the proper course of action would instead be to invite those engaged in the development and use of such technologies, in the course of their activities, to reflect upon and observe what appear to them to be the boundaries of acceptable and unacceptable conduct, and to codify these by consensus and agreement as the principles of what would be termed best practice in their fields. Indeed, what international relations and policy experts sometimes term emergent norms regarding ethics, legal jurisdiction, compliance, and appropriate degrees of consent and accountability for all the stakeholders already have been implicitly established. What is urgently needed at this juncture is a clear summary of the results of these ongoing discussions and debates that would, in turn, help to codify what we seem to have proposed or agreed upon in these matters, as distinguished from what requires still further deliberation and attention. Toward that goal, I present the following guidelines.

Voluntary Guidelines for Engineering and Research: Precepts and Principles

I The Principle of Mission Legality

A military mission that has been deemed legally permissible and morally justifiable on all other relevant grounds does not lose this status solely on the basis of a modification or change in the technological means used to carry it out (e.g., by removing the pilot from the cockpit of the airplane, or replacing a submarine crew and commander with demonstrably reliable software) unless the technology in question represents or employs weapons or methods already specifically proscribed under existing international weapons conventions or in violation of the prohibitions in international humanitarian law against means or methods that inflict superfluous injury or unnecessary suffering (or are otherwise judged to constitute means of warfighting that are *mala in se*).

II The Principle of Unnecessary Risk[19]

Within the context of an otherwise lawful and morally justified international armed conflict or domestic security operation, we owe the warfighter or domestic security agent every possible minimization of risk we can provide them in the course of carrying out their otherwise legally permissible and morally justifiable missions. We owe third parties and bystanders (civilian noncombatants) caught up in the conflict every protection we can afford them through the use of ever-improved means of conflict that lessen the chance of inadvertent injury, death, or damage to their property and means of livelihood.

[Comment: This precept combines the original insight of Strawer's principle of unnecessary risk with Arkin's sense that military technologists should feel obliged to exercise their expertise to lessen the cruel and antihumanitarian aspects of armed conflict.]

III The Principle of the Moral Asymmetry of Adversaries

No obligation of fairness or symmetry of technological advantage is owed to opponents or adversaries whenever the latter are unmistakably engaged in unjust or illegal use of force, whether during the commission of domestic crimes or when involved in international criminal conspiracies (e.g., terrorism).

[Comment: It is sometimes mistakenly asserted that in international war and armed conflict, at least, there is some such obligation, and hence that one moral objection to the use of remotely operated systems is that the other side doesn't have them. Technological asymmetry is not a new phenomenon, however, but rather is an enduring feature of armed conflict. No such constraint is imposed on domestic law enforcement engaged in armed conflict with, for example, international drug cartels. Likewise, no such obligation of symmetry is owed to international adversaries when they are engaged in similar criminal activities: for example, violation of domestic legal statutes within the borders of a sovereign state, defiance of duly elected legal authorities, indiscriminate targeting of civilians and destruction of property, kidnapping, torture, execution, and mutilation of prisoners, and so on.][20]

IV The Principle of Greatest Proportional Compliance

In the pursuit of a legally permissible and morally justifiable military (or security) mission, agents are obligated to use the means or methods available that promise the closest compliance with the international laws of armed conflict and applicable rules of engagement, such as noncombatant distinction (discrimination) and the economy of force (proportionality).

[Comment: This is another implication of Arkin's assertion of an obligation to use remotely operated systems whenever they might result in greater compliance with international law and in the lessening of human suffering in war. Neil Rowe advanced a similar principle regarding the choice between cyber weapons and conventional weapons. In this case, the implication is that nations involved in armed conflict must use the least destructive means available (whether these be robots, cyber weapons, precision-guided munitions, or nonlethal weapons) in pursuit of military objectives that are otherwise deemed to be morally justified and legally permissible.]

V The Arkin Test

In keeping with Precept IV, an artifact (such as an autonomous unmanned system) satisfies the requirements of international law and morality pertaining to armed conflict or law enforcement and may therefore be lawfully used alongside, or substituted for, human agents whenever the artifact can be shown to comply with the relevant laws and rules of engagement as (or even more) reliably and consistently as human agents under similar circumstances.

[Comment: Moreover, from application of Precepts II and IV, the use of such an artifact is not merely legally permissible, it is *morally required* whenever its performance promises both reduced risk to human agents and enhanced compliance with laws of armed conflict and rules of engagement.]

VI Prohibition of Delegation of Authority and Accountability (Meaningful Human Control)

The decision to attack an enemy (whether combatants or other targets) with lethal force may not be delegated solely to a remotely operated system in the absence of meaningful human oversight, nor may eventual accountability for carrying out such an attack be wholly abrogated by human operators otherwise normally included in the kill chain.

[Comment: This Precept is indebted to the work of philosopher Robert Asaro of the New School (NY), cofounder of the International Committee for Robot Arms Control (ICRAC). It also brings professional canons of best practice in line with the requirements of the U.S. Department of Defense guidance on future remotely operated systems, stating that autonomous remotely operated systems shall not be authorized to make unilateral, unsupervised targeting decisions.][21]

VII The Principle of Due Care

All research and development, design, and manufacture of artifacts (such as lethally armed and/or autonomous remotely operated systems, AI-enhanced cyber weapons and operations, and so on) ultimately intended for use alongside or in place of human agents engaged in legally permissible and morally justifiable armed conflict or domestic security operations must rigorously comply with Precepts I through V. All research and development (R&D), design, and manufacture of remotely operated systems undertaken with full knowledge of, and in good faith compliance with, the foregoing Principles (such good faith at minimum to encompass rigorous testing to ensure safe and reliable operation under the terms of these principles) shall be understood as *legally permissible and morally justifiable.*

VIII The Principle of Product Liability

Mistakes, errors, or malfunctions that nonetheless might reasonably and randomly be expected to occur, despite the full and good faith exercise of due care as defined in Principle VII earlier, shall be accountable under applicable international and/or domestic product liability law, including full and fair financial and other compensation or restitution for wrongful injury, death, or destruction of property.

[Comment: This practice mirrors current international norms as practiced by minimally rights-respecting states in the case of conventional armed conflict. When combatants accidentally or unintentionally bring about the injury or death of noncombatants, the responsible state acknowledges blame and offers apology and financial restitution to the victims or to their survivors in the aftermath of an investigation into the wrongful death or injury undertaken to determine any additional criminal liability.]

IX Reckless Engagement or Criminal Negligence

By contrast, R&D, design, or manufacture of systems undertaken through culpable ignorance or in deliberate or willful disregard of the foregoing principles (to include failure to perform, or attempts to falsify the results of tests regarding safety, reliability of operation, and compliance with applicable law and rules of engagement, especially in the aftermath of malfunctions as noted earlier), shall be subject to designation as war crimes under international law (e.g., according to the Martens Clause, at minimum) and/or as reckless endangerment or criminally negligent behavior under the terms of applicable international and/or domestic law. Individual parties to such negligence shall be punished to the full extent of the law, to include possible trial in the International Criminal Court for the willful commission of war crimes, and/or civil and criminal prosecution within the appropriate domestic jurisdiction for reckless endangerment or criminal negligence. In domestic jurisdictions providing for capital punishment upon conviction for the occurrence of such mishaps within that jurisdiction, such punishment shall be deemed an appropriate form of accountability under the Principles mentioned earlier.

[Comment: This Precept incorporates the concerns and addresses the objectives of critics of military robotics pertaining to wrongful injury, death, or destruction of property by remotely operated systems in which a human combatant, under similar conditions, could and would be held criminally liable for the commission of war crimes. The precept allows imposition of the death penalty for such offenses when guilt is ascertained within legal jurisdictions permitting capital punishment.]

X Benchmarking

Testing for safety and reliability of operation under the relevant precepts shall require advance determination of relevant quantitative benchmarks for human performance under the conditions of anticipated use and shall require any artifact produced or manufactured to meet or exceed these benchmarks.

[Comment: This operationalizes the otherwise vague concept of the behavior of human beings under similar circumstances as in the Arkin test, requiring that this be ascertained and sufficiently well-defined to guide the evaluation and assessment of the requisite performance of unmanned systems proposed for use in armed conflict.]

XI Orientation and Legal Compliance

All individuals and organizations (including military services, industries, and research laboratories) engaged in R&D, design, manufacture, acquisition, or use of remotely operated systems for military purposes shall be required to attend an orientation and legal compliance seminar of not less than eight hours on these Principles, and upon conclusion, to receive, sign, and duly file with appropriate authorities a signed copy of these Principles as a precondition of their continued work. Failure to comply shall render such individuals liable under the principle of criminal liability (Precept IX) for any phase of their work, including but not limited to accidents or malfunctions resulting in injury, death, or destruction of property.

Government and military agencies involved in contracting for the design and acquisition of such systems shall likewise require and sponsor this orientation seminar and facilitate the deposit of the required signed precept form by any contractors or contracting organizations receiving federal financial support for their activities. Federal acquisitions and procurement officials shall also receive this training and shall be obligated to include the relevant safety/reliability benchmarks of human performance along with other technical design specifications established in requests for proposals (RFPs) or federal contracts.

[Comment: One frequently raised objection to the concept of soft law and governance according to emergent norms questions the degree of sanction and normativity attached to the enforcement of these norms. Inasmuch as the Principles themselves define a sphere of criminal behavior and establish the bounds of jurisdiction pertaining to criminal activity in these cases, this final Principle ensures that affected stakeholders deemed to be bound by these Principles are fully cognizant of their content, interpretation, and prospective normative force and that the orientation provided and conducted be such as to pre-empt or prevent the reduction of same merely to a bureaucratic exercise, absent any real understanding or commitment on the part of those agreeing to and complying with this governance.]

Conclusion

My intent in offering these principles is to suggest areas of consensus and agreement discerned among contending stakeholders and positions in this debate and to suggest the norms emerging from this debate that might serve to guide (if not strictly govern) the behavior of states, militaries, and those involved in the development, testing, and manufacture of present and future remotely operated systems. I likewise believe that discussion of the meaning, application, and refinement of these precepts as soft-law guidelines for proper use of remotely operated systems would be substantially more efficacious than further moral debate over their potential risks, let alone a rush to enact poorly conceived legislation that would have both unenforceable and unintended harmful consequences.

Some of the foregoing principles are obviously specific to military robotics (e.g., Principles V and VI, pertaining to the Arkin test, and prohibition on delegation of authority to remotely operated systems, respectively). This general approach, based upon mutual consensus regarding emerging norms, and many if not most of the principles, however, would prove useful by analogy in other areas of technological development, such as nonlethal weapons, cyber warfare, projects for warrior enhancement, and other military and domestic security technologies.

In the case of cyber conflict, for example, Principle I pertaining to mission legality would likewise suggest that, in any situation in which a use of force was otherwise deemed justifiable, justification would extend to the use of cyber weapons and tactics as well as to conventional weapons and tactics. Moreover, by the Principle of Greatest Proportional Compliance (Principle IV), in an instance in which the use of force was otherwise justifiable, and given a choice of cyber versus conventional weaponry, the use of the more discriminate and less destructive weapon (presumably the cyber weapon) *would not merely be permitted, but would be obligatory* (under the general international humanitarian law principles of military necessity and proportionality). This principle also dictates the use of less lethal (nonlethal) weaponry when the effects otherwise achieved are equivalent.

★ ★ ★

In sum, I believe there is far more consensus than we have been able to discern among adversarial parties arguing about ethics and law in such matters than we have heretofore been able to discern. That emerging consensus, in turn, points toward a more productive regime of governance and regulation to insure against the risk of unintended harm and consequences than do rival attempts at legal regulation or moral condemnation. I urge that we move on from these contentious, divisive, and thus-far unproductive debates by amending, adopting, and encouraging the principles and procedures outlined earlier.

Notes

1 See: https://nammo.com: With more than 2700 employees, 28 production sites, and a presence in 12 countries, Nammo is one of the world's leading providers of specialty ammunition and rocket motors.

2 This comment was in response to my specific question to him regarding his role and reasoning behind DoD Directive 3000.09 following his presentation at the McCain Conference in Annapolis on 21 April 2022, https://usna.edu/Ethics/Research/McCain/RegistrationInformation.php. The presentation and our discussion should be posted shortly on the McCain Conference playlist, https://www.youtube.com/user/TheStockdalecenter/playlists.

3 This widespread and indiscriminate proliferation of such weapons, we recall, is the chief fear of military conflict expert, Professor Audrey K. Cronin of American University in her book, *Power to the People: How Open Technological Innovation is Arming Tomorrow's Terrorists* (New York: Oxford University Press, 2019).

4 Interested readers are invited to "google" this controversial topic, but I would recommend beginning with the accounts found at the International Atomic Energy Agency website, https://www.iaea.org/topics/spent-fuel-management/depleted-uranium. Section 6 describes the relative advantages and disadvantages of DU and tungsten in military weaponry. *For more information on the military uses of depleted uranium* see: http://www.gulflink.osd.mil or http://www.nato.int.

5 Readers will find numerous references to and descriptions of this stubborn fallacy cited in the index of *Ethics and Cyber Warfare* (New York: Oxford University Press, 2017): 179. This is a nod to a small but significant movement within my discipline called

experimental philosophy, in which members of my tribe increasingly turn to studying and understanding what real people actually believe and do in lieu of placing hypothetical persons on or near colliding trolley cars. But that is another topic. The foundations for this approach lie in an earlier work on metaethics by the eminent moral philosopher Stephen Darwall (e.g., *Philosophical Ethics* (Boulder, CO: Westview Press, 1998)) and in a number of practitioners of moral psychology, principally in the United Kingdom. For a sample discussion, see Hagop Sarkissian, "Aspects of Folk Morality," in *A Companion to Experimental Philosophy*, eds. Justin Sytsma and Wesley Buckwalter (New York: John Wiley & Sons, 2016): 212–224. The author describes *folk morality* somewhat less charitably than I as "the way that ordinary, philosophically untutored folk view the status of morality."

6 See G.R. Lucas, Jr., "Engineering, Ethics & Industry: The Moral Challenges of Lethal Autonomy," in *Killing by Remote Control*, ed. B.J. Strawser (New York: Oxford University Press, 2013): 297–318. For a similar approach to the parameters for design success, see Robert Sparrow, "Building a Better Warbot: Ethical Issues in the Design of Unmanned Systems for Military Applications," *Journal of Science and Engineering Ethics* 15 (2009): 169–187.

7 See his description of the irrelevance of JWT and LOAC/IHL in "The Ethics of Cyber Warfare," *Journal of Military Ethics* 9 (4) (2010): 384–410, and my alternative proposal subsequently that would retain these, in G.R. Lucas, Jr., "Just War and Cyber Warfare," in *The Routledge Handbook of Ethics and War*, eds. Fritz Allhoff, Nicholas G. Evans, and Adam Henschke (Oxford: Routledge, 2013).

8 R.C. Arkin, "The Case for Ethical Autonomy in Unmanned Systems," *Journal of Military Ethics* 9 (4) (2010): 347–356; N. Sharkey, "Saying 'No!' to Lethal Autonomous Targeting," *Journal of Military Ethics* 9 (4) (2010): 299–314.

9 See the ICRAC mission statement and list of personnel at www.icrac.net/members/ [accessed 14 May 2022].

10 The discovery and strategic implications of the Stuxnet worm, against the backdrop of three prior cyber conflicts in Estonia (2007), Syria (2007), and Georgia (2008), were given a preliminary and (at the time) incomplete summary in G.R. Lucas, Jr., "Permissible Preventive Cyber Warfare," in *Philosophy of Engineering and Technology*, eds. L. Floridi and M. Taddeo (UNESCO Conference on Ethics and Cyber Warfare, University of Hertfordshire, 1 July 2011) (Dordrecht: Springer-Verlag, 2013). A subsequent and complete retrospective account of the project, "Operation Olympic Games," in which the Stuxnet worm and Flame espionage malware were a part was provided in the New York Times columnist David E. Sanger's book, *Confront and Conceal: Obama's Secret Wars and Surprising Use of American Power* (New York: Crown Publishers, 2012).

11 See, for example, Pauline S. Kaurin, "Non-lethal Weapons and Rules of Engagement," in *Routledge Handbook of Military Ethics*, ed. George R. Lucas (Oxford: Routledge, 2015): 395–405; also "With Fear and Trembling: An Ethical Framework for Nonlethal Weapons," *Journal of Military Ethics* 9 (1) (2010): 100–114.

12 Accounts of the military uses of "smart dust" (nano receptors) and the possible environmental result of "grey slime," the potential impact of runaway "nano-viruses," and other nightmare scenarios from nanotechnology are outlined and discussed in F. Allhoff, P. Lin, J. Moor, and J. Weckert, eds., *Nanoethics: The Ethical and Social Implications of Nanotechnology* (Hoboken, NJ: John Wiley, 2007).

13 For example, Maxwell J. Mehlman, "Captain America and Iron Man: Biological, Genetic, and Psychological Enhancement and the Warrior Ethos," in *Routledge Handbook of Military Ethics*, ed. George R. Lucas (Oxford Routledge, 2015): 406–420.

14 The degree of futuristic speculation involved in such efforts is indicated in the Arkin–Sharkey debate, cited earlier (n. 8). For an account of the formidable challenges entailed, see: R.C. Arkin, *Governing Lethal Behavior in Autonomous Robots* (London: Taylor & Francis, 2009). For an account of recent progress, see: R. Arkin, P. Ulam, and A. Wagner, "Moral Decision Making in Autonomous Systems: Enforcement, Moral Emotions, Dignity, Trust, and Deception," *Proceedings of the IEEE* 100 (3) (2012): 571–589.

15 In addition to proposals to outlaw armed or autonomous military robotic systems by ICRAC itself, see the much-cited report from Human Rights Watch, "Losing Humanity: The Case Against Killer Robots" (2012), www.hrw.org/report/2012/11/19/losing-humanity/case-against-killer-robots [accessed 15 May 2022]. While unquestionably well-intentioned, the report was often poorly or incompletely informed regarding technical details, and it was highly misleading in many of its observations. Furthermore, its proposal for states to collaborate in banning the further development and use of such technologies would not only prove unenforceable, but it would likely impede other kinds of developments in robotics (such as the use of autonomous systems during natural disasters and humanitarian crises) that the authors themselves would not mean to prohibit. It is in such senses that these sorts of proposals represent seriously flawed governance. Finally, as we have documented in this book, there have been no serious proposals to move this agenda forward in the ensuing decade.

16 G.E. Marchant, B. Allenby, R. Arkin, E.T. Barrett, J. Borenstein, L.M. Gaudet, O. Kittrie, P. Lin, G.R. Lucas, R. O'Meara, and J. Silberman, "International Governance of Autonomous Military Robots," *Columbia Science and Technology Law Review* 12 (2011), https://academiccommons.columbia.edu/doi/10.7916/D8TB1HDW [accessed 15 May 2022].

17 https://sustainability-innovation.asu.edu/research/project/consortium-for-emerging-technologies-military-operations-and-national-security/.

18 There I summarized from extant literature that (1) use of a cyber weapon against an adversary is justified whenever there is a compelling reason for doing so, (2) toward the resolution of which every reasonable effort has been expended with little likelihood of success, and (3) in which further delay will only make matters even worse. Resort to cyber conflict is only justified, moreover, (4) when the weapon is directed purely at military targets, (5) would inflict no more damage or loss of life on these than would be reasonably proportionate to the threat posed, and, finally, (6) the use of which would pose no threat of harm whatsoever to noncombatant lives or property. In other respects, these Precepts of cyber conflict are similar to, or can be straightforwardly derived from, several of the Precepts regarding the development and use of uncrewed systems as summarized in this chapter.

19 First formulated by Bradley J. Strawser in "Moral Predators: The Duty to Employ Uninhabited Aerial Vehicles," in *New Warriors and New Weapons: Ethics & Emerging Military Technologies*, ed. G.R. Lucas, Jr., *Journal of Military Ethics* 9 (4) (2010): 357–383.

20 Note that this is not an explicit rejection of the doctrine of the "Moral Equality of Combatants," an essential element in what Michael Walzer defines as "the War Convention" (in *Just and Unjust Wars*, 1977). Rather, it is a repudiation of a misplaced notion of "fairness in combat," according to which it would be unfair for one side in a conflict to possess or use weapons or military technologies that afforded them undue advantage. This is sometimes cited in public as an objection to the use of drones in warfare. It seems to equate war with a sporting competition, after medieval jousting fashion, and, upon examination, is not only patently ridiculous but also contradicted in most actual armed conflicts of the past, where maneuvering for "technological superiority" was a key element in success. In any case, no such argument is made concerning legitimate domestic security operations, as noted earlier, and does not obtain either within the realm of wars of "law enforcement" or humanitarian intervention.

21 Department of Defense Directive 3000.09, "Autonomy in Weapons Systems," 13 (21 November 2012), www.dtic.mil/whs/directives/corres/pdf/300009p.pdf.

References

Allhoff, F.; Lin, P.; J. Moor, J.; Weckert, J., eds. *Nanoethics: The Ethical and Social Implications of Nanotechnology* (Hoboken, NJ: John Wiley, 2007).

Arizona State University Global Institute of Sustainability and Innovation. "Home Page," https://sustainability-innovation.asu.edu/research/project/consortium-for-emerging-technologies-military-operations-and-national-security/.

Arkin, R.C. *Governing Lethal Behavior in Autonomous Robots* (London: Taylor & Francis, 2009).

Arkin, R.C. "The Case for Ethical Autonomy in Unmanned Systems," *Journal of Military Ethics* 9 (4) (2010): 347–356.

Arkin, R.C.; Ulam, P.; Wagner, A. "Moral Decision Making in Autonomous Systems: Enforcement, Moral Emotions, Dignity, Trust, and Deception," *Proceedings of the IEEE* 100 (3) (2012): 571–589.

Brenner, Joel. *America the Vulnerable: Inside the New Threat Matrix of Digital Espionage, Crime, and Warfare* (New York: Penguin Press, 2011).

Clarke, Richard A; Knake, Robert K. *Cyber War: The Next Threat to National Security and What to Do About It* (New York: HarperCollins, 2010): 64–68.

Cronin, Audrey, K. *Power to the People: How Open Technological Innovation is Arming Tomorrow's Terrorists* (New York: Oxford University Press, 2019).

Darwall, Stephen. *Philosophical Ethics* (Boulder, CO: Westview Press, 1998).

Department of Defense Directive 3000.09. "Autonomy in Weapons Systems," 13 (21 November 2012), www.dtic.mil/whs/directives/corres/pdf/300009p.pdf.

Human Rights Watch. "Losing Humanity: The Case Against Killer Robots" (2012), www.hrw.org/report/2012/11/19/losing-humanity/case-against-killer-robots [accessed 15 May 2022].

International Committee for Robot Arms Control. "Mission Statement and List of Personnel," www.icrac.net/members/ [accessed 14 May 2022].

Kaurin, Pauline S. "With Fear and Trembling: An Ethical Framework for Nonlethal Weapons," *Journal of Military Ethics* 9 (1) (2010): 100–114.

Kaurin, Pauline S. "Non-lethal Weapons and Rules of Engagement," in *Routledge Handbook of Military Ethics*, ed. George R. Lucas (Oxford: Routledge, 2015): 395–405.

Lucas, George R. Jr. "The Ethics of Cyber Warfare," *Journal of Military Ethics* 9 (4) (2010): 384–410.

Lucas, George R. Jr. "Engineering, Ethics and Industry: The Moral Challenges of Lethal Autonomy," in *Killing by Remote Control*, ed. B.J. Strawser (New York: Oxford University Press, 2013): 297–318.

Lucas, George R. Jr. "Just War and Cyber Warfare," in *The Routledge Handbook of Ethics and War*, eds. Fritz Allhoff, Nicholas G. Evans, and Adam Henschke (Oxford: Routledge, 2013).

Lucas, George R. Jr. "Permissible Preventive Cyber Warfare," in *Philosophy of Engineering and Technology*, eds. L. Floridi and M. Taddeo (UNESCO Conference on Ethics and Cyber Warfare, University of Hertfordshire, 1 July 2011) (Dordrecht: Springer-Verlag, 2013).

Lucas, George R. Jr. *Ethics and Cyber Warfare* (New York: Oxford University Press, 2017): 179.

Marchant, G.E.; Allenby, B.; Arkin, R.; Barrett, E.T.; Borenstein, J.; Gaudet, L.M.; Kittrie, O.; Lin, P.; Lucas, G.R.; O'Meara, R.; Silberman, J. "International Governance of Autonomous Military Robots," *Columbia Science and Technology Law Review* 12 (2011), https://academiccommons.columbia.edu/doi/10.7916/D8TB1HDW [accessed 15 May 2022].

Mehlman, Maxwell J. "Captain America and Iron Man: Biological, Genetic, and Psychological Enhancement and the Warrior Ethos," in *Routledge Handbook of Military Ethics*, ed. George R. Lucas (Oxford: Routledge, 2015): 406–420.

Sanger, David E. *Confront and Conceal: Obama's Secret Wars and Surprising Use of American Power* (New York: Crown Publishers, 2012).

Sarkissian, Hagop. "Aspects of Folk Morality," in *A Companion to Experimental Philosophy*, eds. Justin Sytsma and Wesley Buckwalter (New York: John Wiley & Sons,. 2016): 212–224.

Scharre, Paul. *An Army of None: Autonomous Weapons and the Future of War* (New York: W.W. Norton & Co., 2018).

Sharkey, N. "Saying 'No!' to Lethal Autonomous Targeting," *Journal of Military Ethics* 9 (4) (2010): 299–314.

Sparrow, Robert. "Building a Better Warbot: Ethical Issues in the Design of Unmanned Systems for Military Applications," *Journal of Science and Engineering Ethics* 15 (2009): 169–187.

Strawser, Bradley J. "Moral Predators: The Duty to Employ Uninhabited Aerial Vehicles," in *New Warriors and New Weapons: Ethics & Emerging Military Technologies*, ed. George R. Lucas, Jr., *Journal of Military Ethics* 9 (4) (2010): 357–383.

Walzer, Michael. *Just and Unjust Wars* (New York: Basic Books, 1977).

APPENDIX

Author's Testimony for the DARPA/National Academy of Sciences Hearings on "Warfare and Exotic Military Technologies"

"Testimony on Ethical Issues of UAVs for National Academy of Sciences"

George Lucas
Distinguished Chair in Ethics, U.S. Naval Academy
Professor of Philosophy & Public Policy, Naval Postgraduate School

Distinguished DARPA/AAS panelists:
Thank you for inviting my esteemed colleague, Dr Patrick Lin, and me to testify before you this morning.

The year 2011 marked the first time that the U.S. Air Force recruitment and training pipeline turned out more RPV/UAV operators than it did conventional fighter pilots. This comes as a dual shock to the fighter pilots. First, it was painful to be asked to leave the cockpit and set aside years of education, training, and experience, to sit at a control station thousands of miles removed from the aircraft itself. Pilots resisted this change, until they saw that they were simply leaving themselves out of the fight: better to be flying Predators themselves, they concluded, than to be replaced by teenagers with joysticks! But then came a further blow: the highly skilled fighter pilots were less adept at learning the ropes and operating Predators than were teenagers with barely a high school education but a lot of video and computer game experience. This is humiliating enough. But one day, one can predict, the Air Force Chief of Staff will be chosen from the ranks of RPV operators. That will provide the culmination of a cultural sea change among members of the military aviation community. How will that community respond? How will it define and uphold its core values in this new mechanized, automated, "virtual" milieu?

Meanwhile, the U.S. Army has spent millions of dollars to set up a new "Army Center for the Professional Military Ethic." No service has worked harder, both to define itself as a community of professionals and to investigate just what the core competencies, skill sets, and core moral values are that define that professional community. But what sense does it make to speak of the Army's professionalism and professional ethic, if an autonomous and lethally armed ground combat robot can do the same job as well or better? Those are the kinds of questions and challenges that new military technologies are presenting to military services now and indicative of the transformative effect they will one day doubtless have on civilian communities as well.

With the advent of these exotic new military technologies and the challenges they present, one hears a familiar refrain:

- "Our traditional concepts of warfare and its justification are outmoded;"
- "Existing laws of war and moral constraints regarding conventional combat are useless;"
- "Our conceptions of both must be either cast aside or radically reformulated."

This can be described as a familiar refrain, because

- one heard this same complaint earlier, with the wars of genocidal violence and the humanitarian military responses launched in the 1990s;
- one heard this in the aftermath of the terrorist attacks of 9/11 and the subsequent rise of simmering "small wars" of counterinsurgency and other varieties of "irregular" warfare over the past decade (2001–2011);
- and one hears this concern expressed now with the advent of exotic new warfighting technologies, particular the prospect of lethally armed and autonomous robotics.

There is some rhetorical value to this stratagem. It serves to startle, alarm, and even terrify those who otherwise don't seem to take the new and very real challenges seriously enough. There is a real danger, however, of threat inflation, exaggeration, and hysteria, as though we are somehow not well equipped to deal with the new challenges, once we have finally awakened to them.

These ethical challenges are very real and complex, but after 2–3 years of sustained reflection, one can predict that the patterns seen here will duplicate the discoveries of the preceding two decades: to wit, conceptions of morally justifiable resort to war, and of the moral and legal constraints on its conduct, are not outmoded.

- One still ought not to resort to force, for example, without a very strong moral justification, in terms of either the threat of harm posed or the harm actually inflicted, sufficient to justify the risk and destruction that will inevitably follow.

- Moreover, any such resort to force ought to be undertaken only after reasonable alternatives to a military conflict have been attempted without success.

Likewise, in the conduct of ensuing hostilities, whether carried out with conventional forces, or alternatively with robots, cyber weapons, nonlethal weapons, or by biologically and/or psychologically enhanced warriors

- one should still not deliberately target noncombatants and civilian infrastructure; and
- one should still not deliberately use more force than is necessary to attain legitimate military objectives.

These four points are defined in the long-standing moral discussion of war as "just cause" and "last resort" (with respect to the decision to engage in armed conflict), and "discrimination" and "proportionality" with respect to the conduct of hostilities. All four are basic and widely shared ethical principles long enshrined in moral discourse and reflected for the most part in international law (LOAC).

The problem instead is that the new military technologies show us that we need to think harder about what these basic concepts mean, and how they translate and apply in these unusual new circumstances. Here are three examples.

(1) Consider the case of UAV/RPV systems, unmanned, but remotely piloted. Suppose that a given mission in pursuit of insurgents would be permissible under law and morality using conventional manned aircraft. Such a mission would not suddenly be transformed in its legal or moral status, simply by removing the pilot from the cockpit. Either the mission is permissible, or it is not. The position of the pilot with respect to the aircraft is not the determining factor in this judgment. Yet many persons think otherwise, presuming that there is something inherently illegal or immoral about such a mission, simply because it is carried out by UAVs. Morality and legality, however, are properties of the mission, not of the particular technology used to carry it out (provided, of course, that the means or weapons technology utilized is not specifically banned by treaty, as causing "superfluous injury or unnecessary suffering").

But if this point is acknowledged, then it must also follow that the mission's legal and moral status is likewise not inherently transformed by removing the human pilot from the equation altogether. Providing the autonomous unmanned system has been proven as safe and reliable in its operation (including demonstration of immunity to cyberattack, loss of control, or unpredictable "emergent behaviors"), then the mission in which it is employed is no more or less legal or moral, simply on its account. Yet their "intrinsic" legality or morality is among the most contested issues with respect to the further development and use of unmanned systems. Clearly, everyone involved in evaluating their development and use needs to think harder and more clearly about this issue.

(2) Cyber weapons are, or have been, routinely designed to target civilians and civilian infrastructure (e.g., as unleashed in alleged Russian attacks on Georgia and Estonia, or in the alleged CIA "logic bomb" used in the early 1980s to destroy Soviet-era oil pipelines). *That's not "new," that's wrong*. That this deliberate, intentional cyber targeting of civilians and their property has only recently been highlighted and criticized is again attributable to a cultural anomaly: cyber strategy is largely an extension of espionage, psychological warfare operations, and sabotage of the sort routinely carried out by covert intelligence operatives, rather than combatants. These communities operate according to different rules and assumptions. Their covert actions are always considered domestic crimes within local jurisdictions, rather than acts of war.

The newly promulgated U.S. cyber strategy has been widely summarized in the news media, in the words of an unnamed military expert: "if you launch a cyber attack against our power grid, we may just put a missile down your smokestack." But whose smokestack (given the difficult problem of attribution)? And how many missiles down how many smokestacks? And what *sort* of smokestacks (defense industries? civilian factories?) Indeed, is a conventional or "kinetic" response of this sort even appropriate as a response to a cyberattack? Would it matter what kind of cyberattack it was: DDOS? Damage to civilian infrastructure? Draining your 401k? And who is a "noncombatant" in a cyber war, during a DDOS, for example, when personal computers the world over are hijacked in numerous and massive botnets that are collectively carrying out the strike? Clearly, all concerned need likewise to think harder and more clearly about this new technological wrinkle as well.

(3) Finally, in quite another context: does the concept of "proportionate use of force" that has always governed the Law of Armed Conflict (LOAC) and specific rules of engagement for combat now dictate that nonlethal weapons should always be used before resorting to lethal weapons? Should militaries use such weapons under existing rules of engagement for lethal weapons (thereby lowering the threat of destruction and damage from mistakes), or should military and security personnel instead expand the regime (or broaden the prevailing norm) permitting the use of force more widely, in light of the presumed "nonlethality" of these alternative weapons? At present, nonlethal weapons threaten to widen the scope of permissible targets, to include civilian noncombatants as well as enemy combatants. *This is not new or revolutionary: this is a mistake*, stemming from failure to think this through. Such an unfortunate widening of the rules of engagement for the use of force has already taken place with disturbing and increasing frequency in domestic law enforcement: the rules governing the engaging of suspects with force has expanded, and so have unintended injuries and deaths stemming from use of nonlethal weapons in situations in which no police officer would have ever drawn his pistol let alone fired it.

These are some of the questions that decidedly challenge, but do not at all "overturn" or obviate, our moral conventions regarding the declaration and conduct of war. To suggest otherwise is extremely unwise and robs us of the resources required to reflect on these (frankly, quite interesting) questions.

Often, such extreme declarations about the "end of war and morality as we have known it" are made by those who know little about the moral conventions surrounding war or who secretly thought them specious, nonsensical, or irrelevant to begin with. Even military personnel, whose underlying professional conduct these moral principles reflect, are sometimes confused by all this or regard such underlying principles as superfluous, irrelevant, externally imposed constraints upon a deadly and dirty business best carried out with ruthless and brutal efficiency by those (like themselves) whom we empower to engage in armed conflict on our behalf.

What goes unrecognized in these attitudes is that military ethics is a species of professional ethics. That is, just like communities of physicians and health care professionals, or lawyers, or journalists, members of the military profession can also be portrayed as perpetually immersed in an ongoing dialogue regarding the nature of their practice, including aspirations for best practice, as well as professional probity and rectitude, defining the boundaries of unacceptable practice.

To those who think the "international law of armed conflict" is an external, legal constraint imposed by lawyers wearing fancy neckties in Geneva (who presumably therefore know nothing of the actual experience of war), it is important to emphasize in response that, in essence, the conventions that such lawyers may finally enshrine in some legal regime actually reflect centuries of philosophical reflection upon justified use of force and reflect the views and intuitions that we find warriors themselves discussing, for example, in Plato's *Republic*, Shakespeare's *Henry V*, or Sun Tzu's classic, *The Art of War*. Such works, and the discussions of warriors they embody, attempt to define what a warrior is about, and what he or she is trying to accomplish, what he or she is willing to do to accomplish it, and perhaps most importantly, what he or she is unwilling to do in pursuit of otherwise legitimate military objectives. This characterization is true, even in a work like Karl von Clausewitz's *On War*, which seems otherwise to warn us against allowing ethical considerations to influence our judgment about strategy. This is because, at this level, as Michael Walzer observed (*Just and Unjust Wars*, 1977), ethics is inseparable from strategy: ethics is, ultimately, a mode of strategic thinking about goals and objectives and the best means of attaining them. Military ethics, just war doctrine, and the laws of armed conflict incorporate the consensus of warriors themselves about the nature and limitations of their professional practice.

In the military case, a reasoned, reflective equilibrium of perspectives among people of action has not been easy to come by. And its results are therefore fragile and easily threatened. It is simply not true that warriors cannot discern acceptable from unacceptable conduct or differentiate justified from unjustifiable and wrong behavior. The consternation reported among many members of the Syrian armed forces over being forced to target fellow citizens during the beginning of their terrible civil strife, or earlier, among the Israeli Defense Forces in Gaza, illustrated this discernment in practice, as do the essays on military ethics written by Georgian,

Moldavian, Turkish, Greek, and other allied officers for ethics classes taught at the Naval Postgraduate School. Whatever a soldier is, military students find themselves agreeing that the soldier exists to protect his homeland and fellow citizens, not to turn his weapons upon them. And in protecting both, he does not rain indiscriminate and disproportionate violence haphazardly on a helpless noncombatant population, not at least without coming eventually to question the moral legitimacy of his undertaking.

Our technological innovations ought not to shatter this fragile consensus, either through their impact on military culture or through their own design and deployment at the hands of those unfamiliar, or unsympathetic, with this way of regarding public security and the rule of law.

INDEX

For Product Safety Concerns and Information please contact our EU representative GPSR@taylorandfrancis.com
Taylor & Francis Verlag GmbH, Kaufingerstraße 24, 80331 München, Germany

www.ingramcontent.com/pod-product-compliance
Ingram Content Group UK Ltd.
Pitfield, Milton Keynes, MK11 3LW, UK
UKHW020008200926
475702UK00015B/2543

* 9 7 8 1 0 3 2 2 2 7 2 8 3 *